A
Spiritual Psychology
For
The Aquarian Age

Other Books By Arthur Lytle

So You Want To Be A Channel!
Beating Tantra At It's Own Game—Spiritual Sexuality

These books are available from New Falcon Publications

And for a complete list of all of our titles, ask for our free catalog:
New Falcon Publications
7025 East 1st Avenue, Suite 5
Scottsdale, AZ 85251 U.S.A.
(602) 246-3546

A Spiritual Psychology For The Aquarian Age

BY

Arthur Lytle Ph. D.

1992
NEW FALCON PUBLICATIONS
SCOTTSDALE, ARIZONA U.S.A.

COPYRIGHT © 1992 ARTHUR LYTLE

All rights reserved. No part of this book, in part or in whole, may be reproduced, transmitted, or utilized, in any form or by any means, electronic or mechanical, including photocopying, recording, or by any information storage and retrieval system, without permission in writing from the publisher, except for brief quotations in critical articles, books and reviews.

International Standard Book Number: 1-56184-052-1

Library of Congress Catalog Card Number: 91-68304

First Edition 1992

NEW FALCON PUBLICATIONS
7025 E 1st Avenue Suite 5
Scottsdale, Arizona 85251 U.S.A.
(602) 246-3546

TABLE OF CONTENTS

What To Expect From This Work And How To Use It 7
To The Reader 9
Dedication 11
Acknowledgments 13
Foreword 15
A Look Ahead 17
An Admonition 19

Chapter One
An Aquarian Age Pyschic Psychology 23

Chapter Two
On Becoming Whole 31

Chapter Three
A Special Meditation 35

Chapter Four
Some Dietary Factors 37

Chapter Five
About Barriers 43

Chapter Six
Handling Psychic Interference 49

Chapter Seven
Insights On Fundamental Man 57

Chapter Eight
More On The Nature Of Thought 61

Chapter Nine
On Becoming Transformed 69

Chapter Ten
On Becoming A Conscious Co-worker 77

Chapter Eleven
Uses of Hypnotherapy 85

Chapter Twelve
Fear As A Shut-Off To Love 89

Chapter Thirteen
Diagnostic Methods For Case Assessment 93

Chapter Fourteen
Electronic Aids 105

Chapter Fifteen
Astro Diagnosis 109

Chapter Sixteen
  Beginnings 127
Chapter Seventeen
  Benefits 133
Chapter Eighteen
  On The Multiple Roles Of The Aquarian Age Counselor 135
Chapter Nineteen
  The Importance Of Centering 139
Chapter Twenty
  Preparing To Communicate Through The Veil 147
Chapter Twenty-One
  On Clinical Practice And Procedure 149
Chapter Twenty-Two
  On Opening Up A New Case 157
Chapter Twenty-Three
  More On Case Entrances 163
Chapter Twenty-Four
  On Session Preparation 169
Chapter Twenty-Five
  On Searching The Time Track 175
Chapter Twenty-Six
  Communicating And Communications Processing 177
Chapter Twenty-Seven
  Voice Dialogue 185
Chapter Twenty-Eight
  On Running Present Time Problems 189
Chapter Twenty-Nine
  On Running Guilt and Fault 193
Chapter Thirty
  On Running Inertia, Bodies, And Death 199
Chapter Thirty-One
  The Transveil Traveler 207
Chapter Thirty-Two
  On Developing Human Creativity 219
Chapter Thirty-Three
  Recommended Reading 233
Appendix A
  Definitions of Terms 241
Appendix B
  A Timely Example of Synchronicity 247
Index 253

WHAT TO EXPECT FROM THIS WORK AND HOW TO USE IT

This treatise explains cogent psychologies and their related therapies by which the dedicated aspirant can get himself up to speed most quickly in a stable and relevant spiritual sense. Using them, one becomes more and more able to read the feelings and thoughts of his/her contemporaries and gradually becomes aware of Higher Intelligence with the ability to communicate with same at will. An additional benefit is reaped through raising ones Intelligence Quotient.

These principles and practices are presented such that they may be used both in the daily work-a-day world and in private sessions with a qualified Counselor. One becomes freed from addictions to his/her systems of attitudes and habit patterns, finding indeed that the heavens are all about, and becomes consciously a co-worker with the Hierarchy in its world-wide efforts to prepare Earth for the New Order, shaking out the error and incrustation of the Old. Great changes are afoot!

As the Aspirant becomes clear, s/he comes to recognize himself as one of those persons who can graduate from Schoolhouse Earth and join its Spiritual Faculty, helping find and prepare other candidates for similar work on both sides of the veil.

You become a conscious Aquarian Age leader yourself by becoming skilled in applying these principles and practices in your own life.

TO THE READER

In this small channeled volume are tools capable of diagnosing and healing the troubled soul through an integration of the Ancient Wisdom with Cybernetic Science, Psychology, Metaphysics, and Religion. Its application as a Life System leads directly to self mastery and improved relationships. Used ardently it leads to Conscious Co-workership with the Guides and Teachers of the Great White Brotherhood. You set your own rate of progress and boundaries.

Two major goals for writing this document are to equip Counselors with efficient tools for alleviating the soul distress so prevalent today, and to provide effective ways to activate the Intuition. Payoffs are refined relationships and to work consciously with The Guides.

Counselor/Facilitators will receive through-the-veil help when working with trainees being prepared for service as Conscious Channels and Co-Workers.

This book is intended to be an Operator's manual for clearing the soul and accelerating spiritual development. While designed for the Parapsychologist, the Holistic Health Clinician and for the Pastoral Counselor, it can be used by Laypersons-in-Training. The methods will be found very effective, and are used on both sides of The Veil.

The approach is to offer ways to discern what the human capacity can be, to find what blocks it, then describing what can be done to express that capability via examples.

Not intended as a cook-book, the practicing therapist may incorporate refinements or specialize. We encourage the Practitioner to study it all and find what works best for him. The greatest value for some will be its diagnostic methods, enabling most effective use of Time and Energy in transforming troubled souls into Conscious Co-Workers with The Guides.

The methods and techniques of this book enable expanding human consciousness into the higher mental and intuitional planes by getting rid of recorded subconscious blocks and by offering practice in two-way transveil communications, establishing a working relationship with Spirit between and across both sides of The Veil. The attainable advancement in Human Evolution made available is usually underestimated.

*The successful Aquarian Counselor will be a clear Psychic. The successful Aquarian Psychic will be a Psychologist. The successful Aquarian Psychologist will be a Clairvoyant. The successful Aquarian Clairvoyant will be a Scientist. The successful Aquarian Scientist will be a Religionist. The successful Aquarian Religionist will be a Psychiatrist. The successful Aquarian Psychiatrist will be a Master.

*The Path to mastery is the same the world over, but that fact is seldom recognized.

*This handbook offers an excellent opportunity for the person who would like to set up to work for and with The Hierarchy as a Conscious Co-Worker, Recruiter & Trainer, and Go-Between through the veil for candidates for The Service.

*We offer here a wonderful opportunity to become really *free* on all levels, to express Life as it was meant to be. After all, perhaps the greatest gift God can give man is Life itself.

*The Aquarian Counselor will be a Soul Mechanic, helping keep the Personality tuned up. His tools are unfamiliar to the Clergy, yet are authorized throughout the Bible. As part of a trinity, working with Holistic Medicine and Physiology he will offer a total service for Body, Mind, and Spirit maintenance and development.

*One Aquarian goal of The Hierarchy is to replace Fear with Love, and here is how it may be done effectively. We are fortunate to have excellent tools to do the job.

*People are more like computer-driven robots than they would like to hear, being run mostly by programming, and little by conscious decision. However little, it enables them to alter their programming, reviewing and revising it to fit new circumstances and goals.

*Anything that bugs you it is a fit topic to investigate and clear. We humans must be free to look at *anything*, even if we decide not to experience it! Most clients just want to be put back on their track and be given a shove in the right direction, not desiring to go on to Self mastery. That is *OK*!

If you recognize repetition anywhere in this tome, you have discerned the point(s) we are trying to make!

DEDICATION

These concepts and processes are dedicated to the enlightenment of mankind and to discharging its deeper ills by clearing obstructed communication channels between the human chakras and their corresponding centers in the Realm of the Human spirit. This enables man to express Life at will between his true home in the Mental-Spiritual realms and his adopted Aspect in the Material-Emotional Universe, where he has presently trapped himself.

ACKNOWLEDGEMENTS

This Labor of Love began in 1953 when Dr. Dorothy Law-Nolte introduced us to the worlds of Marriage and Family Counseling and Metaphysics. Seventeen years of intensive electronic psychometry study and research under Rev. Dr. Donald R. Schaffer were followed by four years of supervised practice under Dr. Cecil G. Osborne. The Rev. Dr. Joan Leo Mallan tied it all together with her clairvoyant studies in the Akasha.

Rolf and her Structural Integration strongly influenced the direction of our work.

Dr. Arthur Janov and Dr. Fritz Perls developed and contributed fascinating and very effective ways for working in the Gestalt.

Scientific legitimacy for this work lies in a recent treatise titled "The Persistent Paradox of Psychic Phenomena," by Dr. R. G. Jahn, Dean of the Princeton University School Of Engineering & Applied Science. His work was jointly sponsored by The McDonnell Foundation, the John E. Fetzer Foundation, The Explorer's Club, The Institute of Noetic Sciences and the Little River Foundation. It was published in the prestigious "Proceedings of the Institute of Electrical & Electronic Engineers," in Feb. 1982, Volume 70, Number 2. Jahn's work formed the basis for scientific acceptance of our doctoral research and dissertation.

Special gratitude is accorded my doctoral Faculty Adviser Dr. Herbert Fong, Ph.D. in EE (USC) and to Dr. Osborne for valuable contributions to the form and content of the dissertation itself..

Special recognition and gratitude are extended to my lovely wife Lora for her consultancy and encouragement..

Without the successful ministry of Love and Patience by my Guides and Elder Brothers Heindel, Gladstone, and Maxwell, this work might been done through another Author/Channel…if done at all!

FOREWORD

Life is an Energy experience. This book opens doors to increased flow of Life Energy, with the creation and enhancement of human intelligence and intuition. It provides a therapy within reach of the practicing counselor-clergyman and the mental-health clinician, and can be understood by the Advanced Layman. This book is the result of cross-fertilization and integration of concepts drawn from Electronics, Computer Science, Religion, Psycho-Cybernetics and the Physiological and Psychological arts. In the form presented this material provides a breakthrough to relief of soul misery through systematic reevaluation and resolution of engrammatic materials recorded in the subconscious mind.

Our research phase used a calibrated electronic psychometer of unique design which identified the presence and magnitude of subliminal body-mind currents, those which are generated automatically by the subconscious mind in response to stimuli of many kinds. We demonstrated that the subconscious self, the Psyche, can be probed scientifically, with repeatable results. A bonus is the apparent enhancement of Life Energy flow.

We found that excellent results are obtainable without use of the electropsychometer, bringing these processes within reach of any practitioner skilled in reading the subtle communications signals engulfing a client. A well-developed Intuition or/and Clairvoyance are powerful aids to the counseling processes. Similarly of great benefit are a well developed receptivity and communications skills to cogent clear channeled information from hierarchical Sources.

This work should prove of interest and value to the pastoral counselor, psychologist and holistic practitioner alike. A superior working model and therapy of the human soul has emerged. A quiet revolution is already taking place in the parapsychological and related field of transpersonal psychology toward the creation of genius.

We seek not to prove whether conscious channeling is or is not valid, or whether a cadre of Angels and Guides exists and communicates with Earthlings or not. We accept both as natural Facts of

Life, available to anyone who undertakes and does the work necessary to attain Self mastery. There is no glamor to what we propose...just a lot of persistence. Dedication to this program attracts the attention and support of Those Invisible Teachers and Guides who seek Conscious Co-Workers for Hierarchical Service. In that sense, this book is a handbook of attainment of that state of being.

A LOOK AHEAD

An Aquarian Science of the Human Soul is emerging, correlating Cause and Effect in new dimensions, reporting findings having common and extended significance. These findings allow balanced study and treatment of the human being as a cybernetic whole. In other words, we humans are accelerating building the Antakaranah, that mystical Golden Bridge between the Intellect and the Intuition, between the right-brain and the left-brain. As these methods become more widely understood and practiced, the lot of Aquarian Age Humankind will transform.

The processes exposed here go beyond those developed earlier by pioneers such as Freud and Jung, by Ross Ashby, and currently taught by The Association of Transpersonal Psychology, the Institute of Noetic Sciences, by Stone and Winkleman, by Deepak Chopra, M.D., and more. They demonstrate that there is indeed a growing opportunity to open up a new integrative field of activity called Meta-Psychology. Each component now is ostracized and operated separately as Religion, Psychiatry, Psychology, Parapsychology, and Physiology.

Required reading is the landmark work of Dr. Robert G. Jahn titled "The Persistent Paradox of Psychic Phenomena," published in 1982. Jahn has collected and reviewed many hundreds of papers and concludes that contemporary Science is looking in the wrong directions, ignoring the proper domains, and is using the wrong instruments to gain what it would accept as scientific validation for Extra Sensory Perception (ESP). Future research must consider the great variation in ESP sensitivities between persons studied, and the great dependence of results of subjective factors presently ignored when making measurements. Jahn legitimized focus on the specific research in psychic phenomena, and pointed directions where so much remains to be done. Psychotronics research is understood to be funded by the A.M.A., the C.I.A, D.O.D, and NASA. Kubler-Ross and other private individuals and foundations are working to invent instruments appropriate to the Energies of Thought and the human Psyche.

By integrating the above technical research with the traditional practices of meditation, building the Antakaranah may be accelerated. Much research by scientifically trained psychic researchers and many doctoral dissertations have yet to be written before the Science of the Human Soul is accepted as a legitimate field of endeavor. That state will probably come about through research for the development of Genius. However it comes about, the result is certain to usher in the age of the "super human," perhaps even the satisfied and fulfilled human, whether it comes about in our lifetimes or not!

Peace on Earth, one of the aims of the United World Religions, can be accelerated via the Applied Soul Technology we are proposing, going on beyond the goals and limits set for the Evolution of Man which typified the ancient Taurean, Arian, and just-passing Piscean ages, moving forward from the Religion of The Son to what will become the Aquarian Age goals, to be called The Religion of the Father. We believe that there is no faster method generally available for awakening your Soul and completing your mystical bridge than through using the methods we herein present for The Aquarian Age and beyond into further Ages and Realms as yet undreamt of by we mortals.

By personal application of these principles and practices we shall be of great help to the Walk-Ins and other non-terrestrial Beings (ET's) to know and to fulfill their Life Purposes, helping Them get started in accomplishing their respective hierarchical missions, in enthusiasm and power.

There will always be more work to do than shall be accomplished. Then truly "As Above, So Below!"

AN ADMONITION

Our invisible Project Consultants expound on Their goal of preparing incarnate humans as Conscious thru-the-veil Co-Workers.

"Give of *your* best to Life down there, Dear Reader, while you are in it, and we shall be thus able to give you of *our* best. To gain realization of that fundamental Truth of Life is absolutely required in order to be freed from the Wheel of Rebirth. It is in overdoing the *desire for the wrong things*, in mistaking desire for the *right things*, and in not recognizing that which *is* right that causes the fundamental disjointed aspect and pain of Earth life.

"Down there (in flesh) it still could be if only and whenever mankind gets the idea of what first things to put first. When he wakes up to that Truth, he will re-orient himself wonderfully well. In the meantime, we have the task of awakening his consciousness through opening up the spiritual perception of those few people whom We *can* reach. Then, for having expanded their perception of Absolute Truth, (compared to the) Untruths and the Relative Truths which have heretofore been accepted, We will be able to pour out the blessings bestowed upon US by The Father. In His overall Wisdom and Love for His Children, of which We too number ourselves, We are blessed beyond our yet ability to comprehend.

"There is always more than you may yet have recognized, as there is a material aspect up here also. It is just that up here, *things* as such are not as attractive as they appear to you because we can see the underlying nature of manifested materiality. In other words, we can see the nature of the sub-atomic particles in action and thus can examine their various combinations, which, while interesting, yet are seen to be playthings. The nature of that which is *truly* interesting up here lies in the mental concepts and philosophies in which we find development so necessary, now that pursuit of things of a material nature is less attractive. Then it behooves they who would graduate into this sphere to gradually relinquish their dependency upon *things* and become attuned with the Mental-Construct or Abstract aspect of the Universe.

"When and as you unfold your perception, you increasingly but very gradually will comprehend what is meant when we tell you these things. An admonition initially intended in a personal vein is to keep going as you are, except that your diet is to become critical relative to attainment of these capabilities."

Here are several factors which the author's Guides gave to him which also apply to all candidate Co-Workers, especially in the later stages of preparation and development:

"There is nothing better than simple basic foods, served raw. In developing the tongue and taste for those proper foods lies your release from the material aspect. There has to be fulfilled that final release from addiction to the pleasures of Earth. For you, it is now release from the tongue and the appetites. When this is achieved, you will find yourself ready to enter this Level of Awareness in full consciousness. Until then, you are left out by your own choices of foods. We would Love to see your victory, as we need you *both* sides of the Veil."

Personal experiment by this author-channel has proved the wisdom in Their admonitions. Further research into what constitutes that proper diet, and then rigid adherence thereto, produces a remarkably clear mind, sharpens intuitive perception, and brings about normal blood pressure and a serene state without medication. That diet involves a minimum quantity absorption from red meat, alcohol, most spices, and sugar in almost every form. Once cleared, ingestion of sugar is easily shown to fog a clear mind within minutes and to institute a state of irritability; all this in a person who has become medically free of any measurable diabetic tendency.

BACKGROUND

CHAPTER ONE
AN AQUARIAN AGE PYSCHIC PSYCHOLOGY
(An Overview By Our Invisible Consultants)

"Our concept of a complete New Age Psychology is a melding of the original aims of Religion, Psychology and Metaphysics as a way to describe and enhance the nature of man. There is much here which, from OUR point of view can be used immediately as a treasure trove of intelligent information. Not considered difficult to comprehend either in theory or in application, it is the result of length, breadth, and depth in experience. *IT WORKS*. We "up here" have been watching you in your travails upon Cecil Osborne's mat and Don Schaffer's couch for many years, so we have confidence that *you* know *how* it works. Anyone who takes the trouble to engage his attention for so many years will surely achieve similar results, and probably sooner! Gradual relief from the pressures of living will be noticed with application of the spiritual technologies presented in this volume by properly and persistently focussing one's attention to resolution of his own akashic and relationship trouble spots, whether incurred in Lives Past or in the present lifetime. It is now time to begin, rather than to dally further with introductions.

"Within the heart and soul of the serious Seeker lies the key to the Kingdom of Heaven itself. It is every person's responsibility to find that key and use it to release the imprisoned splendor that lies within. Diligence is rewarded. We have absolute confidence in the potency of our prescribed methods of treatment by which the human Soul is the recipient and the Spirit is the beneficiary.

"Rather than freeing man from a devil, it is necessary to free man from the webs of his own making. Not always easily done, but it does require examination of his mental and emotional structures. That our concept can even be contemplated at this time is a tribute to the growth of Humanity during the preceding Piscean Age!

"A little known fact is that we were and still are direct participants in the design and development of Humanity as known today upon the Planet Earth. We are therefore absolutely familiar with the principles and practices of functioning in Human Mind, Soul and Body. There is little we do not understand about Earth Life, as we ourselves have lived many lives with you and among you. We probably have met and resolved every conceivable relationship available to incarnate Mankind. Compassion should then be numbered among our virtues, if indeed there be any virtue in having lived upon The Earth at all.

"Earth Life is conceivably God's greatest gift to Mankind, having provided flesh for man in which to experience Immortality consciously in Materiality, while having instant access to the Gods themselves. As has been proven by our individual experiences Up Here, there is no reason why it is not possible for any who will take the trouble to do so to return directly and all the way up to the Throne of Our Father, even while embodied in flesh. That it has been done is common knowledge among those Earth-folk who look to Jesus of Nazareth as an example and forerunner for the Piscean Age. Others expect The Second Coming for the Aquarian Age, and some today see Divinity in Sathya Sai Baba of India. To us it is surprising that more members of the Human Race have not taken upon themselves finding the short but not too difficult climb of which the Avatars speak. Admittedly a vertical ascent, every step requires conscious decision and individual responsibility for self. One may experience agony, for the burden is heavy at first. However, as each step toward release is taken, the burden is lifted significantly, so that ultimately the remaining few steps upon the ladder become easy.

"Witness the pain of death upon the Cross of man as experienced by The Christ in Jesus's borrowed physical body. There is probably the All-time and ultimate in suffering needlessly, except that the ultimate freedom of mankind rested upon that personal sacrifice. He Himself did not need the purging but He did succeed in freeing Mankind of its accumulated karma to the extent that mankind is now able individually to finish clearing his own karma, whoever wills to do so [Revelations 22: 17 and Heindel COSMO]. (Reference #9.)

"It is intended through the forthcoming information that the techniques we use and the reasons why we urge their use shall both be provided, that true understanding of the process is available for maximal effectiveness. We promise that persons who diligently and intelligently apply them shall begin to *find* the relief as well as the release from travail. Improvement usually becomes apparent first to the Seeker's associates or family, noting that some sort of transformation is being accomplished. Let it be understood that every hour spent in applying our method(s) will have its own subtle reward.

"If it seems to be taking too long to find relief, please consider that it may be partly because one's sensitivity is increasing to the point where items that formerly escaped notice are now assuming significance as obstacles into the subtler realms. Consider also that the method may not really be well enough understood, that it is being improperly applied, or that it is being resisted. Much time has been spent in perfecting development of each technique, but its method of application sometimes must be modified to be accepted by or to work around a particular set of barriers in some clients."

"Any person who is aware that another is undergoing treatment by our methods will be inclined to look carefully for signs of change. By certain profile tests personality changes can sometimes be measured, but electropsychometric means are most rapidly capable of revealing the transforming capabilities of our techniques, Usually the seeker is the last to recognize his own changes, but he or she will notice changes in his associates!

"Lest it be claimed that it is no longer possible for the old biblical miracles to be worked upon individual members of Human-Kind, let us set the record straight. It was then and still is our present intention to free Mankind from the Wheel of Rebirth (reincarnation), since this planet is not considered to be the ultimate home of the genus homo sapiens. Nor is it likely ever to be forgotten that *WE* "up here" have a *duty* to expedite the release of Earth-bound pleasure lovers, and those other recalcitrant members of Human Society who consider themselves immune from the need for salvation in the usual religious sense.

"There are still a few religious sects upon the Earth which consider they have already been "saved" from the end-days, from Hell's Fire and Damnation. If those same people, instead of seeing themselves so exalted, would take the effort to recognize their actual spiritual condition, they would be the first ones to cry *foul*, claiming that they have been deceived by the Anti-Christ, masquerading in the guise and trappings of the priestcraft. It may be true that such a being there may be, for every sort of deception is now being practiced upon the Old Earth. but, it is part of the growth in spiritual strength to learn proper recognition and mastery over those lesser forms of Life Energy, thus to attain to the actual status achieved by those few of us who have gone before. We could ignore those humans who are left behind, but certain few of us are determined to release even those laggards who now consider themselves immune even from the *need* for assistance from any element of God's Kingdom corporeal or non-corporeal not recognized by their church group.

"Enough has already been given here to paint the necessary picture that Release lies within the grasp of anyone who, in his own life, will undertake the equivalent twelve Herculean labors. Clearing the subconscious mind is symbolically every bit as strenuous as was cleaning out the Aegean stables, even to directing the River of Life, sluicing it through the subconscious mental stables as part of what must be done to free himself to return to The Father's House 'white as snow,' to explain a parable from your Christian Bible a bit.

"Ignorance is no longer a sufficient reason for a person to hold back from the final leap God-ward. For the nonce, let it be announced that the forthcoming Earth adjustments (see Cayce, Solomon, Montgomery, Peebles, et al) will undoubtedly befall the human race, whether inwardly psychological or also in part physically. Yet, with that travail is provided a way out of and over and through the difficulties. While many persons will have little to do other than attend to physical survival, there will still be time and opportunity to do the things attendant to spiritual overcoming and release.

"It is time that the methods in *Esoteric Psychology* (Reference 6 et al) (AAB) and our Applied Spiritual Technology be recognized and put into practice over a wide portion of the Earth's surface. That these methods are coming out first in English is not coincidental, as the means for typing them and then getting them into print is most easily accessible to us in English. There are more channels willing to undertake such activity in the U.S.A. than perhaps anywhere else except the United Kingdom and with the future exception of Russia and China. China's political structure does not permit such overt undertakings as yet, but its populace is otherwise open to the ideas we find required for the release of the Human Soul-Spirit.

"Opportunities are being provided for everyone who truly wishes to find and study those blessings rarely found before the present time. They will be found in daily life upon Earth through clearing one's individual case-load of engrams and hang-ups, of addictions to the demons of bad habits, of poor attitudes and bodily ills, and of all forms of disease which plague incarnate Homo Sapiens. There is not yet generally available, to our understanding, an *instant* release from one's ills.

"There is sufficient reason to justify the above statement. It has taken Mankind, individually as well as collectively, hundreds to thousands of Earthly incarnations to evolve into his present state of development, entrapment, and bondage to earlier-forged chains, as manifest in his present conditions. Even to take the trouble to identify and catalog those many categories of involvement would require years but for the fact that these ills are common to the Human Race. Therefore there are few indeed, if there be *any*, who have escaped much of Life in the Material Universe.

"For having discovered the universality of the problems of clearing the human mind and soul, we are able to define and wholesale parts of the curative process. Indeed, some of the curative processes have been reduced to handbook level. But, because these methods of clearing are straightforward to apply, their potency is likely to be appreciated only when tried over wide areas of Space and Time. Once reported upon and accepted openly, a new profession will arise to champion Psychic Psychology as a worthy cause, perhaps to be vaunted as an arm of the Aquarian Age Religion.

"Some members of the mental healing arts who discover the benefits of its successful application will seek to hide its existence from the rest of their colleagues. That situation shall not prevail nor long be permitted. That is largely why it has been written in its present form and level, so that no one limited group among mankind can ever again gather unto itself the very methods by which the whole human race could be released.

THE BIG PICTURE

"Up here we see "the big picture" in detail, and how this publication effort fits into the Grand Plan. We see with clarity sufficient that it is not difficult for us to begin promulgation of Aquarian Psychic Psychology *now*, and subsequently to broadcast it over the remainder of the globe. It has taken quite some expansion of the human intellect to develop and to unfold its concepts tothe practicing humanistic psychologist, even though it should be among that select group to take up our cause and champion it before the eyes of the waiting world. Such widespread acceptance is not soon likely to be the case. Therefore, please bear with us as we outline the gist of the technology, perhaps giving it in layers as in peeling an onion, so that it is understood *how* as well as *why* it is possible for mankind to be so ready for and so amenable to relief.

"We foresee groups forming in small centers around the world dedicated to promulgation of these methods. There will come that time when such practice is commonly accepted as just a normal part of the educative curriculum and process in several generations. As this work becomes commonly understood and therefore commonly accepted, we find each family, church, and schoolhouse having specialists dedicated to teaching this as our New Age Psycho-Religion. After many generations have experienced these processes, the case-load of incarnate humanity will be so lightened that it will be possible, and indeed will be observed, that a new level of spiritual functioning has come over the Earth. It is this condition which we seek to manifest, and to this end that we write. Therefore, we intend to make certain by all avenues now available that these principles be announced and put into practice upon the face of the Earth, ushering in The millennium.

"In the U.S.A. several small groups already have gained access to parts of this technology. Each has found a part of the elephant, and each swears that it has the only proper understanding of the elephant. It has ever been thus. As with the sciences, when enough general agreements have been reached, when enough of the principles are understood and practiced, the art of release of the human soul will become common domain instead of being restricted to the inner domains held in certain ivory towers, or hidden behind the robes of some new class of ecclesiastics as has heretofore been the world situation. For airing our technology thusly, it is anticipated that the common man will eventually understand that none stands between him and God except ignorance of that fact. It is our goal that enough of Humanity shall understand us sufficiently well so that what has been locked away in the towers of the occult as too dangerous shall be released, so that no further need for hidden treatment remains to cloud the release of Humanity. This will hasten reformation of our present well-intentioned but overly protective earthly hierarchies.

"Admittedly, today attempts will be made to hide these materials from the profane, as the average human being is considered by your self-ordained elite corps of doctorally-gowned practitioners. At first there will need to be the usual process of discovery by the elite, requiring time to recognize what it is that we here are presently revealing, and thus time to fall back and regroup. Then, as more and more of the professionals pick up the thread of Truth presented herein, the more each will seek to establish a school of his own and to cultivate a following. To prevent recurrence of that same phenomenon which has led to the present confused state of multifactioned theological affairs upon the Earth, and has led to the domination and subjugation of mankind by a light cadre of religious and psychological specialists, it is necessary that these principles be made available to everyone who can read. Hence, there is much you can do, Dear Reader, to become an expert!

"Perhaps it is fortunate, in a way, that more of the world's population cannot read nor even cares to learn, and that conventional religion has gained such a grip upon the minds of Humanity. However, it is from the present small cadre of potential Psychic Psychologists that the first glimmerings of recognition may be expected to appear, initiating application of the techniques on a broad front. But the general public is not yet aware of its entrapment, nor is it therefore interested in being released from a condition in which it has become comfortable, lulled into spiritual lethargy by its own theologies.

"To achieve these, our short-term and long-term hierarchical goals, requires that We work through that present small, confused, but available cadre of professional psychologists, counselors, and open religionists plus the many interested lay groups to make our first inroads to salvation or relief of the Human Race. Members of those select groups do not yet acknowledge a common goal, and certainly do not recognize man's common problem, nor even its common origin! If any recognition exists of our concept of an Unified Knowledge of Man, and of the possibility of an integrated approach, it lies in the works of certain renegades at the Esalen Institute in California, the Neuro Linguistic Programming people, their associates at The Institute For Transpersonal Psychology, the people, Noetics, and various others groups and individuals working in the San Francisco Bay area, and springing up around the world.

"Many are having varying degrees of success in hewing out methods for clearing the human mind. However, not until the Big Three of Religion, Psychology and Psychiatry become aware of and are willing to admit their common ground, can they commence to integrate and unify into one powerful, simple and inexpensive teaching and methodology. Once that state has been reached, we can focus more attention on training more individual Co-Workers for Between Lives work. Potential new Co-Workers through the veil should find that of sufficient interest to become Master Practitioners on both sides of the veil.

"It takes Us great effort to get something like this going down in the Earth planes, partly because it is difficult to arouse interest in studying the deeper Nature of Man. Incarnate life seems to take so much time and energy just to keep body and shirt together so that man has little time to contemplate his own Divine Nature, or the nature of God and his fellow man. Between lives, most persons are only interested in how to do more of what they were already doing down there in the flesh. In your own way you will become a Channel such as this embodied coauthor, who has developed the technical background and interest and has devoted half of his life to studying the processes of self-mastery. He has become sensitive enough, is interested in the close relationships between the planes, and has made Time and the necessary economic adjustments to be available for us even to begin to get off the starter's blocks.

"Do you now see how difficult it has been, and why The Hierarchy is restructuring Its approach to be truly effective in working through the veil to recruit and train Conscious Co-Workers? We therefore openly invite your interest and active participation in our program!"

"We move along!"

CHAPTER TWO
ON BECOMING WHOLE

"Be ye made Whole" is yet another admonition carried over from the Ancient Wisdoms of Lemuria and Atlantis via the Bible [KJV John 5]. Its appearance there has given it a religious flavor, but increasingly books are being published and groups are springing up rediscovering ways to help the Human to become an integrated being, to become whole, through advances in what we are calling Psychic Psychology, a new technology.

As a person becomes integrated within his attitudes and the social system, i.e., becomes complete or made whole, he is able to live life a bit more energetically, abundantly and joyously. Each author and inventor of a "new" therapy addresses somewhat different aspects of the complex human personality, benefitting the client and society-at-large. It goes without saying that the more aware and integrated a therapist becomes, the more effective he or she is in integrating disjointed psyches in private practice.

The more astutely a Practitioner understands the human psyche, the more readily he will know where the individual therapies and techniques should be applied, and the more efficacious he will be in restoring his clientele to be fully functioning as Spirit in Flesh...being made whole in the biblical sense. He need not fear running out of clients and losing income by "clearing" the personality too rapidly, as the Public will learn of his or her effectiveness and will pay any price for those services. Eventually even the churches will beat a path to his door.

It is recommended that professional therapists, facilitators, pastoral counselors, and lay leaders alike become well versed in each of several schools of therapy, working directly under an established practitioner in each field. One thus gains firsthand knowledge of the pros and the cons of each method. Each potential Therapist/Counselor thus can become an integrated person himself by putting together an approach which fits him and works for him.

Thus, positive client needs and gains are observable relatively quickly.

Study of these methods is also recommended to public school teachers, bank tellers, preachers, salespeople, medical personnel, to anyone working with people over a wide range of temperaments and pressures. Richer relationships can be built from the pulpit and in the Counselor's and the holistic mental health professional's chambers. None is immune to the benefits accruing to recognition and practice of the processes for cleaning up his own case... including those who consider themselves as already "saved," "under Grace," or "born again," since *all* fall short of the Glory of God, to be found in KJV John 3:3.

Becoming an integrated personality pays benefits beyond those introduced here. For example, while living in subsidiary life roles of professional flutist and teacher, this author-researcher became aware of the importance, the vital necessity for students to become a whole person as prerequisite to becoming a better or even an excellent musician. It was found straightforward and effective to meld awareness techniques into teaching flute. These had originally been learned while doing research in the field of personality-development therapies for relief and release from inhibitive barriers and programming. Gentle applications practice augmented the phenomenon of projecting one's presence as an aid to attaining audience rapport. Of course, mastery of a student's particular instrument is still required for becoming an artist! Needless to say, your author was the greatest beneficiary, having learned much about the means and *methods of application* of these principles in his own life, also having learned how to pass them on effectively and unobtrusively.

To become truly a master in *any* field, as contrasted to remaining a skilled but low-profile technician, one must empty himself as much as possible of all factors which act to *prevent* him from being a *Master of Life*. He *must* become simultaneously and objectively able to see what he is looking at, to have the perspective to perceive accurately what effect he is producing, and to feel intuitively into each performing situation to the fullest extent of his total self. All of this in addition to mastering a host of intricate body-level specialized activities for becoming one with his instrument.

The would-be musician-artisan's activities include reading notes, learning the fingering associated with each note, learning the proper body stance, timing, expression, projection, being a feeling channel...all this while viewing objectively the total effect being created in the physical, mental, and emotional-intuitional planes.

A special exercise is appended to Chapter 26 to develop perception of the effect being created on and in any audience by his efforts, and conversely observing its interrelated effects upon him. He cannot be "hung up" psychologically in some area without it detracting from his ability to channel the core spiritual message. Any performer will succeed in communicating his message to the same degree he communicates with the audience on the Inner Planes or feeling levels.

Of course, this applies equally to everyone in any endeavor, for we all are performers of one kind or another on the Stage of Life.

The message of our discourse is that Life can be lived more abundantly when barriers to perception and expression are discerned, resolved, and the soul is awake and functioning in an integrated manner. Again, this is truly equally applicable to *all* walks of human life in the planet Earth.

In other words, to become truly a *whole* person, we must have no *holes* in our holiness. Our spiritual armor must be without voids in our character, having no gaps, seams or patches, smudges or barriers in our Golden Wedding Garment (Heindel).

CHAPTER THREE
A SPECIAL MEDITATION

While many methods of meditation are practiced, some are perhaps better suited to the practice of Psychic Psychology than others. One specific technique is recommended for the special purpose of establishing a working contact with the Inner Self, establishing the serenity which should be the normal state of being. In that state one consciously responds to the Intuition and/or Guidance issuing from the Higher Self, the Inner God-Self, or from Discarnate Intelligence in the role of Guides, Teachers, and Elder Brothers on the Other Side.

From learned application of this approach a person can prepare himself for instant sleep, for out-of-body travel, to pervade his situations, associates or clients, and to communicate telepathically with others similarly spiritually awakened.

One may begin by being comfortably seated and closing his eyes to avoid distraction from the objects in the room. Take a few maximum lung-capacity breaths and slowly release them. An excellent way to develop the present-time processes and to release the random thought processes that often seem to keep the mind stirred up is to focus attention on the air as it passes in and out of the head.

Now, project an invisible line of communication to the upper left rear corner of the room, and just hold it. Let yourself examine it to sense its texture, color, flexibility, and temperature. Just observe it and do not judge it. Then let it disappear.

Again shift your attention and organize a similar line to the upper *right* rear corner of the same room and establish its reality as you did to the other corner just previously. Note that you can change its color and heft, strengthen it, and make it disappear and reappear. When doing that becomes comfortable, establish both lines as before, and just hold them for approximately twelve minutes, or until you and they feel stable.

Now, gradually wiggle your fingers while holding on to the corners. When this is comfortable, also wiggle your feet, slowly adding your legs if it is still easy to hold the communication lines. Slowly continue expanding your attention by feeling the weight of your body on the chair. Allow yourself to hear the room noises. Slowly rotate your head, and gradually open your eyes, noting that it will become possible for you to speak with your Counselor or Facilitator, and that your speech is somehow deeper.

Note, when having your eyes open and holding the two corners, that you feel spread out, perhaps even having a Centered feeling.

You now have a different perspective than before you started the two rear corners exercise. This is akin to the normal spiritual perspective, and you will develop it gradually with practice, and from later extending it to the other six corners of the room.

Please consult Chapter 10 for further insights on Meditation.

CHAPTER FOUR
SOME DIETARY FACTORS

A short discourse is appropriate at this point on Our findings relative to the definition and importance of a good diet to an effective psychosomatic catharsis.

"In order for the Genus Homo Sapiens to function ideally in the Earth plane as his body-mind vehicular structure was designed, certain orally ingested chemical elements must be present in certain balanced amounts and ratios, else unwelcomed psychological and mental disorders and physical indispositions result.

"We take this opportunity to call your attention to modifying certain erroneous concepts presently in vogue versus what constitutes our view of an excellent diet. Views accepted by the contemporary and unthinking or misinformed majority of Earthlings are due for an abrupt change in a few years anyway. The urgency to make sweeping dietary revisions at this time is then dependent mainly on whether one desires to live well through the coming Earth changes, and/or wants to attempt realization of his fullest potential in the immediate future and perhaps thus escape or rise above these changes.

"Adequate preparation for the forthcoming social, economic and geoidal changes requires reversion to certain well-known groups of soil products which, when ingested in minimal quantities, will assure restoration of that blood chemistry balance which is so vital to full incarnate awareness and proper functioning.

"We start by declaring "off-limits" chemically processed food stuffs, especially those which are fabricated from refined sugar. There is no doubt that overuse of sugar in the typical diet seems to enhance tastes of otherwise bland-charactered foodstuffs. In excessive amounts it starts other processes less well accepted by the human body over the long term. Additive sweeteners generally would not be needed if proper and fresh foods were available and ingested, as most ripe fruits and vegetables are already tasty enough to assure proper chemical processing in the human thermodynamic aspects of food carburetion. Carburetion of foodstuffs parallels carburetion of automotive fuels, involving "burning" carbohydrates with oxygen to produce heat, carbon dioxide, water, and fibrous waste products.

"When subtle human taste has been jaded by prolonged heavy use of spices, condiments, and other strong liquids, finer essences which originally would produce a hearty salivary response are no longer able to induce the required digestive and gastric juice flows and peristalsis. Hence, the foods enter the body as an excess of undesirable bulk substances which can do nothing but produce bulk fat, if digested at all, in the tissues of the human body. Also overlooked is the equally important factor that these same foodstuffs, if ingested *raw*, would prove very satisfactory as appetite quenchers if ingested in smaller amounts, eaten slowly and savored.

"For the benefit of persons who seek the proper way through the diet dilemma we would say that one must and can begin to revise his acquired tastes via a program of gradual substitution and insertion of small quantities of fresher green materials, ideally picked just minutes before, fresh out of the field, lawn or garden. No amount of preparation save washing is therefore to be required. Eating three to four varieties of the darker or darkest leaves should be followed by intake of one, or two at the most, of rooted tubers, orange or yellow in color. If seasonal, gourds or squashes of similar color inside or outside are good as substitutes.

"Provide yourself, then, with a simple lawn-garden capability and conduct this experiment for several weeks, during which you should take particular care to avoid ingesting *any* kind of strong seasoning, drink or solids that would mask the delicate beauty of fresh raw produce of the soil.

"We volunteer the observation that persons who will conduct this simple experiment will find to their amazement and delight that vegetables freshly cut and prepared are superior to store-purchased produce in attainment of the clearheaded state that is widely lacking today. That insufficiency is due to loss of the vital Life Forces of the Vegetable Kingdom, which are similar to the vital currents flowing in and nourishing the human mind, and which come from the same Ultimate Source.

"When changing to a vegetarian diet it is well to consider what needs may have been provided from the animal flesh or products previously eaten. Riboflavin, taken as a food supplement, can suffice in small quantities for its loss of meat products as its source. However, when beef, pork, and chicken are first eliminated from the diet it is often noted that certain chemicals, adrenaline and stilbestrol, are needed temporarily, enough so that withdrawal symptoms are minimized. Withdrawal symptoms may be assuaged by very limited intake until the need for temporary supply has ceased.

"Rather than to eat red or even white meat, we would suggest that certain softer yellow-white cheeses be substituted. A natural yellow color indicates presence of sulphur compounds. Products of animal origin which contain traces of those substances usually can be eaten without producing the side effects generated from consumption of fleshy tissues, such as a high uric acid level often found in the blood of the sedentary human body.

"Animal tissue and human flesh are similar enough so that whether to eat one or the other is determined by conditions other than dietary. Human flesh is better for average consumption than is animal flesh, but deprives a higher order of the Divine Gift of Life than does consumption of the flesh of our Younger Brothers of the Animal Kingdom. In an absolute sense, neither is acceptable when used as a food source [Genesis 1:29, 30 and Leviticus 3:17].

"It will be found sufficient that yellow cheeses and cottage cheese replace meats entirely. The use of unfertilized eggs from chickens or other fowl is also to be preferred to meat intake for several reasons, including the fact that no formal life process has as yet been destroyed or denied; large scale egg production prepares vehicles of potential occupancy rather than providing bodies which are first occupied and then later slaughtered and eaten. Preferably, one would select to eat the unfertilized eggs to perpetuate the life strain of the egg-producing fowl or other creature. Turtle eggs, being rare and a delicacy, are sought nearly to extinction, and therefore at present are not recommended for human consumption.

"Certain other factors merit consideration at this time, having relative importance to diet versus ability to function in mental and higher spheres. Those spheres or planes are often recognized by other names such as the "astral," or "first, second and third Heaven Worlds," as states of consciousness, or more correctly, as 'realms.' There are even those heavier aspects of cheeses that clog the very portals of mental and spiritual perception, the chakras themselves, through which we humans are able to contact, cross over into, and function in both the Heavens and the Earth. Earth-folk who would investigate those "higher" levels of experience can do so only by awakening themselves through opening the chakras, usually long closed due to general misinformation, lack of understanding, due to certain traditional habits of thought and eating, and/or desire to focus attention in the three-dimensional world [9, 16].

"Before early man became flesh-eating he was wiry, physically active and resilient to the near extreme. Biblical Man found no difficulty in obtaining enough labor to remove all traces of excessive protein combustion products, mainly the urea products, from his blood stream. However, unless special care is taken, it is not likely that today's vegetated and sedentary life is able to exercise a body enough to be rid of those products, which results in urea crystals directly formed in those portions of the body which receive least circulation. Those tend to be the less-used bony junctures or joints, toes, fingers and in some cases are found resident in spinal interstices, creating arthritic conditions.

"We note with consternation the disintegration of the presently-occupied human bodies, especially those used mostly by the intellectually-oriented races, sedentary as never has been seen in all past evolution. Not only has Man's physical body deteriorated [look at your aged], but so has his ability to respond to spirit signals from and to participate in the activities of the now Unseen Realms. That causes serious concern for the backward trend we observe among those otherwise elite persons who should be nearly ready to leave Earth's schoolhouse and its training programs permanently for the unseen or Higher Life."

Our Unseen Consultant wound up his dietary discourse with a lengthy admonition, as follows.

"To all who would strive to function in these higher realms, we say to open yourselves and your chakras through greatly purified diets consisting of fresh greens, orange-yellow roots and gourd-squashes, nuts and fruits, eaten sparingly without garnish. These foods fresh enough and grown without particular use of strong fertilizers, will be found quite thoroughly satisfying.

"Fasting accelerates the attainment of those changes which it is possible to make. We would drink copiously of freshly obtained pure mineralized water and of the diluted fruit and vegetable juices while fasting, as the body's mineral and vegetable requirements are thereby satisfied.

"No further dietary admonitions are necessary in this treatise, as simple bread products do not contain excesses of sugars. Nuts, dates, raisins and even semi-dried fruits imbedded in bread-dough are tasty and give life to an already useful staple food. Minimal use of honey as a sweetener is well considered, as excesses of sugar also can build up, again with loss of mental balance caused by chemical interference with mental energy flows.

"Conditions of economic austerity favor proper dietary practices. Therefore, fret not such changes in or to the Earth as will close the market places or interfere much with the transportation of foodstuffs from exotic or far away lands. Eat that which is found locally. Begin to cultivate broad-leaf vegetables and to learn of their flavors. Savor those in your own lawn and garden much as do the nomads. Study of nomadic ways, and observe nomadic practices to learn what one may find and do and thy reward shall be large, great with Peace and Clarity of mind.

"Then, when cometh the Earth turmoil of the late 1990's and early 2000's ye shall not suffer for having prepared thy House [body] for that day. In that day, not so far away, The Lord shall return to enjoy His Own...they who can see and hear and commune with Him. In that day there shall be great rejoicing among those who have prepared themselves for His return. Great tribulation awaits those who have heard but have not yet begun their preparation, for the Preparation Period is apt to consume all the time remaining [but twenty years until the Millennium]. [Cayce, Solomon, Montgomery, et al]."

"When a person has his dietary factors under control, he will need but about four hours of sleep per twenty-four, best spent in two periods of about two hours each, leaving much time for meditation on human Self and its place in the higher aspects of The Universe. We would recommend a balanced program of meditation and exercise as means for best development and Service 'above and below,' as appropriate to the one concerned, coupled with a reasonable program of body exercise for well-rounded maintenance of your body-Temple, to keep it serviceable per the Grand Design."

To which we add our AMEN!

Post Script: Additional information related to diet versus spiritual functioning may be read in Ruth Montgomery's book *Threshold To Tomorrow* in Chapter One, pages 30 to 40. The full effects of dietary content on human performance has not received merited consideration.

CHAPTER FIVE

ABOUT BARRIERS

When a person earnestly attempts to clear his case he can expect to contend with varying degrees of inner resistance. Barriers to contact of painful or festering inner programs seemingly abound in the normal person. Fortunately, every barrier has an electrical equivalent circuit which, if contacted properly, can be employed to enhance "psychic trouble shooting" and alleviation by electrical means, much as in repair of conventional electronics and computer equipment. We found ourselves able to employ parallel concepts for "trouble shooting," for isolation, study and repair of trouble spots, and have included a block diagram to assist.

There may be high "psychological resistance" to entering a heavily troubled area, requiring a "high voltage" or a highly intense level of "desire energy" as subjective pressure to break into it. Low-level or easy entry is accomplished by having the proper computer file address or a psychological key phrase which is not threatening to the client's input sensor protective programming or circuitry, therefore allowing access to the recorded feelings and pictures with minimal ego opposition.

One of the more common blocks or barriers thrown up by the strongly intellectually-oriented client, the "head tripper," is the familiar "cop out." Barriers to feeling which are erected by the head tripper for ego protection frequently extend into partial or even to habitual shutdown of feeling at body level and can account for and be known as the "cold" personality.

Knowledge of the human psyche common to the familiar fakir permits the seeming ability to walk across a bed of hot coals without pain or damage, and to run a needle through a sensitive part of the anatomy without pain. One such capability results from learning to cut neural communication between the mind and the sensory devices governing the concerned part of the body, per the familiar principle of 'Mind over Matter.'

The ability to cut communication can be developed by persons willing to experiment and enables impressive demonstration of the power of the human mind, whether at the unconscious or subconscious levels. The same process can be applied to eliminating the pain of dentist's drills, trauma in childbirth, accident wounds, burns, superstrength and so on, and can be a form of self-induced or autohypnosis.

A method more useful for restoring damaged communications is to learn to confront an event in its *total* aspect when it enables life to be experienced gainfully, rather than being avoided.

Central to the success of this discourse is elucidation on the fact that old programming, whether called Religionist's Demons or the Psychologist's engrams, can be discharged or neutralized by fully reexperiencing the emotional energies contained in each recorded original and related experiences ridding self of them for all time.

The review and release process is done in *Psychological Real Time*. In other words, the event is happening *now*! Sometimes all that is needed for a physical release or response is an outpouring of tears, a siege of physical thrashing around, or perhaps a violent outpouring of defamatory verbalization, or more often, states between those extremes.

Barriers in "feeling" people are created most readily in one's childhood, as when an upset or distraught parent or elder can think of nothing but punishing an unprogrammed child for crying, for spilling the milk, or failing to accomplish any of the myriad of things typically tried with less than total success by the very young. Crying, if properly attended, is often therapeutic in the child as well as in the adult who is fortunate enough to be able to use tears in private, as in counseling sessions or publicly in the so-called adult world, regardless of its social appropriateness.

Frequently observed by the student of human behavior is the formerly over-disciplined child who learned to bottle up his hate and revenge feelings and became oblivious to them, only to find them resurfacing in adult life in some inappropriate act, attitude, or psychosomatic illness. A excellent current publication in this area is Janov's "The Feeling Child." (See References)

When the therapist or counselor is able to find an unguarded entry point into a client's programmed defense patterns and can "trick" the client's egoic sentry or to blow up a few defense-system barriers, subsequent contact in that area becomes increasingly easy. When that condition exists, and when a major block has been removed, the subconscious Programming Department reintegrates and reorganizes itself. Similarly, when a therapist finds an unresolved need and then intellectually and prematurely exposes it to the client before formally attempting processing that area or need, the client's egoic sentry may erect an even stronger or impenetrable barrier to prevent further approach in that sensitive area. Ergo, the wise therapist will be careful to observe much and to speak little, *leading* a client to 'discover' his *own* engrams through knowing what they are and perhaps what to expect.

Some blocks, barriers and engrams are so well buried as to seem impossible to discover, contact and defuse with a direct reverie approach, but yet they are set off by recognized social stimuli. It is usually necessary to begin the search for and release of the hidden explosive charge in a protected area by subtle and prolonged nibbling around that general area, looking for unguarded spots, cracking the foundations by building feeling responses.

Sometimes, acupuncture probes gently inserted into a troubled area will produce the desired contact. This approach also permits "leaking off" the charge, much as discharging an automobile battery over a weak short circuit. When the charge has been dissipated, the old battery plates will still be there but the battery is incapable of supporting a demand for a great burst of defense energy when later called for by the usual stimulus or switch-ON program.

The conclusion to be drawn is that it is only possible to approach and release some barriers and blocks by slow and gentle probes over a long period of time. Indeed, use has been made of little subjective golden darts tossed into a known block for several hours to soften it up enough to allow a Reverie Review. Sometimes it is possible to go in and "hit the panic button" often enough to trigger an explosive primal release, if you know where the panic button is!

How much of what to do depends largely on how much the therapist actually knows about the engram itself, on how well he can remain focussed on it with stability. Success can also depend upon his resources for measuring its intensity, on whether he has and can use brainwave equipment, or an electropsychometer. It also depends upon the nature of the individual barriers and on the susceptibility of the engram to approach—that is, on how well it is protected. Release also can depend upon how much distress the recorded engram is causing the client. Much indeed depends on his level of determination, on how much enthusiastic energy, time and money the client has available to bring to bear upon the problem of release of the engram.

In the attempt to soften up a tough psychological area for entry much value may attend utilization of various forms of inner meditation, perhaps aided by contemporary brainwave analysis equipment used in the Theta range. If a person will dedicate the time and effort, meditation sooner or later will provide the requisite insight and release. Rajah Yoga [King of the Yogas] is available to the public. Kriya Yoga is effective but personal instruction is usually available only through affiliation with the Self Realization Fellowship of Los Angeles. The seeker is adequately supervised, receiving careful attendance and guidance. It is possible for an unaffiliated and unsupervised chela or an unwary beginning student to contract pneumonia through overly-zealous practice of certain yogic breathing exercises. Caution is advised, even when "Practicing the Presence of God."

All methods of meditation require persistent practice. In return, all will eventually bring about essential changes and the required unfoldment for the dedicated student. However, for he who would storm the gates of heaven, s/he who has need for rapid relief and has but little time to devote, we recommend application of the specific technologies of Esoteric Psychology introduced by AAB and as presented herein, working with your Guide(s), as perhaps the fastest route to release now available to incarnate humanity.

This Psychic Psychology Technology seems best to fit the Western temperament. For overall balance, meditation still should be used as an initiator of broad-front and longer-range spiritual unfoldment. To be most effective, meditation is engaged thrice daily. Best times of day include approximately on arising, at high noon, and again between about midnight and two A.M. For many people, doing half an hour of meditation just before going to sleep is an excellent practice. Durations of perhaps fifteen minutes minimum to half an hour maximum each are excellent for most people. Keep the spine vertical to assure that consciousness is not lost in sleep during each period.

WHERE BARRIERS ARE FOUND AND INTERRELATE

The discussion here is referenced to Figure 3. That figure diagrams portion of the human consciousness that have to do with

A Spiritual Psychology For The Aquarian Age

impediments and barriers to energy flows in and out of the chakras, and where the current flows become involved in enabling the typical human to function, to operate in the world of flesh and mind.

Starting at the top, we note inputs from the sensors which connect us to the world around us. These include the functions of Hearing, Smelling, Touch, Seeing, Thought waves, and other ESP signals. In essence we have displayed the chakra system along the top of the diagram, because it is through them that we do or do not communicate with the world of our associates and the world above.

The individual chakras are attached to the spinal column and the endocrine system(s), as can be learned in greater detail in many excellent resource books on Aquarian Age medicine [see Chopra, et al]. If one or more of those chakras is not open fully, or is blocked for whatever reason, the entire human incarnate structure and system is handicapped. Note that the Sensor System output signals are shown going to a box called "Sensor thresholds." It is here that we do or do not communicate, or are permitted to interact with the world about us. Some persons will appear much less sensitive to stimuli of a particular sort, while others, having their Sensor System tuned up or opened up in that area, can seemingly do miracles. The thresholds we imply here have to do with the level we have programmed or allow, or can accept. In the presence of a high threshhold, it takes a loud or strong stimulus to cause us to respond. In some cases we have shut off the sensor so we shall not be bothered by the clamor from a particular area or function. Many persons have shut off their ESP Sensors so they can focus their attention on their immediate physical universe and life problems. Their sensitivities usually can be readjusted.

Those same sensor threshold controls are branched and sent to the *EGO* when some predetermined threshold has been exceeded. It is then the option of the *EGO* to decide whether and how to respond. In some cases there is also a level of attention which, by previous automatic caretaking activity is overridden, so the *EGO* has opportunity to attend only the major operations and activities.

When it is determined that a particular response or reaction is to be taken, the corresponding Program is activated, so that automatic bone and muscular activity is initiated to cope with the trouble. Note that it is also possible for muscle action to be inhibited at will, and also for the body functions to be sent up to the sensors and inhibit them from accepting any further input. Hypnosis fits that description for us, when we *decide* to relinquish control from our little or Personality ego to another Personality ego.

We add here that once control has been relinquished to the exterior *Ego* it is possible to program almost anything into the original program files, and to interfere with others already present.

Once a program has been activated, it will usually run its course unless overridden again consciously by the Personality *Ego* The program activates those bones and muscles and processes using them, as appropriate. The fundamental problem is then that of gaining feedback even while the programs are running. He or she who is on top of the battle scene is then usually able to do a more credible job and win oftener than they who fight only from their program(s). And of course, it is important to note that it is always possible for a program to be triggered into activity under false or inappropriate circumstances. It is these latter programs that we usually need to find and remove. In the process of finding and releasing them it will usually be necessary to relive the trauma which were the cause for creating the programs, usually defense or sometimes attack programs, to prevent or cope with future complications in the world of relationships.

Every line connecting two boxes is a fitting place to find barriers to the flow of signals, controls, and commands in the body-mind complex. Of course, the Real-Life diagram of the Human is more complicated, but the Figure 3 offers places to hang what we are trying to tell you, well enough to guide you in understanding the nature of our processing structures and how they all fit together.

CHAPTER SIX

HANDLING PSYCHIC INTERFERENCE

Here we treat a phenomenon originating in the Chakra system, especially from the first center to the fifth. Persons trained in transveil communication (with Spirit) recognize where their feelings, thoughts, spoken words, and intuitions come from and communicate intelligently at any or all of those levels. Not being trained to recognize what is happening permits the phenomenon of psychic interference. Unwanted effects are commonly observed in the mass confusion of World mind, evident in the middle East, in the major political capitals of the world, and distressingly so even among the general populace of Brazil and even in the United States of America.

Whence cometh this mental confusion, this cross-purposeness of psychic dimension, and from whence comes the designation 'psychic interference?' What need we to know and to do about it?

Looking into the dictionary for meanings and applications of the word "psychic" is to discover *Psyche* as the mythological Greek Goddess of Mind, of soul or the mental life, and that aspect of interconnectedness by which *all* mankind is united on an unconscious level. In addition to the Personality mind we humans experience our deeper interrelationships to each other through Race mind and Divine Mind, that is, through individual subconscious mind connected via our superconscious minds.

Forms of psychic communication include hearing voices from people or sources who are not physically present! Another is to carry on 'head talk' with other incarnates who may be inches, or many miles away! One way that Spirit gets *our* Earth-mind attention is to cause the telephone to ring loudly, waking you or me from a deep sleep, except that nobody else hears it, and your telephone recorder is not activated! Not all such psychic communication may be desired unless controlled.

Not all members of Humankind are equally awake, and except for audible communication using mouth and ear, Man is not yet aware of its extended nature. Nor is man aware of the extent to which thought energy from the environment and from Race mind courses through his chakras or brain-mind aspect. He is sometimes aware that Thoughts flit through his mind, but unaware of how much his emotions are steered from outside himself. Few people, contrasted to the multitudes who have heard of telepathy, are aware of how often their moods and general attitudes are established telepathically, subliminally or subconsciously by a thought held strongly and/or persistently or projected to them, whether it originates in the immediate vicinity or not. If the nature of a powerful thought-form is such as to trigger a sympathetic or subjective response or pattern into the psyche of anyone in the vicinity, it is powerful enough to set the general tone for an entire area. Anyone in the area is likely to be mentally and/or emotionally subject to fall victim to the prevalent mental thought pattern...unless strongly self-determined or is unusually self-aware.

There are beings, incarnate or discarnate, of little, average, or high motivation, who are aware of the above possible use of mind. Many use their knowledge fully, consciously and deliberately to control the minds and actions of their peers and associates on a wide scale and in several dimensions. In the U.S.A., for example, deliberate use is made of subliminal suggestion by the Communications media to influence the minds and actions of key segments of the population, as well as of entire sectors of Earth. Conscious application of mind control technology is widely practiced for national and international political and economic gain, or to foment discontent and rebellion. The depth of an economic recession tends partly to be the result of collective attitudes which reflect the intensity of the views held by the affected populace. Retrenchment from free trade follows naturally upon the lack of individual willingness or ability to participate with trust in "The System," and yet in its turn The System consists of the aggregate of collective thought and attitude. Therefore, *individual* attitude can be and is manipulated to feed upon *collective* attitude in large measure.

Just look at the money and time spent in building *image* by everyone from food venders to senators and statesmen! The psychic interference process follows a *law* which is non-evaluative of good or bad intentions, and therefore is responsive equally to thoughts and powerful thoughtforms originated by saint and sinner alike. Then...when an aware person or being determines to spread an

A Spiritual Psychology For The Aquarian Age

attitude or doctrine, he does so easily over a wide area through the simple expedient of a thought strongly held, or even by a weaker thought held with constancy over a sufficiently long period of time by a group of like-minded beings. As those nearby simpler souls of uncontrolled intellect intercept and accept those mentally impinged fields and their contents, the original thought or attitude is multiplied in strength, increasing exponentially in power as it gains adherents. Eventually the *original* thought or attitude becomes the prevailing thought, and whole nations or/and mobs can be moved to action accordingly.

Thus it is that initially small movements like Christianity and Communism gain adherents. When a few minds agree consciously upon a principle or an attitude, and dwell upon it, "mind waves" or psychic entities known as "Thought Forms" are quite literally created and energized. Sometimes these become ensouled by Elemental Spirit(s) and when released or launched, find adherents the world over, far beyond the simple physical confines of the originating group mind [16].

Another indication of the subtle but powerfully pervasive Mind Control process at work is the simultaneous occurrence the world over of particular inventions, one such being the invention of radio in the minds of Popov in the U.S.S.R., by Marconi in Italy, and by others in the U.S.A. Other group-mind action would include the automobile, airplane, video games, and so on.

Divine Intervention could account for the simultaneous appearance and wide acceptance of timely and innovative ideas. However, such simultaneity by Divine Intervention, while existent, is of less frequent occurrence than might be expected; We Guides believe and hold as our "official upstairs policy" that the affairs of man shall be left in the hands of man, except where certain trends need to be initiated, countermanded or averted.

We are able even to prevent the recurrence and spread of certain ideas formerly well known and widespread over the ancient Earth, like the great Atlantean Crystal, which would solve your present and long-term energy crisis. However, to resurrect certain anciently discovered principles would probably lead again to near worldwide destruction by the hand of Man as it did in earlier prehistory (Read Edgar Cayce on the great Atlantean crystal and other technologies). Until that time when Man is again ready for an infusion of such ideas by having generated within himself sufficient degrees of the traits of compassion and concern, We Who are responsible for Planet earth shall prevent rediscovery of those simple but powerful ideas. If necessary, we would prefer to let Man go back to his recent agrarian existence rather than to see our last habitable planet destroyed. Such is the power of external thought control and manipulation over Earth.

Perhaps the greatest protection the world population has is its own lack of ability to hold and stay focussed long term on any thought, even and unless the thought touches upon some fundamental need or injustice, as when economic and social inequities are so great as to be able to generate mob response. The less developed and controlled is the mind in any human being or society of like humans, the more susceptible it is to control by those in whom mind *is* well developed and disciplined. The world political, religious and economic structures stay in power by use of that very same principle, controlling the mass mind via its public communications medium by coloring, releasing and withholding information accordingly and effectively.

Now...a being, incarnate or discarnate who is *aware* of the Laws of mind can utilize that Law for *any purpose whatsoever*. Being a *law*, it is as dispassionate as the Law of Gravity. The Laws of Thought (Boole, Korzybski, et al) as such are now widely used for attracting potentially supportive persons, one after another, creating situations and circumstances desired or feared.

Like attracts like. Strength draws support. Weakness attracts confusion and exploitation. "Verily I say unto you: unto him who *has*, more shall be given. From him who has *not*, even that which he has shall be taken away from him." This restatement as a Law of Thought has been adapted from Matthew, 13:12.

To free one's self from such pervasive subliminal subversion and exploitation one must become a stable point of reference in a sea of confusion. To be a master of Self is to rise above the noise of the Race mind, and up out of frustration and non-accomplishment. To do this it is possible...nay *vital*...that one examine his entire subliminal mental-psychological structure, his entire system of conscious and subconscious beliefs and attitudes. Only in that way does one identify whose thought and feelings he is experiencing, gradually learning the art of *conscious* non-resistance in the face of undesirable mental fields, principalities and powers [Ephesians 6:12].

Here lies the way to freedom from psychic interference of *any* kind and every sort and source, person or institution. Building more barriers or mental blocks to reduce sentience to such communications is to reduce one's inherent ability to function in our mental universe. Better then by far to learn to *confront* Thought and Feeling, trusting Intuition and responding consciously only as it is to the advantage of the recipient...to *you*...to do so.

DIAGNOSTICS

CHAPTER SEVEN
INSIGHTS ON FUNDAMENTAL MAN

"We were discoursing on arrangements which need to be made in order to enable The Big Three of Religion, Psychology, and various manifestations of Mental Health Disciplines once again to become effective in fulfilling the charters originally sequentially given them, which, of course, was spiritual guidance and alleviation of the ills of Mankind. Their task is simple when properly done, but long ago any such simplicity was lost when We, as incarnate Teachers and Prophets, withdrew from the Earth into the Heavens.

"It is no longer possible for any particular member of the Laity to address members of those hierarchies (The Big Three) to ask simple questions and to receive simple answers. Many of the questioned individuals lack an in-depth understanding of fundamental truth about the nature of the human being. The problem arose long long ago, not then being a product of the Twentieth Century, but having been openly in evidence as long ago as Atlantean times. In that fargone era we decided to leave the Earth plane for better pastures, since many of us had, by then, discovered the nature of the Earth plane and its attractions sufficiently well so that we could see the payoff. It was clear, even then, that entrapment was the end-product of random living down there. We had little difficulty in determining where lay our best plan of action.

"Rather than being able immediately to leave our bodies and depart, we had first to invent ways to become "clear" ourselves. We then had to put them into practice before we could become freed from Schoolhouse-Earth's attractions so we could graduate, forever thereafter to remain up here. We and several associates decided to take ourselves in hand and actually buckled down to the task of self-mastery and liberation.

"The methods by which we became liberated were recorded in papyrus, stone, clay tablets, and the Akasha, were published and widely taught, and for a time were put into action by many among you even now present in flesh. That includes yourself, for you too were incarnate among us at the time. Those records and activities were the original of the Ancient Wisdoms, and became the early religions, the repositories of all the knowledge of the human soul and the incarnate human spirit. Embodying all that had been discovered about the soul, it was complete enough so that We had no difficulty understanding what had to be done to overcome the powerful pulls on undeveloped Mind by the attractiveness of the games which still flourish down there. You may be amazed to find that there is nothing, absolutely nothing at all, that you are doing in this present time on Earth that we have not experienced. You Earthlings are still trapped in what we decided, yes, *decided*, to abandon *long* ago, but We *did it*, and *so can you*!

"If you and your fellow Earthlings would similarly determine to free yourselves, you could do so in a generation, or within the lifetime remaining for most of you. The time remaining is sufficient for whomsoever will take it upon himself to learn of us, of our methods, put them into practice, make great gains, and to overcome.

"A person's accumulated Karma need not stand in the way of fulfillment of the purposes of Life at all even when it is considered that interpersonal karmic relationships are still the primary reason for interrelating at all down there. Other reasons include gaining experience in the Principles of Love, the abandonment of greed and sexual lasciviousness, and the attainment of Mental Growth via practice in use of the abstract Laws of the Mind. Humanity would learn that Earth is ideal for experiencing what is not really possible nor practical for Man, as now being constituted, to learn Up Here in a discarnate state. While it is possible for anyone built in the Image and Likeness of God to learn the lessons originally intended, we do not see it as being the usual lot to experience Earth without having become addicted to one or more of its joys and pleasures.

"There is so much astral junk-energy or desire-stuff on the planes of Earth Life that we are amazed when anyone decides to leave the Earth plane. That usually does not happen until a person has become so enamored of physical life that he forgets where he is and gets over-committed, whence trouble really begins to manifest. In other words, when man loses his identity as Children of God he begins to work outside the Laws of Life and reaps accordingly.

"It is not that there are insufficient strengths built into genus Homo Sapiens where lie the fundamental causes of his downfall. Rather, it is along the lines of parting with one's Source, forgetting one's basic affiliation and purpose, where lies the cause of the Fall of man. Man, as originally built, is able to manage the pleasures of the Earth plane, because experienced equally, everything is pleasure. But Time does strange things to the values-perception capability of the mind. The payoff for Earth-life discipline is seldom recognized immediately in any particular line of activity. That factor alone is sufficiently disarming so that no immediate punishment is felt for having transgressed in any way, so that the possibility of any long-term payoff or settling of accounts ceases to be recognized. There, we too, as well as your own self and acquaintances, have fallen victim to the indefinite or delayed payoff.

"Divine Punishment per se was not the intended result of transgressive action down there, but what is important is the fact, but seldom recognized, that punishment manifests cumulatively as *loss of freedom*. It lies in that direction, recognizing the threat of loss of further freedom, that lies your own best incentive for controlling, or even of desiring to control your own destiny. When it is finally recognized that specific lines of action result in lessened future privileges or pleasure, then and only then do we see Mankind coming around to take charge of himself. Therein lies the clue to begin emancipation of the Human Race. Without following up on that particular clue there would be no salvation! Then let us delve further into those methods of rescue and salvation!"

CHAPTER EIGHT
MORE ON THE NATURE OF THOUGHT

"Thought is a most peculiar process, with energized thoughtforms as the essence or product of thinking. The usual thinking by free association is little beyond scanning records held in mind. Creative thought, seldom experienced by the typical human, is a synthesis of integrating existing thought forms with intuitively derived insights to provide new answers to old (or new) problems. Because mind is Universal, the Thinker is not necessarily limited to Planet Earth and its resources. To be useful, Thought is provided means whereby spirit is enabled to contact and make use of certain material aspects of the Universe that are required for *spirit* to create effects in the dense or matter aspect of Creation, to play and to build.

"Stated in another way, nascent spirit has only *being*ness. For it to become *functional*, to be at cause-point and create effects in any lower plane, it must have a substantive means to *communicate* Energies and manipulate Matter.

"The Human was designed and experimental models were developed via incorporation of lessons learned on evolving various other Life Kingdoms of earlier milieus. The biggest problem The Creators faced was to formulate means enabling Spirit to influence matter, to perfect a method whereby Spirit could make matter conform to its dictates.

"In other words, some sort of transducer was required to enable energy from the higher-frequency realms of Consciousness to flow into the lower frequencies of physical Consciousness. We identify that ultimate transducer as *mind*. *Mind*, and only *mind* has the ability to intermediate for a spirit throughout the full range of life frequencies from stone to throne, so to speak. However, for mind-stuff to be able to control the material aspect of the Universe, it was first necessary to have infused *life* into every material aspect of our now mental-material Universe.

"In other words, it was necessary to infuse matter with Life, i.e., with the latent dimensions or elements of *consciousness*. Thus, all in the Universe is alive and imbued with consciousness of varying degree, from the atom on up through stone, plants and vegetables (AAB, *Consciousness of the Atom.*).

"The nature of fundamental matter is most readily understood by visualizing the basic molecular structure of Hydrogen, in itself a wondrous substance, as it is constantly being created out in free space and is thought therefore to be the original Force that causes the Universe to expand. All other molecules of matter throughout this galaxy, about 135 different kinds of them, are variations of the basic Hydrogen atom. The complex structures of the heavier molecules are vibrating at lower and lower rates relative to the basic Hydrogen atom.

"Through integration of the seven superimposed spiritual bodies of the human, the desired activity of 'spirit in matter' has so far resulted in the perfection of the fleshy bodies you and I know as the Human Race. We humans differ from our little brethren of the animal kingdom mostly in our degree of evolved *mind* or consciousness.

"Following the successful marriage of Spirit and matter in the Human, it was necessary that Spirit acquire experience in learning how to function in matter. It has taken us all of Time since Creation to develop conscious control of our presently exhibited capacity for thought. And before we as Units of Humanity have "earned the right" to return to the Heavens as having overcome and mastered the various addictions to Earth embodiment, we shall have developed certain strengths in the employment of its various intermediary higher vehicles as well. Along with Love, Wisdom, Integrity and Compassion these strengths include the ability to direct and to control our individual application of intuitive consciousness. Perhaps the most difficult of all lessons, we must become emotionally stable and one-pointed in our conscious use of mind as a Creative Power.

"As Man learns to be sufficiently perceptive, as have a few forerunners of the Human Race, he will see for himself that on an individual basis, he uses Thought as the medium by which he maintains control over all the recordings made in his own memory units or cells, and of others who also use those same cells similarly. He will become aware that he has the gift of Intuition and Telepathy as aspects of *Mind* through which he contacts other Beings, as well as with the universal recordings of All-Time represented as the Akasha.

"Akasha is a word of Sanskrit origin and implies "mind recordings," having been known even 58,000 years before our meager recorded history [records of the prehistoric and pre-Atlantean periods were destroyed in the great library fire in Alexandria during the Roman conquest of Egypt]. The development and nurturing of mind is then worthy of all the care and dedication of which mankind is capable. Without proper use of mind, Man is little more than a neurotic animal. With the ability to use mind, he can contact any part or aspect of the Universe, traveling and gaining access to all the places and knowledge contained therein. He assumes the Image of his Divine Creator.

"Before we leave the subject of the birth and development of *mind*, let us consider a related frame of reference.

"Mind has another aspect, sometimes labelled in the religious frames of reference as *soul*. Spirit operating in Matter does so via the mechanism of the religionist's *soul*, thus giving substance to the concept of the Triune Being. In tangible ways, then, it can be considered true that we *are* made in the image and likeness of our Creators; the Father concept, the Great Spirit of the American Indians, worked in the Original Substance, "of which all things are made that are made" [St. John 1:3]. The substance is called "The Holy Ghost," in which He synthesized and gave birth to HIS Creative thoughtforms. By analogy to our galaxy, we can indeed be considered representative of the physical body of God, in a much larger and more powerful sense than normally accepted.

"The creative process supports analogy for Human understanding that the religionist's Trinity is duplicated in the Human Body, Soul and mind. Our human level of performance at this time then bears a scaled resemblance to that Trinity, reflecting our fitness for functioning at this present level of Life. When we shall have developed *mind* and *soul* sufficiently, we can rejoin our Creators at their higher level of manifestation, in Spirit, in a body less dense than that offered and required by Earth life [9, 16].

"Let it still be remembered that we are obliged by the Theory of Rebirth [reincarnation] to stay on or to return to Earth only as long as we require it to learn our few lessons. Then, with acquisition of this new concept, let us be about our proper business, that of clearing and building more effective means for the development and nurturing of *mind, soul,* and associated qualities, using whichever label and reference system you prefer.

"It is found that there is a Law of mind, and a related Law of Thought told of in both the New Testament and the Old Testament of the Christian Bible. These have to do with the power inherent in Thought well-formed in Mind Stuff and firmly held over suitable periods of Time. As it is found in *any* beginning, a thought firmly held will manifest in the physical plane sooner or later, in direct accord with the power, the clarity, the stability, and the duration in which it is held by The Thinker. In the Old Testament, Job is quoted as having said, "That which I feared has come upon me." [Job 3:25] Other Biblical references to the conscious use of thought can be found by the user of a Concordance [see Strong]. The O.T. has expressed it several ways also, but perhaps the most easily understood and certainly best known, is "As a Man thinketh in his Heart, so is he" [Proverbs 23:7]. Perhaps equally well known is the admonition, "Where two or more are gathered together in my Name, it shall be done unto you" [Matthew 18:20] and "whatsoever they ask, it shall be done unto them" [John 14:14]. In our use of biblical symbology, "name" means "nature of."

"In other words, a thought held strongly, reinforced as by several other minds joined in maintaining that thoughtform shall surely manifest in its kind. We are now dealing with a fundamental and potent LAW, which may be seen to be an impersonal *process*, used with equal effectiveness by the Just and the Unjust alike.

"When observing the effects of collective human thought, held in the Race Mind as presently manifest on Earth, all seems to appear as chaos, to be random with respect to any common goals with the sole exceptions of concern for food, sex, and death. We find human Thought, per the Bible, is a power available to all, equally in principle if not in fact. Each Thinker, whether neophyte or expert, will probably have developed different levels of ability to use his portion of Universal mind in and of which his mind is but an interrelating element.

"Then *clearing thought forms* from the mind becomes a most important function if a person is to rise above traditional human limitations, aches, and trauma!

"We see concentrated use of mind when technological, economic or political groups band together consciously for accomplishment of some specific purpose. Each member adds his little mental powerhouse to the total mental power of the group. When group objectives are formulated coherently in mind, and are stated precisely, such as were the founding principles in the Constitution of the United States of America, those principles become increasingly powerful. The *thought power* of our Founding Fathers is abetted by the minds of a nation of similarly dedicated followers, supporters, and thinkers. As a nation, the United States of America shall maintain a position of world leadership only as long as we cling individually to the vision and value system built into our hearts and our Constitution..

"These examples indicate the power in the idea of focussed thought on attainment of some goal. One then recognizes that the collective force of the Mental Universe is thus totally responsive to a clearly defined purpose, and that the randomness of thought loosely held elsewhere is subservient to strongly held *group* thought.

"Thus we have seen several applications of the Laws of Thought as used in the Realm of Human mind to have been taught and practiced with success in Biblical times, and practiced in the founding of the U.S.A. We find it as well in evidence throughout History at the Bastille Rebellion in old France, when some *Cause Celebre* captures the minds of a large number of people. We saw it again during the Gold Rush days in the U.S.A., and even when some fool shouts *"Fire!"* in a crowded theater, or when fear precipitates a rush on the banks and creates instant panic as during the early 1930's Depression in the U.S.A.

"There is additionally another realm in which the same fundamental law is expressed, but in other units and perhaps in other dimensions. In the science of electrical communication, performance of a television channel is partially characterized from the ratio of coherent signal power to the noise power in the channel. In Psychic Psychology, Signal Power is directly related to consciously purposeful Thought Power, considering that Thought Power *does* have strength when it is clearly and coherently formulated. Electrical noise power is analogous to random thought power, having little or no common coherent or purposeful reference. Then random thought is indeed the analog of random electrical noise in terms of Cause and Effect, opening doors for our approach to handling the lower mind.

"In other words, in electronics, when the mathematical correlation process is applied and a small but self-consistent signal is overlaid with itself repeatedly, the coherent signal power adds linearly, while the noise power in the same channel adds randomly (or root mean square), thus creating an increasingly higher ratio of signal power to noise power. The greater that ratio, the greater is the possible idea or data communications rate, and the lesser is the probability of error in the messages sent. By the Law of Analogy, we can express processes of each discipline in terms of *one* mathematical law. That one law is Universal, differing only as the variable quantity's units change, and thus should be expected to relate effects in the Universe of mind to effects in the Universe of Electrical Communication through the kinship of their adjoint processes, no matter what mental or psychic planes are in use.

"Because we are legitimately entitled to be drawing together these two observed processes as deriving from a common source, ANY thought dwelled upon consistently in the presence of the randomness of the world population's thought helps explain the mechanism for fulfillment of *our* observations, of what *we* dwell upon. It now awaits some interested Social Scientist to formulate laws of mass behavior based upon appropriate applications of the associated Laws of Thought in terms of Statistical Entropy.

"Thought, then, has *power*, works by knowledgeable *law*, and its proper use must therefore be mastered by he who would accomplish anything of lasting value on any level in this Universe.

"*We have made our case!* Then he or she who masters Mind can master anything else. We have used mathematical and scientific principles and logic to prove statements observed and recorded in the Bible! Then that which interferes with clear use of one's mind must be rooted out, reviewed, and corrected or eliminated.

"Dwell on your case cleaned up and give thanks that it is done!" Mark II: 22, 23, 24 is a Biblical paraphrase credited to The Christ in answer to a query on how to pray. We too are dealing with the same Universal Laws you are. To succeed in this Universe we have but to learn the Laws of our Being, becoming expert in applying them, including the Law of mind, in our daily lives.

"We aver that what you may have known as "Prayer" constitutes a powerful, even if seemingly gentle, application of the Power of Mind. When the Conscious mind is aligned with the Subconscious mind, we have available the fulfillment of the criterion "where two are gathered together" [Matthew 18:20] for potency in use of that given Law of Functioning in all our interrelationships on a grand scale. You thus have known the right words all along, and have heard them come from the pulpit all our lives, little suspecting the tremendous potency available in them. Perhaps we have not been familiar enough with terminology, with the meaning of which we are here offering.

"Now that we have reaffirmed the Power of Mind and of the necessity for control of individual thought, and for observation of our feelings as processes in the individual Human, you have tools with which to work. It is now your personal responsibility to take charge of unraveling your own case. Each person is ultimately responsible for obtaining salvation from his own misuse of the Power of Thought, having now been shown the fundamental processes involved.

"Fear not to apply what has been heard and seen above. Rather determine to study and to practice its application in your life. The element of *decision* is now all that is required, sustained by lifelong follow-through. Individual christing is your reward!

"Then *Bon Voyage*! The Universe and an Abundant Life await your success. We shall be happy to aid you in your quest. Unseen though we be, we yet are able to abet you with constant gentle reminders of your goal, for *your* goal is now *our* goal, which is the release of Mankind from the trap of limited visibility and understanding. You have access to the Power of the Universe to aid you, for you are aligned with the purposes of God, as are We.

"Amen."

CHAPTER NINE
ON BECOMING TRANSFORMED

"Repent Ye...be Ye transformed by the renewing of your mind" [Romans 12:2].

How often have you heard that command...and have you ever wondered how to do it? Do you know anyone who has done it, or who is even trying to find out how? This is an age-old instruction, but who has taken the trouble to determine what it means?

The Nazarene also is credited with having admonished His Disciples to "Go forth and preach the gospel and heal the sick" [Matthew 10:7]. Few of the conventional religions seem able or minded these days to comply. However, we are of the opinion that The Master of masters would not have issued such commands unless it were possible and expected of attainment. Then perhaps there is some way in which we humans fall short in our understanding or in our approach, preventing compliance with His dictum.

Some people say Jesus was able to do these things only because He healed with a Higher Source. We *do* hear quite a bit these days about spiritual healing, or faith healings, medical healings, naturopathic healing, healing of the memories, psychological healings, remote healings, and healing by laying on of hands. We call them the 'Healing Arts,' being unable to find clear-cut definitions and/or differentiations of methods that will stand so-called scientific scrutiny, or find general acceptance. Many medical healings are difficult to reduce to scientific laws, often treating the symptoms by herbs, pills and formulae, doctors recognizing some other "Healing Force" besides the knife or the pill. We all appear to be working with a Beneficent Force, aiding in creating favorable conditions for "It" to work.

Why do we not hear more about *cures*? Many healings seem at best temporary, so what IS healing? Perhaps we should look at our criteria for determining who or what is sick, and look even closer at what sickness is, and at what it is *not*.

We seem to have good general agreement that a victim of bronchial pneumonia or leukemia is "pretty sick." We generally write off a morning-after hangover victim as "merely indisposed." We agree that a broken leg is not an illness or a sickness, but an injury, still meriting special attention. Traditionally, we admire the loyal hard working "always on the job" person who never has a sick day in his/her life as some sort of an ideal, as a paragon. But what if that paragon goes home and kicks the dog, or abuses family members, whether with words, attitudes, or with actual blows? We seem to agree that there is a malady of some sort, even if we disagree on how to effect a cure!

And there is the Psychopath, and the Schizoid personality. And what about the person who is perpetually afraid for his life, or who is afraid of losing his/her job, of being passed over for promotion, or who is extremely jealous? Are not these persons in need of help, perhaps sicker than any of the previous and simpler cases? How about the ulcer victim? Many people fit these circumstances, but we do not yet accept them as normal, as par for members of the human race.

Perhaps there is a tie-in here with the biblical admonition regarding "renewal of the mind" of Romans 12:2. Let us briefly explore implications that there may be a correlation between misuse of mental process and what we might call social indispositions, physical distress, ailments, and epidemic illnesses of the body or/and mind.

Increasingly, leaders in contemporary psychology and medicine recognize a definite relationship between subconscious thought and attitude patterns with body-level or psychosomatic manifestations [Ashby, Chopra]. Clear correlation has been established between personality types or attitudes and ulcerated stomachs, for example. Many popular publications present articles pointing up the cause-effect link of attitudes and over-eating of the wrong foodstuffs, calling attention to the body-mind downward spiral of obesity. If not reversed, obesity leads further to diabetes, followed by cataracts and blindness, accelerating further bodily disintegration and often to an untimely death. The Reader may have observed these processes in his own family or circle of friends.

Some doctors readily admit that they have neither the time nor much incentive to treat causes, as the usual patient is poorly cooperative. There is getting to be too much for one M.D. to know in depth, with a corresponding rise in groups of specialists. Therefore, about the best an overworked M.D. can do is to practice medicine in his specialty, treating the side effects as they are recognized.

"Alternative Medicine" has caught the attention of a few researchers among the A.M.A. Especially noted at this writing are Doctors Deepak Chopra, A. Stoll, Richard Gerber, McGrady and Kubler-Ross, examining the entire Human as a complex of chemicals and electrical fields, integrated and operated by the human Spirit. They are making significant if not fascinating progress in learning how to experience perfect lifelong health. Their work has dimensions seemingly consistent with the biblical injunction to transform the mind. But we need a better understanding of what *Mind* is! Evidently it is much more encompassing than we humans had believed!

Avant Garde psychologists Janov, Perls and Sutphen have developed effective and interesting methods for obtaining substantial relief from recorded mental root-causes, accelerating obtaining the "clear" mind that eventually leads to and marks an integrated or whole being. The late Dr. Fritz Perls made his breakthrough in Gestalt Therapy. Janov made remarkable strides in treating clients with his "Primal Therapy." Both men triggered a ground swell of successful parapsychological-imitators. And before they came along, L. Ron Hubbard started the popular Dianetics movement about the year 1950, now expanded into the worldwide Scientology movement.

The Truth about Homo Sapiens may thus be seen to have many facets, no one contemporary source or channel thereof possessing it all. Truth is then where you find it, and may be recognized as that which is true for *you*. A few religionists are beginning to explore and promulgate a similar message. Earnest Holmes, founder of the Church of Religious Science, teaches proper recognition of the interrelationships between the spiritual, mental and physical aspects of Man. Mary Baker Eddy's Christian Science Church also teaches Quimby's views of these body-mind interfaces from the vantage point of Man as an element of the mind of God. Gifted individuals Ambrose and Olga Worral and Oral Roberts document highly successful *cures* through invocation and prayer, and laying on of hands, yet disclaiming personal participation other than to being channels for a Higher Energy or Power.

Some claim that The Higher Power is impersonal and is available to all who learn to use it for good as well as for "not so good" purposes. The above trio and other agencies are strongly united on the point of view that said Power works through *law*. They aver that most people use that Law unconsciously and therefore improperly. As a traceable result, they bring upon themselves the ills of which they so obviously suffer. And yet, people blame an improvident Deity rather than their own lack of understanding of how Deific Law works, through their individual misuse of Mind.

The interested person can prove this for himself. Many books, secular and religious, discuss use of "The Power" that is available to *every* human being. Popular works include Dr. C. G. Osborne's book *You Are In Charge*, Emmet Fox's *Stake Your Claim*, Robert Schuler's *Possibility Thinking* Terry Cole-Whittaker's San Diego-based television ministry, and long-standing Norman Vincent Peale's *The Power of Positive Thinking*. Proper and sustained use of that Power tips the scales of the typical Human-Humanoid experience to victory over Life down there on Earth. If you cannot find ready answers from these popular authors, consult other philosophical resources listed in the bibliography. Perhaps the most profound are works by A. A. Bailey and those by H. P. Blavatsky. That old standby, The Bible, says, "Ask and Ye shall receive," and "Ask aright, giving thanks that you have already received that which ye ask and it shall be done unto you" [Matthew 7:7]. Whether the "Power" or the "Law" is personal or impersonal, the results are available to every seeker, but work best when used consciously.

Several psychic or mind-related approaches to alleviating distress include so-called "Faith Healing," or "Healing by Laying on of Hands," and "Absent Treatment." Each is widely practiced with demonstrable success. Perhaps first documented in the Bible, such methods of healing are increasingly recorded in the annals of growing charismatic or/and religious groups. Psychological and physiological healings persist among New Age groups in spite of quasi-official doctrine that The Church has lost such gifts. And yet the Bible itself is replete with healings by Touch, the Spoken Word, and by other simple acts involving belief or faith, indicating that such should be commonplace in contemporary society.

Each of these methods recognizes the element of participation of Spirit in or for their workings. Both the Healer as the Channel of Healing and the Recipient of the healing process and energies are required to accept, i.e., to 'believe,' or *know* the possibilities and their effectiveness. Per mark 9:23 "It is done unto you as you *believe*" [Mark 9:23]. Apparently the word "belief" must be related to "experience," or to some meaning stronger than its conventional interpretation! The biblical "As a Man thinketh in his heart" also requires further consideration, in that the phrase "thinketh in his heart" refers to what is programmed in the *subconscious mind* of the Believer, rather than to an intellectually accepted or verbalized 'lip service' or to the heart muscle itself.

In contemporary mental health literature. the *heart* of which the Bible speaks is becoming increasingly accepted as the subconscious or "inner mind" of the Homo Sapiens. A person need not be a psychic, just skilled even a little bit in human relationships to "read" rather quickly what is transpiring in that "heart" of his fellow communicant. Even without using the principles of Neuro Linguistic Programming he can gain insight rather quickly into another person's programming, knowing what it probably will produce in the outer life of that other person.

Then, to be a skilled Primal Facilitator, Therapist, Pastoral Counselor, Marriage Counselor, Transactional Analyst, or any other of the variously titled mental health practitioners, one must soon learn to discern and identify enough of a client's inner workings to know how to help the client to begin helping himself, and thusly to make socially-significant or transformational changes in the client and hence relevant to that client's personal world.

For some of our readers, the key to understanding and using much of the above may be more readily recognized if put in Biblical phraseology. The Christ is quoted as having said, "Repent Ye" [Acts 3:19]. Theological interpretations of what was meant by that short admonition do indeed abound, even though action in accord with the resulting understanding seems uniformly less than alacritous.

According to Webster's Collegiate Dictionary, "repent" has the connotations of regret, contrition, and revision of one's attitudes, conduct, or actions. To be truly of lasting value, changes must be accomplished on the level of the subconscious mind, i.e., in one's programming. Perhaps the most rapid change possible is to discharge the energy in counterproductive programming or recorded engrams, because the original experience is not negated or lost.

What seems to be missing when most people go about trying to repent as a way of renewing their mind is recognition that their reactions seldom originate from conscious mind considerations alone, but are controlled directly from their subconscious programing, lodged in their 'heart' or programs. Therefore, change should not be expected until the person becomes no longer a slave to his automatic stimulus-response patterns, these which reside below the decision-making level of mind. If people *really* seek understanding of and on these points, they can *know the truths* that will set them free, per John 8:32. That promised transformation by renewal of their programs is available to anyone who sincerely desires it, with all his heart, soul, and mind.

This particular example of biblical backup offers further evidence that the scribes of our Ancient Wisdoms were perhaps better informed about the causes and removal or modification of unworthy character traits than those many seminarians who today seek to establish and legislate how the originally intended meanings shall be interpreted.

Our social code has made most religious people uncomfortable using professional psychological help and methods to rid themselves of their troublesome traits. Through centuries of flawed doctrine they have come to believe that to have any sort of psychological distress means they are demon possessed or influenced by principalities and powers, all "things of the devil." Alas, many people fear social ostracism from admitting that they have any personality problems at all. One would think that the Christian churches would espouse the more esoteric meanings contained in the very teachings of The Master upon Whose Life they claim to be based. Instead, some seminaries openly train their pastors that the above formulae for release by transformation of the mind are of the devil. Others teach that such methods died with the Disciples.

Doctoral dissertations continue to be written, and Master of Divinity degrees are still awarded on studies of the characteristics of the human spirit. As if to seek proof that we humans are not responsible for our frailties, these learned researches often are biassed to show that *our* assertions of psychosomatic or psychological healings made were indeed lost to the church, scarcely speculating upon possible causes for such loss. Instead, each such thesis is used to bolster further the positions held by the prelates and their supporters and superiors that each of them is correct as defended and even by the latest dissertative rehash of that tired theme. It is interesting to note how widely healings occurring within the Charismatic Movement cut across denomination lines and controvert the very assertions of those same doctoral theologians and seminarians.

At the root of the difficulty in clinically verifying attainment of the promised transformation is perhaps an inadequate understanding of the principles and promises involved in making any changes to or within the human psyche. Even inside the psychological perspective there is a fundamental lack of understanding of that which is not known about the human soul, and since so much is not recognized it is not acknowledged to exist in the first place.

To enhance resolution of that very problem, this publication is dedicated to introducing a working understanding of the human mind, to providing examples of means by which he who reads and understands may identify and heal the nonconstructive or reactive mental processes stashed in the depths of his client's subconscious mind. We have already considered that certain dietary indiscretions also are known to cloud the human mind via interference with body-mind and blood chemistry.

The well-rounded and equipped therapist, therefore, should be able to converse openly with his client regarding any aspects of his case, regardless of whether that client is religiously oriented, psychologically oriented, is steeped in today's high technology-oriented world, or is ignorant of it all. This is admittedly a tall order!

To assure an optimal working environment for the Aquarian or Psychic Psychologist or Mental Health Clinician, we find it advisable for said practitioner to have accumulated a considerable amount of supervised experience, plus assiduous practice in recognizing that which is optimum for working with subject energies and awareness. This much work is required so that salvation of the human race from mental or soul entrapment and enslavement is avoided. Anything less than proficiency will doom some larger number of Guides and Guardians to watch over incarnate slaves with whom They cannot communicate. Such is not a pretty picture of the George Orwellian outlook for World Mind Control.

"Go, then, about Our Father's business, doing as best you can with the assurance that We shall be right in there with you, pitching for you, and even pitching *with* you if you Ask aright [Jer 8:6]. In this sense, 'asking aright' implies some degree of understanding of the processes involved, enough so that mere belief in the process is replaced by *knowledge* and *experience* that the request is honorable, and effectively yielding genuine gratitude that the request is even *now* being manifested in the ethers, and will shortly be manifested in the material universe. Proficiency is gained by such study and trial."

CHAPTER TEN
ON BECOMING A CONSCIOUS CO-WORKER

The following items are major elements in the Ancient Mystery School teachings. They appear in The *New Age Fellowship, Inc.*, responses to your Dear God Letters, as when a person asks how to prepare for conscious participation in the Hierarchical Service. When put into practice these elements cleanse and strengthen the body and mind, and relieve the subconscious mind of nonconstructive patterns of thought and programming. Over the long term, they offer additional payoff by way of improved personal relationships. Candidates for out-of-body training have different talents and service potentials, but access them similarly, especially in the beginning.

1. Detoxify your blood stream to clarify your mind, to become receptive and responsive to the Universal mind in which we are already immersed. Enhance body resilience through exercise. Elimination of the processed sugars and spices makes the mind maximally receptive at the higher levels. Replacement of red meats and commercially prepared foods plus chemically produced food substitutes and preservative chemicals, and their replacement with natural foods both builds endurance and keeps the fires of Youth fired up, but also permits the Candidate Co-Worker to enter the Spiritual Out-Of-Body schools and activities not otherwise available. This process continued leads gently to a simplified diet on which the person can survive and survive well from being able to ingest products of the soil, tree, and vine. One becomes able to live off the land, truly a free soul.

2. Rid self of counterproductive attitudes, enabling the soul to be responsive to the life situation(s) at hand. Thus, know directly what constitutes Right Action for each circumstance by being in subtle communication with one's feeling environment.

To learn what needs to be cleared from Mind, make a list of the personality traits you *admire(d)* in specific persons you have known. Consider each parent, relative, teacher, friend or other influential persons. Make a second list of all the qualities you *disliked* in them or others, from your earliest days until the present. Add to the lists as persons come to mind, reliving the feelings you do *not* like and those you *do* like. By doing this you gradually disconnect from the negative things, which will disappear from your life, and you will increasingly multiply and manifest the good traits. You will also gain more disposable energy and Peace of Mind.

3. Again with pen and paper, list what you would do with your life if you had all the Time, Money, Health and any other needed resources you desired. Review and revise your list from time to time, studying the items, setting priorities, allowing enthusiasm to build for particular item(s). Pray asking to understand your Highest Good. Visualize yourself happily making goals and plans, happily-doing them, getting yourself in gear and moving forward.

4. A high quality computerized natal horoscope based on your place and time of birth can provide access to your accepted prebirth Life Plan. It can identify your talents and your liabilities, helping you understand yourself. Transits and progressions can provide you with a working knowledge of the various forces available to you for your entire lifetime. The quality of the insight also depends on your intuition, and on the perceptiveness and wisdom of the astrologers you consult.

5. Take care to become aware of your feelings, to sense where the seat of an ailment feels to be. You may be surprised to find yourself unwittingly picking up ailments originating in the body or mind of an associate, believing the problem to be your own! Untrained sensitive persons lose much energy and time in trying unknowingly to resolve problems that are not theirs to solve. They also deprive the ailing person of opportunity to learn confronting and solving their *own* problems. Such persons need to learn to say *no*, and how to direct hangers-on to ways to solve their own problems. This is a difficult role for Big Brothers, Big Sisters, and for Universal Mothers to learn.

6. This item is similar to Item 5 above, in that many persons pick up the *thoughts of* another person while believing they are thinking their *own* thoughts, not noticing who is thinking what! In communicating with other humans one needs to learn what is possible when using all of one's senses. This ability is gained by practice in observing the effects caused on others by your own words, movements, and thoughts. Similarly, practice observing

what effects the signals from your associates have on your *own* feelings and thoughts. Learn to read responses and reactions, and to keep track of whose are whose. An interesting result is that you will be considered clairvoyant, a natural born psychic, being very intuitive. What you are *really* doing is learning to read and use the signals that have been and are there all along!

7. Much more remains to be told regarding developing your ability to communicate telepathically, without trance, with beings not presently occupying physical bodies, also with others who are embodied but located elsewhere. Also, much remains to be taught in making use of Creative Energy in Healing in the sense of awakening the Chakras, and in working directly with one's Guides and Teachers. Much necessarily is left to individual instruction, done via subsequent personal communications. We of the *New Age Fellowship* are engaged in channeling such matters for The Guides until the Student/Aspirant is able to receive and trust himself or herself in the channeling process. The overall goal our New Age Fellowship Teachers and Guides have for us is that each Student shall learn to stand on his or her own spiritual feet, relying on personal direct contact in working with Them. We thus each are becoming stepping stones...we are therefore, a springboard activity here. We trust each of you will accept us in that role and become a Conscious Co-Worker with us.

We now introduce formal development exercises that will enhance spiritual growth and expansion, and perfection of the personality self. One benefit to be gained immediately upon reading is a partial listing of what can be done and what becomes available for clearing major portions of one's psyche of blocks and barriers, for having developed a high level of psychological stability. The ideas and processes are not usually something the Man on the Street would be given. The manner in which we prevent and discuss them will make sense to persons who are already even somewhat aware of the existence of a spiritual technology. We now itemize qualities that await the advanced aspirant-seeker, items not fully treated elsewhere, and which are available to persons who understand us well enough to discern directly and heed our instructions.

Gaining spiritual perspective...knowing the Big Picture.
Advanced energy flows, their development and use.
Traveling consciously in body-mind space.

Pervading another person's space.
Conscious channeling—without trance.
Diagnosis and resolving problems outside of Distance and Time.

PREPARATORY EXERCISES

No matter what you call it, traveling through the veil, "being on the other side," astral projection, and out-of-body travel whether one is physically deceased or not...most are known but are not available as out-of-body states of being to many persons. The requirements to be mastered to partake of the pleasures of "flying" out-of-body are found in mastering one's habitual focus of attention. Or put in slightly different words, if a person is able to see clairvoyantly, the *travel* aspect of OOB functioning becomes as simple as just *being* where you want to be! As a matter of fact, many persons leave their body frequently but are not conscious that they are doing so. Most other people are seldom entirely within their body-mind space, hang around half-in and half-out. Such latter people are likely to be considered 'spaced out' or in a perpetual daydream state or fog, and miss much of life on either side!

The key to doing all this is to *become aware of being aware*! And how does a person do *that*? Read on, Dear Reader, *Read On*!

To become aware that a person is being aware is a simple thing but requires dedication and practice. One such exercise is called "Spotting Spots" and is detailed in Chapter 21 on "Ending a Session." The process of spotting spots requires that the client put his attention in rapid sequence on a series of points in the space around him in body or in the space around him, establishing communication with each one of them on command by the Counselor-Facilitator. When a person can do that, s/he is usually in complete control over his/her thoughts and observations and so is fully 'in present time,' i.e., is psychologically stable.

When a person becomes able to be completely in present time, s/he next learns to move his focus of attention around inside his own body-mind structure at will. In doing so, he then becomes able to sense, to perceive, how well his inner-self-body is functioning. In that state of being able to move around anywhere inside his own skin, so to say he can discern where healing may be needed, and can supervise said healing processes by bringing energy into an area that has been blocked off from the/its normal health maintenance and healing energy flows. Said blocks may have been erected by physical injury, but also may be collected trauma and engrams built to isolate unresolved psychological threats. The person may then be unable to keep his body-mind in perfect health through loss of communication with the afflicted area.

The New Age Fellowship, our parent organization, uses a technique called "The Elf Self" which goes into further detail regarding traveling around within Total Self for diagnostic and healing purposes. When the person has learned how to visit any portion of his or her own Space, whether of mind or body he will discover that he can enter into the body-mind space of a companion or client. It may require that he (you) sit with your eyes closed to discern and maintain your location and feelings without interference. Later will find yourself working with stability, even with the eyes open and talking normally to the other person. All states between are available. The Counselor will, in fact, notice that there is little to discern as to where each party (person) starts and stops, where the boundaries are of the two persons are to be found. One begins by identifying his own limit of self-expansion to cope with being interconnected with the people in his volume of space at any one time. This can be seen to require a tremendous state of Psychic Stability, including the capacity for functioning three feet behind his own head, as to find himself at will three feet behind anybody's or *everybody's* head.

Perhaps unfortunately, the soul and intellect of most of today's humans are not well enough developed to handle all the information and emotions and thoughts and energies which abound, else such person would be overwhelmed, confused by it, and would become mental basket cases without understanding how or why s/he got that way. We address what is perhaps the greatest factor involved in why the mental institutes are filled with people who are sensitive but do not know they are, nor are their corresponding professionals aware that there is such a world as their 'crazy' clients are experiencing but cannot describe or function in with stability and hence credibility!

To become a useful Channel requires only that a sensitive person be able to focus attention for long periods of time to particular selected wavelengths of Intelligence. He and she will find themselves necessarily rising above the 'spiritual noise' of the general populace, then becoming receptive in the higher planes. How he or she arrives at the ability to rise above the world's various religious and philosophical noise is then consistent with our central theme, that of becoming healed of blocks, barriers, psychic wounds, evolving into a spiritually stable being. The quality of the material thus received by many contemporary channels is then a direct measure of their freedom from Ego and Earth Mind, and is likewise a direct index of how well they are able to hold attention in the abstract higher levels, above the Astral Planes, for example.

Perhaps we need not dwell extensively on why we hold trance channeling a bit in disdain, less desirable than Conscious channeling. We view trance channeling, or possession not necessarily as being a spiritual thing but a *psychic* thing. Then one necessarily must listen to and check out the *quality* of what is received. "By their fruits shall ye know them," knowing the *good* Sources by their performance rather than solely by their oratory or claims to have been one former grand being or another. Aye!!

Perhaps one of the greatest favors we can do for most of our readers is to make the point that it is vitally important that a person become increasingly and more fully aware of his own thoughts and feelings, knowing that they are originating within his or her *own* private fields...in the sense that we are not picking up and solving the thoughts and feelings and problems of other persons in our vicinity/space.

A person becomes aware of what another person is thinking and feeling by gradually gaining recognition of his own sense of Self, and this is done only by gaining proficiency in the arts of meditation and contemplation. One literally *must* learn to go within, shutting out the noises of the world *mentally*. At first it may be necessary to become detached from the man-made noises of the world by going to a quiet mountain top, or to some quiet place, or wakening perhaps at 3:00 A.M. while the world around is asleep. But there must come that time when, as the Bible says, to "enter thy closet and there commune with God."

That element has not escaped transmission from The Sacred Word down through all religions, all Wisdoms, and all Ages...one must learn to commune with God Within...not God out there, but *GOD WITHIN YOU*. Another Man can intercede but only temporarily. A priestcraft is needed only for those who do not recognize their own essential Divinity. There will come a time when you can go directly to "The Boss" (the Teacher, your Guide, The Christ, etc.) and there work consciously, engaging in the resolution of world problems as your interests and talents enable you to do so. In the least and still vitally important sense, you will become a Harvester of your Fellow man who is ready and perhaps is willing to take his next step godward in his own evolution.

No more can we ask than that you shall awaken yourself, overcoming the ego-self so the *EGO SELF* can operate fully uninhibitedly in the Earth and overcome it...graduating from Schoolhouse Earth, perhaps becoming a Faculty member thereof! You will never run out of students nor budget!

We rest for the time being.

CHAPTER ELEVEN
USES OF HYPNOTHERAPY

This chapter airs several factors and points of view on using hypnosis as a tool in clearing nonconstructive engrams, traumatic recordings or alleviating other troublesome programs of the human psyche or soul. We believe there is a definite time and place for use of Hypnotherapy, but because of its broad power, hypnosis is *not* recommended as a regular tool except by a spiritually-oriented expert, a clairvoyant who can SEE the side effects being created. *Most* hypnotherapists lack the spiritual perceptiveness, the basic qualities and training in psychotherapy, and do not understand the limits to be trusted in attempting cleansing the psyche by hypnosis.

Most neophyte hypno-practitioners, however well-intentioned, are limited to using hypnotherapy by cookbook procedures, oblivious as to what is going on in the client. Precious clues are often lost. The therapist must be expert at following the fine line between directing and being in a position to direct the client in using his or her own perception on his trek through the client's inner worlds. The usual hypnotist is unaware of how to explore the subtle insights that key into the network of recordings that bedevil the troubled client by controlling his stimulus-response or reaction patterns.

When used by an expert, Hypnotherapy can be a fine blockbuster in cracking open heavily blocked areas of the psyche, following through with subtler approaches to release the locked-up emotional energy. Even so, the ideal therapist still needs to know when and how much to use his heavy artillery over using the delicate shades of perception that provide the more subtle awareness and entry into the higher planes.

Just getting rid of a traumatic block is then not necessarily the entire consideration involved. Unskilled use of Hypnotherapy exposes the client to risk losing a vital life lesson, an unresolved learning experience contained in the troublesome recorded engram. Then, rather than just helping said client to be cleared of an incident or traumatic event, an important growth experience is made unavailable, and its lesson probably incapable of being properly tracked and eliminated or neutralized in that lifetime.

Our Controller-Ego-Self is so efficient that it has the ability to construct cross-references from one sort of trauma to related others, so that threat situations tend to generalize, resulting in the personality always being uptight, mobilized for attack. Seemingly irrational responses become triggered through the cross-filing system. Each ego has developed different cross-filing rules, so that when a hypnotist looks for some relationship trauma to discharge, it is likely that he will instead contact and trigger some cross-filed reaction and miss the original process! But that can be good...if followed through.

Hypnosis may become a useful tool when it allows a client to do what he/she cannot do with normal regression therapy. Until a Counselor-Facilitator-Hypnotherapist has been through hundreds of hours with an expert therapist, learning at first hand how it works, he should not use it on anyone else. We are claiming that there is too much danger of modifying the inner akashic recordings, making them inaccessible for subsequent study, or causing loss of important life lessons by working with an inept facilitator.

One fundamental problem in developing the human mind and Soul is to overcome *illusion*, to learn to *whom*, *what* and *where* are real. Creative Imagery coupled with Hypnosis is one of the fastest ways to create and amplify illusion. The power of the human psyche to create illusion goes unrecognized, except by The Media and Advertisers. Seldom appreciated is the extent to which subliminal hypnosis can generate desired illusion by teaching, by suggesting, by programming that one is communicating with angels or hierarchies, or out-of-town big-name Masters. Such Beings do exist, but too often only in the emotional and astral planes, in a person's mind. All the platitudes known to man are being "sent through" various psychics by illusion-generated entities. Indeed, at least one very large metaphysical organization is based on using the glamor of illusory personages who spend inordinate amounts of time mouthing inanities. There are indeed many such thoughtforms feeding sensitives, claiming to be Jesus of Nazareth, who are mouthing some of our teachings, but which are plainly inconsistent among themselves, let alone disagreeing with what knowable discarnates, the real Teachers and Guides offer. If you would separate the good ones from the pretenders, study to discern how they work with the Hierarchy in solving world problems through perfection of the individual. "By their fruits shall ye know them!"

We are suggesting that aspirants to Conscious Co-workership and Self Mastery be cautious when dealing with hypnosis, as the human mind will generate whatever is demanded of it. Undoing one's illusions is indeed likely to be difficult, painful, and may extend over several lifetimes. We suggest 'testing the spirits' to avoid being karmically involved in undoing what damage we did to the minds of those clients who are taken in by the beckoning of Illusion.

For the serious Student there is little better than learning to work consciously and *at will* in the reverie state. Hypnosis as a form of Directed Reverie Therapy is best used more for short-term research than for Spiritual Development. For best results one still needs to work consciously to bridge meditative reverie while learning how at will to look around to perceive, to hear and feel everything about a personality or some subjective or a recorded scene while in Present Time. By extending one's awareness, one develops proficiency enough so that he can do it for himself. When you can do *that* you can read the Akasha directly, work consciously with Divine mind, and can sort Illusion from Reality, and work with illusion at higher levels.

Criteria by which to test a potential Hypnotherapist include understanding the motives of one who would invite you into a hypnosis session with offers to seeing behind the veil (which you can do!), doing out-of-body travel (which also you can do!), and/or controlling whether ants and flies will leave your domicile (which also can be done). But leaving well-enough alone is beyond most amateur would-be-practitioners, until they have experienced trouble and have learned to avoid it entirely.

Yes, it is possible to use hypnosis to tune in on Past Lives and to other Planes, but the risk is great for people who merely dabble in curiosity and irresponsibly. Any real shortcut to Heaven is still a bit rough and demanding, as the barriers have to be transcended either way! If you still want to try or test it, take plenty of time to observe the effects being generated while your therapist is at work on somebody else first!

"In closing we aver that the price for risking damage to a fine human mind is not worth the karmic setback and mind derangement it can cause. If there be any gain available from employing hypnosis, it lies in offering quick trips into the psyche, and even

then its use is discouraged by anyone except spiritually oriented professionals.
"We rest."

CHAPTER TWELVE

FEAR AS A SHUT-OFF TO LOVE

The importance of clearing a client of Fear recordings and programs can hardly be overemphasized, especially when compared to all other psychological barriers to the incarnate Human Spirit. Rationale for that claim is now discussed. Without being free of Fear a person cannot Love!

Psychic or mental Energy is required to maintain the human subconscious Programming Department. The heaviest users of that energy are those programs of literal instructions and orders having to do with assessing sensory inputs and mobilizing defenses and/or counterattacks for any sort of estimated danger. In addition to issuing feelings of warning and mobilizing our available forces against unseen dangers, that same Programming Department contains programs for playing piano concertos, for walking, breathing, etc. Most of the time the Piano Concerto Program cannot be considered a potential source of danger. Some programs operate around the clock, especially those dedicated to protection from real or learned threats and subsequent mobilization for Fight or Flight, all in preparation for potentially ensuing battle.

We all have known people who were taunted by the name 'fraidie cat' back in childhood, and perhaps have known even more adults who are habitually uptight an inordinate percentage of the time. When a person is 'running scared,' patterns of constant mobilization build up into what becomes 'essential hypertension,' somewhat suppressible by diet, exercise, meditation, medication, and through attention given to resolving psychological or attitude problems. Untreated essential hypertension leads to gradual body-mind disintegration and lessened creativity, hence to acceleration of the death processes.

The nature of man's design is such that self-preservation is his highest order of priority. To that end the human subjective energy flows have been trained or programmed to focus on evaluating all sensory inputs, filtering and shunting control signals to defense patterns appropriate for coping with whatever is recognized as a threat.

In other words, the human sensory system monitors and sorts out all the inputs the sensory system receives, including the basic five senses, and the higher senses as extensions of the basic five. The typical human personality is relatively slow or even blocked in reception and evaluation of his sensory perceptions. Conditionally speaking, the little ego-self is much faster, with the result that the incarnate spirit as the Personality is unaware that it is being controlled by the stimulus-response patterns psychologically and psychically *built* into the human soul and lodged in what we can call the accessible Subconscious Program Department, our individual psychic Department of Defense.

The energy demanded by the Programs Department to fulfill its functions is proportional to the degree to which Fear and Protection dominate the person's attitudes and thought processes. Persons ridden with Fear have little surplus energy for sustained physical, mental and creative activity. On the other hand, persons with little or no Fear or Protective Programming tend to be those same persons who are aflame with life, bursting with the Energy of Creativity.

Without going deeper into operation of the human psyche in defending our observations, we state that of the greatest problems a client is likely to come in with, fear-dominated programs are most likely to be at the root-cause. And high on the list of recordings will be incidents deemed traumatic by the client, regardless of what lifetime they originated in. Then the Practitioner can beneficially use *fear* more or less as a standard entry category in his effort to begin improving Life for the aching client.

In other words, We offer this chapter to call attention to a category of psychic disorder that is almost always good for at least one session. Fear is insidious in that it almost always is cross-filed as Fear of Failure in any Life activity that requires risk, taking a chance in the unknown. It thus negatively influences one's competitive spirit, and can even prevent experiencing life at all. More aspirants are confined to the monastic life through simple Fear than were ever so dedicated by Love of God!

Then, when observing a client to find some way to restore his verve for living, you may approach the client with suggested threats, making some use of those already operating in his career environment, family and finances, mocking up hypothetical threats and observing how the client attempts to confront or to hide. Then take it from there by going into the usual reverie review process. That approach yields productive session time while also doing the client a big favor.

Fear eliminated or defanged is Life Energy restored, and the ability to Love released.

CHAPTER THIRTEEN
DIAGNOSTIC METHODS FOR CASE ASSESSMENT

Every person on Earth experiences some level of discomfort. It is a part of the Practitioner's job to assess the nature of what is ailing his client and to administer the treatment in accord with what the Practitioner finds as the root-cause, whatever the origin(s). By fitting the treatment to the ailment one expects greatest case gains, least wasted energy, and greatest satisfaction for himself and the client. We do not offer medical services, working on the subjective levels. Medical matters are referred appropriately for professional treatment.

We have successfully used several different approaches to case diagnosis with varying results, depending on which particular area or aspect of said client is blocked off or troubled. Persons of an intellectual orientation, those most right-brained, are skilled at hiding their feelings behind barriers of rationalizations. These are usually the most difficult to open up when the problem is of an emotional nature. We then use techniques best fitted to approach the egoic intellect, letting it 'believe' that it is being protective according to what it has programmed, or what it has permitted to be programmed. To learn what a person's ego and its programs permit or calls for we can use tests, some as simple as looking at other people, and going on to talking about more abstract things, things more of an emotionally uninvolved nature.

The methods available are broadly enough based so that one Practitioner may not equally skilled in their application. Then the process of matching the punishment to 'fit the crime' suggests that a candidate for clearing will do well to find and to work with a variety of specialist therapists, counselors and facilitators. And we say this without prejudice.

Another factor to be considered in the processes of diagnosis and treatment is that all and each Therapist, Counselor, and/or Facilitator are not equally clear, and hence are not necessarily equally responsive to a particular client's needs and/or character and programming quirks.

Our purpose here is then that of alerting our Earthlings to the magnitude of the task of becoming clear, and why it is oft-times found necessary working from behind the Veil as We do, to be in close control in session when administering to the needs of our particular Trainee-Candidate Conscious Co-Workers through-the-veil.

As will be noted below, the gamut of available techniques for the contemporary mental health clinician ranges from Testing to Tea-leaf Technology and from Divination to Detailed and Documented Discourse. Each has its applications, benefits and limitations such that the well equipped practitioner will specialize in several complimentary approaches. In any case the place of a well developed and trusted Intuition cannot be underestimated.

USEFUL DIAGNOSTIC METHODS

We now discourse on about a dozen diagnostic approaches that have been used with varying degrees of success. The level of achieved success depends on the proclivities of both the counselor and the client. In each category we will attempt to offer enough information to enable the reader to apply the technique, or where to look ahead for further enlightenment. Some border on the Psychological Sciences and others border on the mystical Arts. Diligent application will require skill in any application! Not at all a simple thing we undertake here in this approach to unscrambling a mixed-up customer!

If there will be difficulty in broadening one's talents to become a skilled Psychic Psychologist, it may be that of taking a right-brain artisan and broaden same to become an intellectual. Perhaps no less difficult is the task faced by a professional or left-brain intellectual to awakening his or her intuition, to learning to accept and trust intuitive inputs.

1. SPIRITUAL ASTROLOGY

In the hands of a skilled practitioner whose Intuition is well developed, Spiritual Astrology is an outstanding tool for gaining insights in working around blocks to the human soul, to the Feeling Self. Not yet widely used for personality investigation, here one potentially finds greatest use for astrological charts, presuming that both the birth information and the chart interpreter are both accurate!

We think enough of Astro-Diagnosis to have invited Susan St. Thomas, a master chart builder and interpreter, to furnish Chapter 15 on Astro-Diagnosis. The reader may gain an appreciation of the extent to which further training is required for an Astrologer to become a Psychic Shrink, and vice versa, but that is not to deny the power in that combination of interests and skills!

2. THE SACRED TAROT

In the hands of an expert, here defined as a Tarot-reader whose intuition is well developed, Psyche Analysis and discernment of a client's personal and social relationships profile by Tarot is available for analyzing the forces at work in the Present, near-past, and near-future. When used for in-depth analysis purposes, the Tarot can provide excellent insights, suggesting what direction a client is likely to respond most productively. We shall not go into the depths of Tarot analysis in this book because several excellent volumes are already available. But, if there is to be a problem in using the Tarot for psyche-analysis, it lies more in the relative skill the card-reader can bring to the card interpretation. It will easier for a typical Tarot Reader to become a Psychic Psychologist than it will be for a typical Psychologist to become an intuitively-led Tarot Reader, but the payoff for the effort would indeed be great, being built on extending availability of the Counselor's Intuition. The Tarot reader can make use of the traditional Celtic Cross, or on other single-card or three-card spreads, first formulating the request for understanding the spread as it offers insight into the question to be answered. Do *not* try to limit your insights to what you find interpreted in a book: use should be made of another's experience only for general guidance, and then only until you learn to trust your Self.

3. "MAKE A LIST"

Several types of list can be made and employed in diagnosing and alleviating the confusion so often found in the ailing human psyche, establishing Divine Order by identifying one's lifetime goals and priorities. One of the first things to do on a new case surely includes clarifying the mind and mental processes akin to combing the snarls out of a tousled head of human hair, as must be done prior to erecting a special coiffure. Diagnosis and case analysis by data taking and profile erection using standard tests and charts and making lists is by no means a new approach to the professional counselor-therapist and is treated elsewhere. However, the primary value for offering our particular approach to unscrambling the human psyche is to make it possible and much easier for the Inner God Self or Ego, for your own Inner Genii, to implement its own Grand Design swiftly and efficiently.

As we shall show, bringing order to the human Psyche by list-making is similar to using a comb and force to bring order to a matted head of hair: making and arranging the list is the combing and brushing. One sometimes also needs to use a shears, but when the hair is straightened, is once again orderly, the fundamental beauty is there to be experienced. Special coiffures then can be designed and implemented to suit any occasion. Because of the order, once restored, it is possible to go smoothly from one tonsorial delight or program and recording to another.

Comparison of combing out a rat's nest of hair is indeed similar to attempting the task of removing the blocks, snarls and interconnectednesses of subconscious programming. As the threads or psychic wiring become organized it becomes easy consciously to revise, remove, and strengthen whatever is found there, whether constructive or destructive or neutral energy-losing programming. Then, for the present we shall call attention to an excellent method for diagnosing more or less directly the status of one's emotional or/and subconscious attitudes and programming by a specific method of "MAKING A LIST."

In the first example of 'MAKING A LIST' one asks his client to scan his memory bank for specific relationships with various standard categories of close people such as parents, teachers, siblings, other relatives, friends and associates. In the first column just list their names. In the second column, to the right, just jot down what you *like* about each of them and what you *dislike* about them. Your list should include at least a dozen people, letting the list include authority figures such as Police, Firemen, Pastors, Politicians, Bankers, etc. The same process can be done beneficially for institutions, writing what you like and dislike about School, your Home, Police departments, the government, doctors and dentists, newspapers, etc. It may take several days to feel that you have found most of them. Let the Counselor-Facilitator study the list, and keep a copy for yourself, imaging a composite person made up of the cumulative traits listed. You may sooner or later discover that said list describes your own personality self. You then have a marvelous lead as to what traits to commence revision and clearing.

A second and very valuable list to make will go far toward identifying what the client would do if s/he presumes having all the money, time, health, and opportunity desired. Organization and study of the list makes it possible for the client gradually to discern how he would spend his lifetime. As said collection of items is reviewed, added to and modified, a close connection will emerge between that list and the intended Life Purpose for one's incarnation! Allow your client to ponder each list at leisure, adding to it or rearranging it at will. Perhaps several weeks will be required for the client to feel he has done an optimum job, and several months may consolidate it into a firm working plan for your client's guidance.

Select healing processes that enable the client to relate to himself, that will be accepted for analysis and clearing by the client. That process needs discussion, with client participation, using Creative Imagery and Free Association in the discussion, helping the client to examine his feelings to make best use of the Self-Image gained from having done the homework. Compare the relative strengths among the common elements rambling through the write-up, finding collected but buried attitudes toward Love, Self Acceptance, Resentment of Authority, Health, Money, and various other character traits as they emerge. From said lists you can derive an excellent compilation of whatever is being a driving force or a reactive inertia in the client. In other words, by guided study of the lists, the client is really drafting a description of himself!

4. CREATIVE IMAGERY

It is necessary that the client become skilled at making use of his or her Creative Imagery, of his imagination, in tuning into the scenes and situations he or she encounters. Encountering himself as the Good Guy or the Bad Guy is an important point so the client can work out the give-and-take that always takes place in one-on-one human relationships. One then becomes able to discern which feelings are his and which emanate from the other person and similarly with picking up the thoughts that stream through the client's mind. One needs then become communicative on a deeper and yet higher level of awareness than is usual for the typical candidate or client. The aware client then more swiftly becomes in charge of himself and his situations and encounters, gaining the upper hand in social-personal relationships and becomes able, as a bonus, to tune in on and receive two-way communication with his or her Guides. Then far from being a tool or instrument of curiosity, Creative Imagery serves the dual purpose of feelings one's own feelings, but as well, learning to sense correctly the feelings of his associates. Of such material are the best Counselor-Facilitators made!

5. DRAW A PERSON

Another effective way to enable a person to glimpse his inner self and give it expression is to allow the client to select crayons and paper and drawing whatever comes to mind. Even a little skill permits discernment and analysis of what the shapes and colors tell about what is going on deep within the client. For example, strong red indicates rage. Black indicates Death or total isolation. Green can indicate abundance. Pink is thought to indicate Love. The colors can be expected to match auric colors, depending somewhat on the shapes and their locations within the drawing.

6. RORSCHACH TESTS

Here is another opportunity to permit the inner mind, the Inner Self, to express Itself without being censored by the egoic or programmed personality mind. Certain standard ink blot sets can be purchased, with handbooks of interpretations, and others can be made up by an enterprising Counselor, letting interpretations be suggested intuitively to the counselor and perhaps to the client as well. It is an excellent manner of avoiding the self-criticism programming that operates so effectively to control and restricts the personality self so devastatingly.

7. GRAPHOLOGY

Many of our readers learned to write by copying the Palmer Penmanship Method in our earliest days in school. As some of us grew up our penmanship began to drift away from the idealized letter forms taught us. In fact, those same changes enable a skilled interpreter to trace the development of our Personality. Much research has been done which correlates certain letter and word formations which form detailed and consistent definition of our various personality and spiritual characteristics. So consistently well documented are the handwriting analyses that courts of law and other historical research societies accept the assessments of certain professional handwriting experts. Hence, handwriting analysis is now an accepted tool of the social sciences now called *Graphology*.

A Spiritual Psychology For The Aquarian Age

This volume recommends that an interested reader should undertake study of Graphology outside this book, as there are many excellent books available on the subject, even if not agreeing identically on all points. To duplicate here the extensive work done elsewhere is nonproductive. One usually can obtain the analytical services of a fine Graphologist for a fee. Even a casual reading and study of our referenced volumes [see Bibliography] will show general agreement among writing styles, but that different graphologists produce varying interpretations from the same fundamental handwriting sample, so it is mete that you, as an independent Counselor, should try the services of several graphologists to determine whose services are most amenable to your own points of view and practice.

8. PALM READING

Shakespeare is credited with observing "What we are shouts so loudly that our words cannot be heard for the din." And so it is with palm reading! Palmistry is another psychological or psychic art. Indeed, many books have been written about what the lines in our hands mean. Interpretations vary from reader to reader, but it cannot be denied that the combination of hand markings coupled with liberal acceptance of intuitive inputs is capable of providing a valuable resource of character analysis. Even better, it is not difficult to discern the nature and timing of some major events throughout one's lifetime, including the Life Plan at birth. What was considered important to the Psyche is indeed reflected in indicators of trauma that were or were not resolved,

For example, one's emotional life can be assessed, to the point where even a casual observation is capable of telling the Counselor-Palm Reader much about the basic inner nature of said client and how he or she confronts the world, about their artistic temperament, and deviations from the original Life Plan. Even such devastating trauma as unresolved childhood molestation and related "secret life" activity is not difficult to identify.

It is recommended that a potential Palm Reader should read several books, perhaps take a course or two, and working with cooperative friends to find for himself what the various lines and signs imply. It should be accepted that different readers will find different messages, each Palmist then tending to observe the client through a filter of the Reader's own making. While Palmistry usually is considered as a parlor trick, to be used only for entertainment, a serious student of the palms and fingers, abetted by intuition, can provide startling assessments of one's adjustment to Life. As with other means of Divination, suggestible persons should not be told anything having to do with coming misfortune, learning then how to be socially amazing or amusing appropriate to the needs of the moment.

So much about the palm's owner can be discerned so rapidly that it is here recommended that each potential Counselor-Facilitator will pick up what comes easily, learning the available signals, and how the message on some portions of the lines and bumps can be validated on other portions of the palm. Said assessment can include the age of the person at the time of any emotionally significant event, past or future. As to reading the future, let it be well understood that the events of the future can be changed...being reflected in changes in the palm line structure. The instrument of change is *conscious decision*. Then, it is possible, even if perhaps not always wise, to be able to identify nonconstructive events likely to befall the client, suggesting the need to strengthen self, to look at possible and perhaps recommended revisions in social and physiological patterns, taking cognizance of where the trends point.

It is often easier to gain insight into future events via Palmistry than through Astrology, although the detail and exact timing may differ. Unless the correct moment of first breath is used as the birth time, the forecasts of occurrence via Astrology in themselves may vary significantly. Then, to permit gaining information in its most useful form, we recommend that a mix of analytical techniques be used. Let it not be forgotten in all this use of different techniques of diagnosis that our initial objective is to learn what attitude and programming patterns are operating that are nonproductive or counter-productive. We then need be perhaps more concerned at first with the client's *past* and Existing programs than of what comes from a glimpse into the future.

In closing up this introduction to Palmistry, let us assure you that use of Intuition is strongly to be encouraged, as the Incarnate Spirit of a client is often imprisoned in its body-mind structure, and that an early form of telepathy is often available in advanced souls, even as the shapes and textures of the hands and fingers indicate more or less clearly the degree of capability of The Spirit to work in its flesh vehicles.

9. COLOR SWATCHES

A method sometimes useful for inciting interest into ways of telling us about ourselves includes use of color swatches. By fondling a collection of colors, perhaps an inch square, a person can often note preferences for certain colors and abhorrence for others. Many colors will be neutral, of course, but it is worthy that a color swatch analysis be undertaken at sometime in the Counselor's work with each particular client. One of the more obvious items is that some clients will exhibit very little response, while other persons are sometimes brought to unexplained tears or anger.

A firm basis exists for including this form of quickie analysis as evidenced by clothing designers and interior decorators, when designing rooms and clothing to produce certain atmospheres in the wearer, or in those who attend meetings in specially colored rooms. It is found that psychotherapy itself can make itself more effective in obtaining or triggering certain effects by various color decors in counseling chambers. Indeed, the pride of nations is often told in the colors and shapes of their national flags!

10. OTHER METHODS OF DIVINATION AND DIAGNOSIS

And while we are telling of ways to gauge the spiritual and social sensitivities of a client, of her/his responsiveness to the environment, let us also include mention of the effects produced by perfumes, by stale or fresh air, and by sounds of all sorts, timbre, and loudness. Become increasingly aware of the effects that background music has on your ability to arouse or create desired effects on your client, as aids in the analysis and the treatment phases of your work.

It should be kept in mind that each client meets a wide cacophony of sights and sounds in his daily living, and each has some effect on how said client will interrelate with that environment and its other human occupants. Great advantage may be taken to manipulate the environmental sounds, smells, and background motion to gain the effect you wish to create in undertaking in-depth responses of a controlled nature, for both analytical and for therapeutic purposes.

Runes are sometimes used with convenience and success to bring about insights into a particular situation. Much indeed rests on the ability of the Counselor-Reader to interpret intuitively what needs to be known and/or acted upon. We tend to use Runes more as a curiosity and interest arouser than as a formal diagnostic tool.

The *I Ching* ranks high on the scale of useful technologies for gaining insight. Much depends on the ability of the Reader to tune in on the intuitive aspects provided in the line patterns. That this is so should be acknowledged when considering that of 64 major categories, there are perhaps another dozen subdivisions, all these to be interpreted as befits circumstances not necessarily pinned down and discussed by that limited number of possibilities. We have found that the *I CHING*, when used respectfully and in a prayerful setting, outstanding messages have been transmitted. As is often the case, however, the Reader does not understand even the clearest message, tending to wish for certain preconceived responses.

11. PERSONALITY PROFILES

The advent of computer science has made it possible for keyboard analysis and diagnosis of personality quirks and characteristics. Programs may be found advertised in Pop Psychology and other professional trade journals, and can be had capable of working on most popular computer types, such as IBM-compatibles and MacIntosh.. Others and more advanced models are becoming available. It is possible for the therapist or client to enter the computer program to display, to read off a particular item or question and respond to it on a scale of 1-5 (with some models, and equivalent in others) for 50 or perhaps 100 questions. This done, the computer proceeds to provide a display of the major traits and characteristics which it has been programmed to provide. While it is not always feasible for a Counselor-Facilitator to purchase a computer for such diagnostic and analytical purposes, it is found quite handy for such to be at hand.

It is also possible for a person to obtain largely the same results by using existing profile determination methods, such as the widely used MMPI. The Minnesota Multi-Phasic Personality Inventory materials can be purchased and are a normal part of the services available through Yokefellows International of Burlingame, California [see Bibliography]. The Yokefellows people have a program of personality diagnosis and improvement that can be recommended to most people. Some such groups use trained leaders already skilled in the diagnostic and treatment field, so that our reason for mentioning it here is to note that resources are perhaps more widely available than many metaphysically-oriented workers are aware.

12. ELECTRONIC AIDS

The advent of transistors and computer technology has made it possible to refine the electronic lie detector and related instrumentation to a high degree. Perhaps the highest generally available instrument useful for and designed for psyche analysis is the E-Meter. Designed and perfected by Volney Matthison and used widely by L. Ron Hubbard, the E-meter has become the basis for determining the presence and the relative degree of clearing any of hundreds of categories of psychological experience, engrams, and trauma recordings. This item is offered more for completeness than to recommend purchase of an E-meter. It is our understanding that to obtain an E-Meter one must affiliate with the Scientology movement, an action not entirely consistent with our objectives.

13. TEA LEAVES AND COFFEE GROUNDS

We do not consider use of tea leaves or related approaches as serious candidates for diagnosis and analysis of the human psyche. Not that a vivid imagination or strong intuition is not valid when working through these devises, but that much better work can be done in general from using the above more refined approaches.

14. THE OUIJA, A SPECIAL NOTE.

We make a strong appeal that a potential Counselor-Analyst scrupulously avoid using the Ouija Board for any phase of this work because of the possibility of spirit possession of s/he who operates the board. Not that good advice and insights are not obtained, but it is too easy for discarnate entities to gain entrance into the psyche/aura of the user of said board. When a strong entity takes possession in the body-mind of a weaker incarnate human, great damage can be done to the psyche and social stability of the weaker person. As reported frequently in the classic metaphysical works, it is too often the case where a Ouija Board user suffers serious setbacks in an evolutionary sense, losing the ability to control his/her mind.

IN CLOSING...

When you later confront your client, you can inform her/him that you have done a preliminary analysis and that you can, on request, discuss it as a basis suitable for guiding your subsequent program of therapy. For being exposed to what you consider grist for your in-depth relief program, usually the client will be more readily cooperative and curious about its implication and application.

To the extent that it seems appropriate you can probably and safely discuss the Personality Profile with the client, but we would be inclined to withhold most of the negatives, temporarily leaving them hidden, allowing same to surface while in session. You will have more than enough material to make use of Seed Thoughts (see later), as providing avenues of approach to case opening and resolution.

The materials already assembled from application of the above approaches to diagnosis may often be used as case openers and for several years of in-depth work and guidance. And of course, once inside the subconscious barriers, many other tie-in side issues may be expected to rise.

There is a direct advantage in using the "MAKE A LIST" approach over Astrology, in that the Practitioner need not be as well prepared or informed in use of Astrology or Tarot, having a direct real-time entry through the insights to his programming already revealed unconsciously by the client.

Take it from there! We move along.

CHAPTER FOURTEEN
ELECTRONIC AIDS

Some clients will benefit from using brainwave analysis as a means to facilitate entrance to their inner mind, to help them to get in touch with their feeling selves. Several good inexpensive models or types of brainwave devices are available with which to develop skill in practice of the meditative arts. In general, we would state that it should become a natural thing to access one's inner mind-self without using electronic devices. We do agree that they can be of merit in working with the troubled soul or mind. When working alone, we suggest that unstable persons be wary in using brainwave machines of the types which appear for sale in metaphysical trade literature.

If you would succeed as an all-around Psychic Psychologist, with a reputation as a high quality Practitioner, you will do well to gain experience in use of contemporary electronic brainwave analysis equipment and to understand its limitations. This note is also written partly as an admonition to the Practitioner to become familiar with the tools of the trade, rather than as an encouragement for the lay user to invest in such equipment.

The well-rounded practitioner will be familiar with the different levels and rates of brain-mind activity. These take place in frequency bands from near zero to four cycles per second (Delta), of 4 to about 8 cps (Theta), 8 to 13 cps (Alpha), and 13 or more cps (Beta). Delta corresponds to the trance or deep dreamless sleep state for most people. Beta corresponds to the fully awakened and exteriorized attention state of being. Alpha corresponds to a stable relaxed condition of internalized attention or daydreaming. The Theta level of awareness is most used while working in the reverie state. Each level or rate thus corresponds to some level of known mental, astral or spiritual activity, even when the client is unconscious, or is unable to communicate from or within those altered levels.

Initially, mind machines are most useful for focussing on a particular state of brainwave activity and maintaining it. Later comes a time when the client and/or the counselor finds it unnecessary to employ electronic assistance to attain or maintain any particular meditative state. Eventually the experimenter or client can assume any particular level of mind-state during fully awakened consciousness. Working in the Delta state with that ability marks the Master. To retain the Theta state outside of session requires that much good have work been accomplished, freeing the soul from 'software' recordings and barriers and other distractive or disruptive free-association influences.

Then far from forbidding their use, we find merit in brainwave electronics devices being used with or by some clients. We wish to be on record as saying that many clients need but little if any use of instrumentation to obtain a cleared subconscious mind/akasha. If electronic brainwave equipment is available for experimentation, we highly recommend that the experiments be conducted under the close supervision of a Practitioner who is skilled in its use.

Perhaps the most useful and sensitive electronic instrument available for enhancing the subconscious mind review process is the Electropsychometer, discussed elsewhere, and often just called the E-meter. The client grasps and holds two electrical points of contact, usually one in each hand. The operator views the meter which displays changes in the levels of the minute electrical currents which are generated as the ego and its associated programming patterns respond to the myriad inputs received by the body-mind "hardware" during Earth living. Those minute signals are the same coded voltages which automatically operate the body protective programs and their respective mechanisms and mind-body functions of walking, speaking, the emotions of fight or flight, etc.

The E-meter circuitry operates rapidly enough to register the egoic response rate and magnitude of any input received from each sensory device, whether from physical, visual, audio, mental and psychic impingements. A trained E-meter operator can profile his client in various categories of typical pleasures and threats, recording the measured relative amount of energy the psyche stores for reaction program execution. But until the stored energy becomes discharged, the measured E-meter response is likely to remain more or less undiminished from one stimulus time to another.

Then an E-meter is perhaps best employed to make an initial engram scan to sort out and identify critical present-time areas of distress, allowing the Counselor-Facilitator to discern the nature of any the threat(s) and how to approach them. Work done subsequently in confronting nonconstructive recordings need not require use of the E-meter. But, said meter is very useful later to discern when the stored engram energy charge has been cleared, at which time the operator gets a 'flat meter' when working a particular engram or traumatic area. In other words, the Therapist-Counselor who has access to an E-meter and is skilled in its use usually can work more efficiently with it than without it.

We recognize that mild hypnosis may sometimes have value in working with people who have difficulty in releasing obstacles to feeling, facilitating entry into the reverie search process when non-hypnotic access might otherwise be denied or delayed.

If there is anything we scrupulously avoid, it is use of mind-altering and/or state of awareness altering drugs of any and every sort. It is our experience that people who depend on drugs to cope with their programming and attitudes *always* lose, regress in awareness, fall in their spiritual status from what is capable of being experienced without them.

CHAPTER FIFTEEN
ASTRO DIAGNOSIS

The following is an invited work written by Susan St. Thomas on the method she uses to diagnose a client's Spiritual Profile, finding the lessons learned and those yet to be learned in Earth-life.

For more information regarding her astrological natal charts and services, contact: Susan St. Thomas M.A., 19 Winfield Street, San Francisco, CA. 94110.

LIFE PATTERNS:THE ASTROLOGICAL BIRTH CHART
BY SUSAN ST. THOMAS M.A.

Natural correspondences exist between Astrology, Numerology and Tarot. They are all integrated symbolic systems of life teachings as well as spiritual tools. While the development of intuition greatly enhances the use of these tools, it is not necessary to be psychic to read charts, numbers or cards. The following information is offered to assist therapists, counselors, practitioners or anyone seeking greater self-awareness through the transformative arts.

From the beginning of recorded time in the development of human life on earth, there is evidence of astronomical observations. Earth people have honored the cycles of the sun, moon and stars because they reflect the cycles of growth and change on the planet and within each individual living here. In the last 200 years, celestial measuring and recording has become very sophisticated, making astrological studies easier and more accurate.

The symbolic language of astrology is a blending of science and religion. It shows the correlation between the movement of heavenly bodies and life on earth. As a system of universal wisdom the symbols of this "science of the stars" offer many levels of understanding about life cycles and our individual roles in the Divine Plan. Even though astrology can be used in the fine art of prediction, its greatest value is in the self discovery process. Our natal charts—the "picture" of the sky at the moment of our birth—

are seed patterns of who we are and what we have come to experience in our lives.

Within the spirit of each of us is a vital impulse that stimulates each expression to fulfill our own purpose. This movement toward purpose is dependent upon other forms of life and is a movement toward wholeness, unity and balance. The individual natal chart is one "picture" in this process.

The life path, as indicated by the natal chart, is not a fixed static destiny, but rather an unfolding process that is constantly shifting and changing. As sparks of the Creator, we are each given the gift of free will to choose our way along this path and to accelerate growth as an option. When we are in harmony with our highest purpose and connected with our inner spiritual direction, we choose the right action for the fulfillment of this plan.

Now the natal chart can be used for self study to obtain a different perspective on ourselves—to understand our natural talents, abilities and character patterns of behavior. When we are ready to look at our true natures, the character patterns, as revealed in the chart, strike a deep cord of affirmation. Since it is said that character is destiny, then if our future is to be any different than our past, we must must modify our patterns of behavior, shift our attitudes and expand our consciousness.

Due to the complexity of astrology, it may take an experienced, trained reader to uncover the complete life patterns in an individual birth chart which are limiting that individual from living in the fullness of his or her expression. We will.however, consider the basic components—planets, signs and houses, which outline themes in the chart. Reading the chart as a whole is something like taking the end of a string and tracing it around the chart until it reveals the "person in the horoscope". The point of entry, or the beginning of the string can be found by first identifying the most important or significant points in the birth chart—the position of the sun, moon and ascendant or rising sign—the sign on the first house.

The planets of our solar system, including the sun (a star) and the moon (a satellite of the earth) are associated with the energies of life or the vibrations. The signs of the zodiac, Aries through Pisces, represent the qualities of expression for these energies and the houses or "sections" of the wheel are associated with the departments of life just as the various departments within a larger company function as a whole to keep the company running smoothly. the aspects are the angular distances between the planets in the birth chart and reveal the flow of energies within the individual—whether these are dynamic/hard or flowing/easy. Planets in the individual birth chart are also like voices which all need to be heard or expressed. They seek to be expressed in the department of life where they are placed by house in the wheel. the aspects between them indicate how they "speak" to each other and consequently how they are expressed in the individual character or personality. If we find a chart pattern dominate by "hard" aspects, we get an individual with conflict and frustration because the voices or planetary energies conflict or challenge one another. Once a resolution is found for these issues, specific needs can be filled without one obstructing or opposing the other. These hard aspects also create dynamic, often magnetic energies within the individual which can be highly creative. A chart dominated by "easy" aspects may bring a life of reward and general contentment but can also produce laziness and inertia.

The placement of the sun in the birth chart by sign and house indicates how and where the individual "shines" to the world—his or her natural abilities, greatest strengths and weaknesses. This is where the individual projects his/her vital yang energies and lights the way for others to follow. The moon's position supports this role indicating where emotional interaction and security will be developed. Whereas the sun is consciousness, the moon is unconsciousness and the storehouse of memories. It reveals the soul's history—the roots of behavior patterns which emerge from past life experiences and are conditioned in childhood.

The sign rising in the east at the time of birth, or the ascendant, is the entrance into this life and describes the natural role for this individual—the one he or she will use to move through life and to fulfill the essential life mission, as indicated by the whole of the chart. This rising sign is the mask which also serves to defend and attract in relationships.

Planets in the first house of the chart should also be considered to be components of the mask or natural role in life.

Before we progress to the twelve dimensions of the astrological language, we must consider the four elements, fire, earth, air and water, associated with the four bodies (physical, mental, spiritual and emotional) and four functions used (hopefully) in being a human on this planet. Each of the signs of the zodiac, Aries through

Pisces, is classified by element (function) and quality (manner). When the count of dominant signs from the chart is taken, it reveals the most prominent functions used by that individual_ To find the element count in a chart, give one point to each of the planets by its *sign*, one point to the ascending sign and sign on the M.C. (tenth house cusp), then an extra point to the sun sign, moon sign and the sign holding the planet(s) ruling the ascendant (called the life ruler) An example of how to determine the element count in the chart is shown in the section on Sophie's chart interpretation. weak or missing element in the chart may be a function which is underdeveloped, not integrated with the others or has been overcompensated. An essential need for healing is balance and the elemental balance or imbalance is a key in determining where the work needs to be done.

A dominant "fire" individual has an abundance of energy, inspiration and a strong sense of adventure. He/she likes to be actively involved in new venture and self-expressive projects.

This individual has an optimistic outlook on life and is willing to take risks but can also be out of step by focusing excessively on the future. A lack of fire creates a reluctance to try new things, slows down the vital forces and suggests a need to develop self confidence, courage, hope and a joyful approach to living. Aries, Leo and Sagittarius are the fire signs. The Sun, Mars and Jupiter are the fire planets.

A dominant "earth" individual has a sensual appreciation for the physical world and an instinctive understanding for the laws of nature. Due to an innate respect for time, he/she patiently works to create order, plans and designs for tangible results. This type of character generally has a keen interest in the body and gives more attention to health but, carried to extremes, may be overly concerned with money, possessions and bodily functions. A lack of earth in the chart indicates a disregard for physical limitations or neglect of health and material support. While this type of individual may have extraordinary talents or abilities in other areas, life can be chaotic and he/she may have difficulty applying these abilities in practical ways. He/she would do well to develop positive health practices, make plans, set goals and stay in tune with nature. Taurus, Virgo, and Capricorn are the earth signs. Venus and Saturn are planets with earth energy.

Air is the element of communication and circulation. An individual with the dominant air element possesses a strong mind and intellect, enjoys social interaction and cultivates relationships easily. He/she can be objective, but detached and may also appear distant at times. "Air" people may live in the mental body—their heads—and lack sensitivity to other people's feelings or not be completely grounded in their ideas. A lack of the air element in the chart indicates an inability to communicate ideas to others, loss-of freedom, problems in social awareness and the possibility of resistance to learning. Gemini, Libra and Aquarius are the air signs. Mercury and Uranus are air planets.

A dominant "water" individual is deeply emotional, very sensitive, imaginative and easily moved by feeling responses. He/she needs to be involved in emotional exchanges and meaningful experiences to be nourished and satisfied. This type of individual needs plenty of time for quiet reflection and meditation to still the churning waters of emotion. He/she may, however, retreat from the world to avoid pain, choosing to remain in isolation and dwell on the past rather than confront the harsh reality of the outer world and work to create a better future. The chart lacking in water can be an individual who is disconnected from his/her subconscious emotional flow until it erupts and he/she is flooded with unresolved memories and dark feelings. Cancer, Scorpio and Pisces are the water signs. The Moon, Neptune and Pluto are water planets.

Figure 1 represents the fundamental chart used to derive and correlate your personality characteristics with the positions of the planets, the signs of the zodiac in which they travel, and their positions in the houses. You are at the center of the chart! The houses represent the departments or dimension s of life and remain fixed as shown by the innermost ring. The outer ring space is used to record planetary positions as they rotate about the center of the chart. The chart rotates every twenty-four hours, exposing us to our entire zodiac of modalities in the course of any particular day. Nobody escapes exposure on one or more levels. We start off Life with the imprint of the skies at our first breath and are subsequently exposed to the lessons of Life by the vast number of combinations set up over the years by the Divine Wheel. How we work with those forces determines our success in life and our overall spiritual growth.

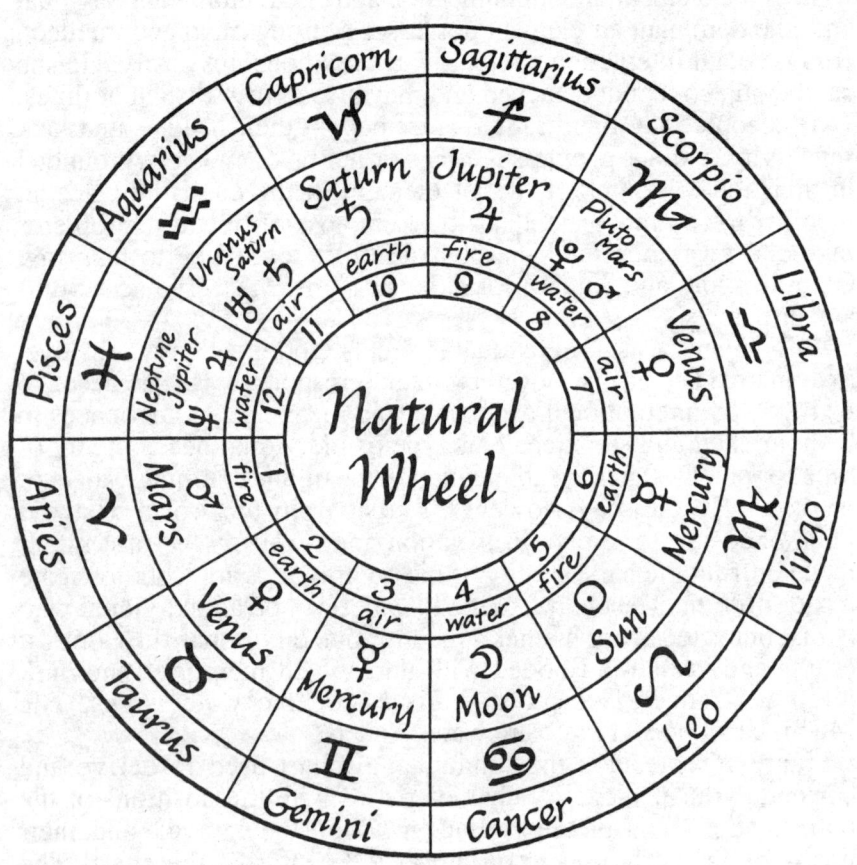

FIGURE 1
THE NATURAL WHEEL OF LIFE

The twelve dimensions of astrology take into consideration the twelve zodiacal signs, their natural house association and their ruling planets. Keep in mind, the planets represent the *energies* at work in the life pattern, the signs show *how* these are expressed and the houses show *where* they are focused in the life of the individual. A focus on one of these dimensions in the birth chart would bring the experiences and lessons of that dimension into the life of that individual as a theme, purpose or intention. More than one focus is shown in each chart. A focus for Dimension One might be indicated by the Sun, Moon or ascendant in Aries, a group or stellium of planets in house one and/or Mars (the ruling planet of Aries) prominent in the chart.

The experiences/lessons of *Dimension One* involve development of the self—the personality, the body and the ability to take an original and unique stand in life. The individual is building self-confidence through action, competition and confrontation. Relationships play a significant role in this process since they are mirrors of the self and provide a following for the necessary leadership skills to develop. Aries, the first sign of the zodiac, and house one are associated with physical development and self assertion or projection into life. Dimension One individuals are frequently attempting to "get ahead" in life. They can be pushy, self centered and abrasive if they have not developed a sensitivity to other people. Aries relates to the head and face—these people plunge headlong into new venture and are often pioneers of new lifestyles. Mars is the ruling planet of Aries.

Dimension Two is associated with resources, values, and pleasures. Taurus is the second sign and house two focuses on the development of talents which can be of an artistic nature. This individual has a good earning power (or at least enjoys spending money) and may possess the resources/talents which other people can develop and use in productive and profitable ways. One of the weaknesses of this pattern is personal over-indulgence in the material and sensual pleasures of living. The Taurus-second house-Venus individual has a keen aesthetic sense but may want to keep all the beautiful things for him/herself. Sharing is a valuable lesson. These people also have the tendency to get stuck in the "comfort zone" of life, becoming unwilling or unable to face challenges. Taurus is related to the neck, throat and ears. Dimension Two people frequently have a strong speaking or singing voice and need to be "heard" in life.

The experiences and lessons of *Dimension Three* are associated with communication and education. Gemini, the third house and the planet Mercury are part of this pattern, indicating that this individual is here to learn, gather information and disseminate it to others. He/she requires a variety of experiences, relationships and contacts in order to build a network of ideas. While this individual is mentally agile and learns quickly, he/she may also be scattered, restless, nervous or aimless in his/her development, not able to apply what is learned or experienced in any practical pursuits. Mercurial specializations may be teaching, writing, coordinating. the hands, arms, lungs and nervous system as associated with Gemini.

Dimension Four is associated with the sign Cancer, the Moon and house four. With this pattern we find an urge to "nest"—to build security, protect, sometimes parent other people and to be cared for *by* others. These individuals are unusually sensitive, imaginative and easily hurt so they frequently build strong psychological defense systems to protect themselves. The family unit, whether it is blood relations or a circle of friends, is important to the life of this individual. They enjoy history, are collectors of just about anything that has value or meaning to them, and will hold allegiance to country, culture or religion. The sign Cancer relates to the stomach, breasts, and all "containers" in the body. The experiences of *Dimension Five* take the individual into the world of creative self-expression, recreation, teaching and entertainment. Children and love relationships become a focal point of their attention. These are "heart" people who tend to invest enthusiasm and vitality into their projects and interests which range from the visual or performing arts to gambling. Leo is the fifth sign, ruled by the sun and is associated with the heart and the spine. The individuals of this dimension need an audience to support their sense of self-importance—they can be radiant stars of loving inspiration or overbearing egotists. If they have an outlet for their creative talents and have developed a circle of loyal friends and loved ones, they will be content.

Virgo, the sixth house and the planet Mercury are associated with *Dimension Six*. The lessons and experiences of this pattern relate to service, work and the refinement of the personality through problem solving and discrimination. These individuals are here to heal and/or help other people. Beginning with their own problems, they develop methods and technique to cope with their physical sensitivities. Virgo is a mind over matter sign. The lessons require an understanding of the connections between mind and body before the individual can live in peace and good health. He/she may choose a life work in the field of health or other technical specialization where correction and adjustment are applied to create a smooth running business, office or home. Acceptance of imperfections in the self and in others is necessary if this individual is to have harmonious relationships in life. The intestines, abdomen and the assimilation processes in the body are associated with this dimension.

The experiences of *Dimension Seven* related to the sign Libra, the seventh house and the planet Venus, involve relationships—one to one or one to the public. A strong sense of justice and a desire for companionship impel this individual to seek support and approval from others. Uncomfortable with discord or dissension, he/she tends to avoid confrontation or will fight for equal rights with charm and sweetness. An important lesson of this pattern is to maintain personal strength and identity while at the same time pleasing others. They limit their potentials by living through other people or by living exclusively for one other individual. The kidneys, filter system of the body, are related to Libra.

Dimension Eight is associated with sharing, bonding and intimacy. The experiences of this pattern involve personal transformation through merging with others. Intense emotional interaction is characteristic of Scorpio, the eighth house and the planets, Pluto and Mars. The individuals of this dimension are deeply reflective, often secretive and seek activities, interests and work where personal power, healing, business and finances or research are involved. These people do not enjoy the trivial pursuits of life and prefer private to public lives. Some type of self-mastery is required to tame the desire nature. Scorpio is associated with the sexual organs, bowels, reproduction and elimination.

Dimension Nine, associated with Sagittarius, the ninth house and the planet Jupiter, brings experiences/lessons related to higher education, travel and exploration. These individuals need freedom to expand beyond their personal limits, whether this is intellectually or physically. The world is their playground and their optimistic outlook on life tends to attract opportunities and good fortune. Wanderlust and the tendency to live in the future can detract from application of all that is learned.

These individuals need to build a strong base of morals and a personal philosophy for living that works for them. Once this is accomplished, they may choose to teach it to others. Sagittarius is associated with the hips, upper legs and the liver.

The experiences of *Dimension Ten* include achievement through hard work and self discipline. Responsibility plays a large role in the lives of these individuals. They are the builders and climbers of the zodiac—they are always in the process of moving to the next higher level of life. The life patterns of these individuals involve a search for security and protection; once found they can give these qualities to others. Finding a fulfilling career or place in the world is an important part of the life mission for these individuals. In the process, they often make great accomplishments and work their way to the top in their field. Good in organization and management, they enjoy a position of authority and dislike taking direction from others. Capricorn, ruled by Saturn and the tenth house of the chart are associated with this dimension. The bones, joints, skin and teeth are related to this pattern. Inflexible attitudes often result in rigid bodies.

Dimension Eleven brings in the experiences of group creative process. Aquarius, the eleventh house and the planets Uranus and Saturn are related. This is a social and humanitarian dimension. The individuals of this pattern seek friends and associates of like mind, similar interests and common beliefs with whom they can work toward progressive or revolutionary change. The lifestyles of these individuals tend to be unusual with plenty of room for freedom and inventive solutions to life challenges. They must find a balance between personal will and divine will if they are to live in harmony with others. Circumstantial upsets, and unexpected turns of event color the lives of these individuals giving them the chance to apply their intuitive insights or inventive solutions. The circulatory system and legs (symbolic of our freedom) are associated with this dimension.

The final dimension, associated with the sign Pisces, the twelfth house and the planets Neptune and Jupiter, relates to universal service and personal self-sacrifice. Once the individual with *Dimension Twelve* prominent in the chart finds balance between soul and outer personality—between giving and receiving, helping and being helped, there is harmony in life. When compassion has been awakened and inspires this individual to move beyond merely personal gratification, he/she is rewarded by renewal of spirit and the riches of heaven. Suffering can become a way of life until the necessary lessons have been completed and the soul awakens. The search for true beliefs is part of the life quest. One characteristic of this dimension is the unusual assortment of relationships and life experiences that mark definite "chapters" throughout the lives of these individuals. Pisces is associated with the feet representing the spiritual foundation upon which we stand. There is a strong need for privacy or sanctuary from the harsh demands of the outer world. These people have delicate emotional natures and often take an escape route rather than meeting life head on—the lesson of Dimension One and the next stage in the circle of life.

Let's use Figure 2 an example chart for a woman born March 11, 1934, 1:00 p.m. in Newark, New Jersey. We will refer to her as Sophie and identify the basic themes in her character, personality, natural talents, patterns of behavior and her life purpose.

To begin, let us figure the element count in the chart. Starting at the ascendant or first house, moving counter clockwise, we find the ascendant and one other planet, Pluto, in Cancer, a water sign (2 water points). Neptune is in Virgo (1 earth point), Jupiter in Libra (1 air point). The Moon, Venus and Saturn are in Aquarius (3 more air points), and three planets are in Pisces (3 more water points). The M.C. or 10th house sign and Uranus are in Aries (2 fire points). Now we give another point to the Sun in Pisces (1 water), the Moon in Aquarius (1 air) and the Moon rules Cancer, her rising sign so we count its sign again (1 more air). The total is 2 fire, 1 earth, 5 air and 7 water. Are you confused yet? Study the Natural Wheel with basic sign/planet rulerships and their relationship to the houses of the chart. The more familiar you are with these terms, the easier it will be for you to find your way around the natal chart.

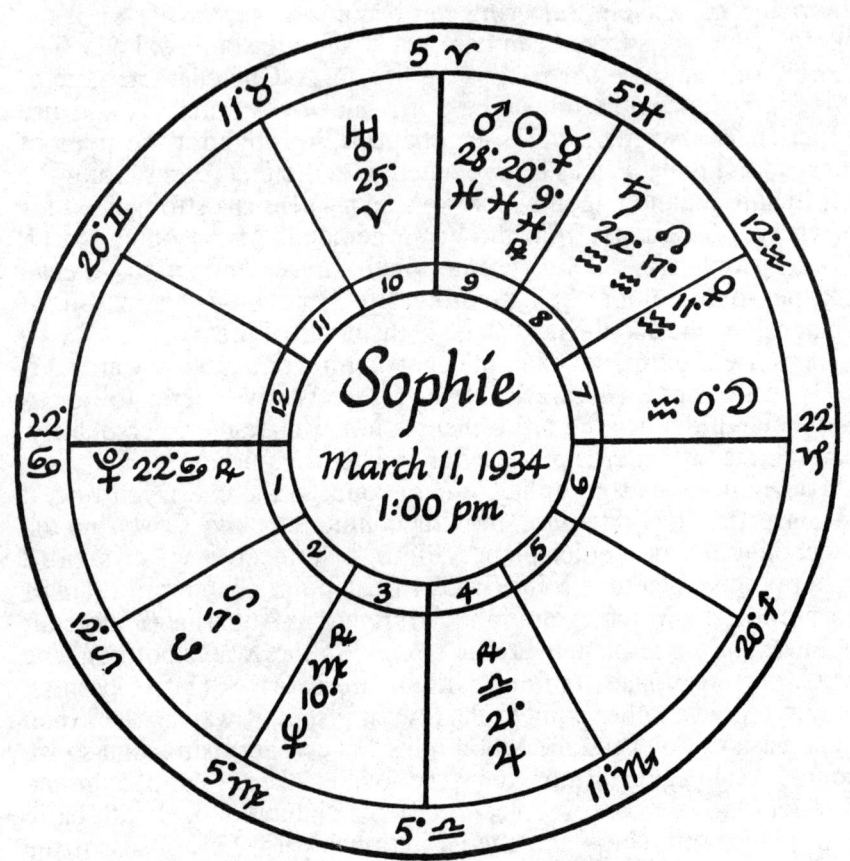

FIGURE 2

NATAL CHART FOR 74° WEST LONGITUDE
AND 40° NORTH LATITUDE

The three most important points in Sophie's chart are her Sun in Pisces, Moon in Aquarius and Cancer rising. Her dominant elements are air and water with only one earth sign and one fire sign represented. As an air-water individual she has deep feelings, rich imagination and the urge to communicate her dreams, visions and emotional needs to other people. She needs plenty of personal quiet time to protect that sensitivity but also plenty of social interaction and intellectual stimulation to satisfy her quest for knowledge. Until she developed her self-confidence, found autonomy and grounded her natural abilities in the professional world she was tossed about in life like a small boat on a windy sea.

Dimensions Four, Nine and Twelve are highlighted in her chart. Cancer, sign four is rising (on the first house cusp), she has three planets, including the Sun in Pisces and they are placed in the ninth house of the chart. Jupiter aspects the Sun.

Sophie's home life supplies a rich, stable foundation for her creativity to blossom. From her first marriage, she has one son, now grown. He and his family are a special part of her life. In addition to her need for a "nest", her lifelong urge to explore has taken her traveling to distant lands many times in her life. Her son even traveled with her for many years while he was growing up.

Professionally, Sophie is an artist/designer and has achieved a number of successes in the development of her career, including a business of her own where she directed 20 employees. She has been married twice with a number of colorful relationships highlighting each chapter of her Dimension Twelve lifestyle. Two major disappointments: a bankrupted business and a broken marriage ending in financial betrayal, taught Sophie to protect herself emotionally and financially. Following these experiences, she was also inspired to design self development workshops and has learned to be an attentive listener.

Sophie's need for security keeps her close to home and to the kitchen where she demonstrates her artistry with cooking. She still needs the freedom outside the home to grow spiritually, intellectually and socially by cultivating a large circle of friends. Her task is to balance these complementary qualities: security and freedom, build self-confidence, hope, faith and to develop a productive rhythm in her work without stifling her spirit.

An in-depth study of Sophie's birth chart helped her to be aware of her individual need for both security, home and family as well as freedom to travel. Instead of denying one for the sake of the other, she now accepts both needs and plans her life to fulfill these aspects of her character. She now has a greater understanding of the unique gifts she has to offer other people, enjoys a rewarding career as a designer and a wholesome companionship.Another category for use of the natal chart is chart comparison of relationship studies. We can "overlay" two birth charts to explore the exchanges between two individuals and to derive insights into the purposes of the relationship. the value in this type of comparison is not to determine whether two people are compatible or incompatible but rather to understand the attraction, common interests and dynamics of the relationship. By comparing natal charts, we can penetrate the surface exchanges to understand essential motivations, needs and potential problems in the relationship.

The people in our lives serve as mirrors to catch a glimpse of our own true natures. Relationships also serve to purify the ego—to refine and polish the character and the soul. Specific personality types will "hook" into our own chart patterns and we will have an attraction to that individual. These relationship patterns are associated with Dimension Seven, the 7th house, sign Libra and the planet Venus, even though the whole chart is used in chart comparison. The 7th house indicates *what* and *how* we share with our partners—basic needs in a one-to-one relationship and what particular traits we "assign" to others or project onto others in the process of transference. Other unexpressed facets of our chart/personality may also be projected onto others. This depends upon the individual.

Aspects between planetary positions from chart to chart indicate the nature of the energy exchanges between two people. Conjunctions (planets at the same position by sign) are cohesive, bonding contacts; hard aspects create conflict but also stimulate excitement. Easy aspects show areas of ease in relating—natural affinities.

Referring to our previous chart example for Sophie, we find Capricorn on the 7th house with Venus and the Moon in that house. Sophie attracts accomplished professional men who give her a sense of emotional or material security, or she works together with her partner to build a secure professional base. However, the contrast of the unpredictable, erratic sign Aquarius often adds the element of surprise or disruption to her relationships, sometimes ending in abrupt separation. She is attracted to unusual, progressive people, both men and women, who share her maverick viewpoints, spiritual and intellectual interests. She prefers independent thinkers who allow her plenty of space to press her own uniqueness.

As we each progress in our inner work and become more attuned to our authentic selves, accepting of our needs and limitations, our relationships become more harmonious.

Accepting and honoring the special gifts within each individual we meet is a sign of our own enlightenment.

Once problems and limiting life patterns have been identified in the birth chart, the work begins. Therapies, meditations, rituals and other resources for personal growth are available. No one is destined to live with a problem for life, unless that is a choice. In time, even a limitation can become an asset. Life is a dance choreographed by the Creator. If you don't like the steps you have been taught, make up a new routine.

PROCESSING

CHAPTER SIXTEEN
BEGINNINGS

"It is seldom possible to find a member of the traditional helping professions from whom one can receive the kinds of services needed to alleviate or to clear an aching soul. This state of affairs results from our difficulty, our alienation, in contacting potential Students and Aspirants to become Conscious Co-Workers, and accounts for the slowness with which we are able to enhance or inaugurate the Kingdom on Earth. Not much can be done in a short time, but this way it is possible for us to get things set up for selected members of this and following generations to become trained counselors. By working with them through the veil we can share their burdens, relieving and readjusting them so that it is possible once again to re-establish The Kingdom in the hearts of key persons, of those whom we can prepare to become Channels. A few thusly trained will make an auspicious start. By becoming adept at making significant changes in their personal lives, other persons will see the results, and will be quick to adopt the methods for themselves.

"Our objective is to find, recruit, and train potential members of the incarnate Hierarchical Church among the religions and from among some members of the established psychological professions, so that their methods should bear immediate fruit. It is only when one has been through the mill as a Counselor will he understand the human possibilities. As slowly as we seem to be moving, only in that way will we make progress rapidly enough for the new Soul Technologies of which we write to find acceptance throughout the mental health world.

"The world is hungry for more effective methods for bringing soul relief and which restore harmony and order in the lives of its inhabitants, especially considering the spiritual vacuum in which the psychological community and its members now find themselves. So, it is our mission to divulge new methods to all practitioners through whom our original objectives are best realizable. Most noteworthy of all is the fact that our Teacher-Counselor-Channels will make the greatest and most rapid spiritual growth of them all!

"It is here made possible for a person to achieve success in the world, even while mastering Life and thus spiritualizing self at the same time. Anyone desiring to perfect his or her relationships can do both! One previously successful attempt at publication is now known as "The Aphorisms of Patanjali" [6]. This and a few others predate the Bible, but so few people were fortunate enough to have been recipients of those instructions that in effect they have been kept an eternal secret. With Piscean Age values giving way to those of the Aquarian Age, Schoolhouse Earth is undergoing a great graduation exercise and reorganization.

"This text then numbers among those being readied for Aquarian Age service. There will be new texts and new teachers ushering in the new lessons for the New Age. Our Father's Grand Plan is being presented to anyone who will listen.

"Intense interest is generated by such writings as these when put before the transformation-oriented Ecclesiastic. Their work can thus be made more interesting, effective, and exciting than it has been to date because it is made possible for General Religion to become more proficient in restoring harmony into Life via the human soul and mind. The typical human can now accelerate his or her spiritual evolution by "Clearing" or "Transforming" the mind. Spiritualization and Self mastery have been occurring so slowly that Planet Earth might as well be forgotten as any other than a pleasure zone intended for the faithful, dedicated to those who give a modicum lip service to The Lord, or as a Hell for the naughty. Most people on Earth seem to want to be rewarded for *good intentions* rather than to be "crowned Above" for getting good grades in Schoolhouse Earth.

"It is typical even if lamentable that human evolution is again mired, but it is not a new phenomenon. Readjustments to the Schoolhouse Earth curriculum become necessary at *every* transition into a new Zodiac sign. Each adjustment, this one included, is a Labor of Love at times when it would seem that there were little point in trying to do anything about those who must reincarnate, who must return again and again to the School. However, even now there are people who could benefit enough from undertaking Special Spiritual Counseling so that significant steps for the Human Race are made available in the lifetime remaining.

"Of greater significance than alleviation of a person's soul aches, however desirable, is that our purpose and approach be implemented well enough so that individual pain is used to show where the steps are in attaining to self mastery. Everything needed is available to persons intent upon graduating from Ye Olde Schoolhouse. One's spiritual evolution may be accelerated *at will* to the extent that some individuals will need reincarnate only when desired to learn the latest zodiacal lessons, to serve as an Specialist-Teacher, or/and as an Invisible Helper or Teacher-Counselor between lives. They will come back to Earth long enough to help shift the World's burdens again toward the spiritual realms, thus using growth-pains as patterns to guide Humanity, as it was intended in the Beginning.

"In other words, we have here a proven approach by which it is *practical* both to relieve distress and to grow spiritually, i.e., *consciously*. We do so by relieving mankind of the same impediments which have tied Man to flesh for millennia.

"That relief is available should be of great impact, bringing joy to Those who have accepted responsibility for salvation of the soul of mankind. Humanity may now collectively regain its balance, permitting and ushering in an era of Growth and Fruition, seemingly overnight as now compared to what has been heretofore accomplished by mankind.

"That such powerful techniques are entrusted to the public at large is not to deny their potency. Traditionally such power has been restricted to the hands of an Elite Corps trained in its proper manipulation, thus preventing powers of darkness from subsequent utilization. While it is always possible for selfish ends to be accomplished by persons who will discover and apply our methods, once they have found power to clean up the ills of the world, even if for the wrong reasons, they will themselves be joined with the overall effort to cleanse Mankind's Soul, thus setting forth more interesting goals.

"We grant that man needs a dichotomy in which to develop the powers of choice. Even so, discovery of and attainment unto newer and higher goals will continue to be found so desirable that even the greatest of misapplications will not long be attractive enough to thwart the Godward evolution of Mankind. Therefore, it is with a clear conscience that we can now reveal the inner secrets which have for eons been withheld from the irreverent or public eye. Let any exploitation-minded practitioner who thinks that here are techniques by which Mankind can further be duped know that a price will be exacted for such misuse. They will be transformed by their own attempts at transforming others.

"Thus is the Golden Age—the millennium—to be ushered in. Once the Forces of Evil find it more interesting and attractive to pursue the Grand Design, They will integrate in a common attempt, even if perhaps as adversaries, for the greatest revival yet seen upon the face of the Earth. It is therefore and thusly that we are now free to reveal, by these discourses the methods by which many shall be preserved. Fortunate are those who are able to be among the early recipients of this documentation, such as the Recruiters and the Counselors, they themselves being and constituting the cadre of those in the avant garde of the Human Race who will prepare the way for the general application of the techniques to the benefit of Mankind.

"It is still required that the Facilitators, Practitioners, Counselors, the Clergy,...the mental health professionals...shall be trained, become skilled in application of the principles, for we are here dealing with power of another dimension, the Power of Abstract Thought, not yet recognized on Earth except by a chosen or fortunate few. Relatively few such persons working consciously through the veil are sufficient so that there shall be normal evolutionary growth in promulgation and application of the techniques. Twenty years hence will show great strides made in their availability, so that we find it both feasible and necessary that our work shall be released at this time."

APPLYING FOR DIVINE ASSISTANCE

"Many Counselors could pick up this book and apply its principles to diagnosis and treatment of the aching soul. A special class of help is available, capable of accelerating human spiritual evolution enough to enable graduation from Schoolhouse Earth in this incarnation and entrance into The Greater Service. This section is designed to help interested Practitioners and Aspirants apply for that Special Help and work with our Special Guides and Guardians Who operate from Behind The Veil. Chapter 12 of *So YOU Want To Be A CHANNEL!* [27] details how to apply for Special Help, but in brief the process is as follows.

"Write a Letter to God, asking that you shall understand your potentials for serving consciously in the Spiritual Service, and how to fulfill your highest good. Let it be clear as to your dedication to that process. Compose the letter to reflect your goals and to describe what you consider your present-time problems. To do this adequately may require several rewrites. On having done your best, write it out and sign it in ink. Also make a copy of it and sign the copy in ink. Keep the original in your Bible or Holy Book.. Mail it to The New Age Fellowship, with your name and address clearly printed on both the letter and its envelope. Mail it in a Self Addressed, Stamped Envelope (SASE) to the author. Just before mailing it, pray that you shall understand the reply. Allow perhaps six weeks for us to receive it, prepare the response and return it to you.

"Know that your activity has initiated much behind-the-veil training activity on your behalf. Immediately you write the Dear God letter you will be taken up out of body during your sleep time and will receive special instruction in Special Schools tailored to your needs, be they of the physical, dietary, emotional, and psychological varieties. Parts of those instructions will also be given you by mail, as much as is feasible for your understanding and implementation. Special reading may be recommended from time to time. Your interests may shift, and you may meet unusual people, and find yourself invited to attend special classes and lectures. Become aware that you are standing on the threshold of a lifelong program of self refinement and perfection. Also be aware that not everyone who enters The Training program will be willing to make the adjustments and small sacrifices in Life Patterns and style sometimes necessary.

Your Teachers and Guides will work with your Counselors and Facilitator(s) to provide the insights you need to revise and/or remove your blocks as needed to open you to greater flow of the Life Force. You will be protected against interference in your spiritual unfoldment, as long as you keep the link alive, and that is done through steadfast adherence to the guidance offered you, via occasional contact with the New Age Fellowship, through which our staff works with The Guides in answering your queries.

"You will not be asked to retire from the world, to work in isolation. Instead, you will learn to master, to overcome yourself, your thoughts and feelings and responses *right where you are*. The Teachers and Guides, the Hierarchy, needs strong conscious Helpers *in the World*, much stronger souls than were generated by living in a monastery or convent! You may not like everything we suggest for you, but we trust you will recognize increasingly what it is that needs be done and will understand the rationale behind it. You will certainly transform your daily relationships and your feelings. You can expect to experience an ever increasing sense of order in your relationships and affairs and become a stable beacon, a rock in the stormy seas for your associates. You will recognize *your* changes through how your associates look and respond to *you*!

"You will gradually become aware of the presence and ministry of your Guide(s) and will someday become a *conscious channel*, a Helper-in-the-Flesh for your associates. You will teach others to become what *you* have become! We trust this offer is attractive!"

CHAPTER SEVENTEEN
BENEFITS

Having the goal of excellent relationships with our fellow humans is of major importance to our success and happiness in Life. Classically a difficult problem to work through, our approach to clearing the sub-conscious mind of nonproductive and/or counterproductive attitude 'tapes' is demonstrably very effective, requiring an ordinate expenditure of Time and Effort.

Another specific benefit from practice of our techniques is a raised level of awareness, enabling conscious work in the Inner or Higher planes. This condition results from reviewing the contents of the subconscious mind, and as a fringe benefit contributes to a well balanced Personality. In each technical approach we draw attention to the primary and the secondary benefits, from awakening or developing some particular character trait or chakra in the fundamental process of clearing The Path for the Spiritual Aspirant and Students of the Higher Life

The methods we describe produce Healing on three levels of beingness, Body, Mind, and Soul, being interlocked, identified as the physiological, psychological and spiritual levels. For example, one can greatly increase one's capacity for Love through elimination of Fear. We develop clairvoyance through practice in observing the recordings in the subconscious mind, so that one can literally study what is written on the Metaphysician's Akasha, known also as "The Book of God." One also attends to development of Direct Knowing, the Intuitive faculty, by clearing the barriers to sensory receptivity, its expression and providing practice in using it for conscious transveil and telepathic communications.

These qualities manifest in the world as increased Energy and Enthusiasm, so we are justified in saying we can significantly enhance human Creativity, it being a manifestation of Intuition.

In resolving human travail perhaps the most oft experienced element of distress is found by using the command "Look for a time when it hurts." This focuses the client's attention in searching the subconscious jungle of Cause and Effect recordings, clearing a pathway by almost literally hacking a way through Pain and Fear recordings. As the major underbrush thins out, is resolved, one becomes able to experience the subtler recordings, observing their cause-effect factors at work in the daytime world.

An excellent way to help a client get started is first to help resolve his day-by-day present-time problems. Little by little the client becomes a stable element in his environment and can spare the energy and focus his attention on the deeper/inner attitudes and barriers. Here then are the principles practices and benefits available from deliberate dedication to going within and exploring the Inner Life as you and your client have constructed it!

This amounts symbolically to clearing the same brush and bramble that the King's Son had to hack through to reach The Princess and free her from entrapment, to consummate the mystical Wedding.

CHAPTER EIGHTEEN
ON THE MULTIPLE ROLES OF THE AQUARIAN AGE COUNSELOR

The roles required of the new Aquarian Age Psyche or Soul Therapist are indeed manifold. They include but transcend earlier listening, hand-holding and consolation into guiding and assisting clients in confrontation and reevaluation of personal nonconstructive programming at deeper levels. The best therapists will be qualified to offer several avenues of approach, as appropriate for bringing about a broader self understanding within his client. All this is necessary for restoring the Aspirant-Client to his true life business, that of Knowing Himself. That person will become increasingly aware that he is Spirit, a "chip off the Divine Block." He will gain facility in wielding the Universal Laws of Relationship, enjoying increasingly the "Land his God prepared for him from The Beginning," thus consciously becoming a Co-Creator with God and a Conscious Co-Worker with The Hierarchy of Teachers and Guides. Should there be any other outcome? After all, is not Man made in the Image and Likeness of God? Should he not grow into manifest realization of that pedigree?

The practicing Aquarian Age soul therapist and counselor should expect to find himself being used as a crutch until his ailing client is able to stand firmly upon his own feet of spiritual self-determination. That same counselor can also expect to be used as a confessor, a confidant, a dart board and sparring partner for testing ideas, an oracle, a model for teaching the client how to interrelate, even being used as a cudgel by one or both members of a marital rift situation. Said therapist may occasionally be invited into a love affair. Of course, succumbing to such offers open the door to blackmail, karma, lawsuit, disease, loss of standing and even worse, causes loss of the Invisible Guides' support. At the very least, sexual liaison with a client invites loss of objectivity and risks loss of credibility.

Any practitioner will do well to learn to play the dichotomous roles of father/mother, boss/employee, husband/wife, parent/child, good-guy/bad-guy, adult/child, priest/devil's advocate, and so on, as required to help the client get in touch with and work through his buried feelings, getting them out into the daylight of Present Time for reevaluation and clearing.

Of the various published and popular contenders for a favored therapy, this author likes best the principles practiced and taught by Dr. Fritz Perls, as expounded rather thoroughly and well in his books "Gestalt Therapy Verbatim" [26] and "In And Out Of The Garbage Pail." Perls integrated and extrapolated the psychological technologies known, including working with Dr. Rolf, Jung, and other contemporary greats. His two books give examples of how he works, well enough so they can be applied by anyone who understands what is happening and who understands the nature and structure of the Humanoid incarnation.

Until a therapist has had enough experience in programming reevaluation on his own case to become stable in his own Universe, he may become drawn into the vortex offered by a very troubled client, could "flip out," or/and further degenerate his client's case. To be most effective, a practitioner will have worked under specialists in each of the various disciplines so that he can evaluate, formulate, and develop his own best techniques. Only thus can he become competent to understand his client's distress and therefore be effective in his own client relationships. He will thus learn a variety of safe approaches to the Pandora's Box often posed by troubled humans.

A competent counselor-therapist will identify the differences between sympathy, empathy and compassion, and hence be compassionate enough to be appropriately "tough" with his client when and as needed. He will then find himself well enough equipped to take or leave a client, "walking out" when a client must be taught to fall back on himself.

It is not always easy for a client to be saved from himself. Nor is a counselor required to solve his client's problems *for* him. The utmost in professionalism does require emotional detachment from the deceptions and devices which clients at times will throw in the way of the successful resolution of their problems. Sometimes it seems that the whole Human Race is bent upon 'going to Hell' or blaming its troubles on someone 'out there' rather than on individual personal release and the biblical "return to The Father's House." Humanity appears instead to prefer playing sick games over even short periods of hard work, or even to confronting life seriously at all.

Without performing a goodly quantity of work upon himself it is not possible for the typical Earthling to join in the Higher Games awaiting him on the Heaven Side of the Veil, or across The Great Divide of Death, if you prefer. Those higher games mastered lead to functioning on even yet higher spheres of which the average human may have heard only via mythology and theological speculation. Activities attributed to The Gods of yore reflect the potential human experience but on a scale grander by far than he has any present means of comprehending.

To find potential trainees and to indoctrinate them as high quality counselors is a rarity to we Teachers and Guides. It is still a difficult achievement, even when considering other higher beings who would help and assist the Human Race on call. Then, let each would-be therapist-counselor begin his/her own unfoldment immediately by working to open and clear the pathway to the Inner Self. Again, this is done by removing the impedimenta now blocking conscious approach and entry to the Higher Life to be found insulated and dormant deep within each human breast. For doing so, he can and will be used to lead others into a larger appreciation for the vastness and joy of an expanded level of consciousness.

CHAPTER NINETEEN
THE IMPORTANCE OF CENTERING

Success as a Psychic Psychologist or as a Psychic trained in Psychology depends heavily on the degree to which one stays centered.

The most important thing you can do toward becoming a master Psychic Psychologist is to become so familiar with the feeling of being centered that you can operate from it consciously at will, as a state of being. A state of being infrequently observed we offer to establish that Being Centered is the evolutionary norm for incarnate spirit, rather than only a religious or metaphysical ecstasy serving no identifiable purpose.

WHAT IS CENTERING? WHAT DOES IT FEEL LIKE?

The feeling of "being centered" carries with it a rich serenity, a feeling of relaxed complete awareness, yet a feeling of being in total contact within yourself and with your environment...even the feeling of being One with God. It has the sentience of well-being, of *I AM*, of total competence, yet not at all in an egotistic sense. By just being, observing without evaluating, while enjoying that state of consciousness, one has true perspective as to what is happening anywhere in his body, mind, and surroundings. This extends to awareness of what is going on in the minds and bodies of his or her associates. One is often telepathic and readily communes with other orders of Intelligence, emulating the old prophets and masters. When centered, one's upper triad of Chakras is open and balanced with respect to the lower triad. The beauty of it is that you can *develop* that capacity and can work from it at will!

For openers, please recall that the human aura is an electromagnetic matrix which interpenetrates the human body and occupies the space surrounding it. Some clairvoyants report that the auric space appears as a multicolored haze of swirling energies several feet in diameter, and that it is most easily seen when the body is viewed against a neutral background. Other persons sense it as an induced or empathetic feeling of heat or pressure, perhaps pleasant, perhaps not. When centered, one feels as if comfortably ensconced in the midst of his holy temple and observes Life from that throne.

Next, consider what happens when a boxer has been "knocked out." His body on the canvas, the aware ego has rudely been expelled from its physical space. On reentering its flesh body, on recovering consciousness, there may be misalignment between some part of the auric matrix of Self and its flesh body due to damage to corresponding physical and psychological processes. A similar and gentler process of dissociation occurs when a person goes to sleep. Again, the auric awareness self leaves (rises up out of) the flesh body, shutting off conscious communication between the Spirit and its flesh sensors...visual, audio, smell, taste and touch. (Perhaps the reader recalls that similar senses operate in his own dream state).

Please observe our claim that it is a normal state of affairs for the spirit and its auric vehicles to separate, to leave and reenter its body of flesh *at will* among those persons qualified..

A commonly experienced phenomenon finds the entire auric vehicle exteriorized, habitually displaced several inches outside the physical body, with impaired awareness of and participation in one's environment. That situation is familiar as "day dreaming" or "wool gathering." This out-of-body or out-of-mind phenomenon also exists when we do something stupid, are on drugs or drunk, as when one is feeling either 'high' or 'low.' Whether the spiritual-auric self is inside or outside the body consciously makes a tremendous difference in how one is able to confront his or her worlds. If we are entirely centered in our space, we are aware of some degree of euphoria. We then perceive the sensations fed to us by *both* sets of perceptic mechanisms, the classic five plus their higher etheric/psychic or auric octaves, with Intuition and Knowing.

And conversely, when we, as Awareness Units, are out of our body as in daydreaming, we usually are at best only partially aware of our surroundings. We then do not see well, nor hear or respond well, so are said to be "out of it," "not with it," or to be preoccupied.

Note carefully that a person can only access the full range of seven senses (whether seven or twelve senses are used merits further examination) when he is cleared of perceptic barriers and blocks, is centered, is *aware* of being aware, and is therefore operating from his fundamental Spiritual Self...from his God-Self...rather than from any one of his or her numerous sub-selves in the Voice Dialogue sense (see Stone and Winkleman). This presumption assures that each perceptic is open, balanced, and that each chakra is passing its proper levels and frequencies of energy. To the degree that these presumptions are met we are alive and can participate in and be responsive to the whole world of activity on whatever level(s) one chooses to consider. On having overcome our emotional and engrammatic factors, on having the Akasha (the subconscious mind) cleared of nonconstructive junk, we find ourselves able to *know* Right Action...God's Will...*anything* and *everything* we focus our attention on with stability. To the degree we are clear, to that degree we they are able to channel consciously, to give readings, and to heal the aching psyche to the same level and degree.

We hope to build acceptance that Being Centered is a normal capacity of the Human as designed, however broadly developed. The main reason that said state is so rarely attained is that few persons in the social, religious, and philosophical communities know anything about it, or realize that Centering is anything other than a mystical experience that should be revered and/or be left to the Gurus and the Masters. *We* claim that the ability to *become* and *remain* centered is an acquirable condition, and that all capabilities attributed to the saints as perfected humans can be manifested to the degree that we are successful in becoming awakened and Centered, in cultivating that fundamental human quality of being integrated from The Crown Chakra to the tips of their toes! We acquiesce that one need not be centered at all times, but the alternatives would seem to consist of slogging through life only partly awake!

PREPARING TO BE CENTERED

One can remain centered with stability as the emotions become stilled, when the mental body is quiet, and on having resolved one's subconscious recordings of trauma, fear and other unresolved issues. While working to clear the subconscious mind, a client increasingly *responds* to the pressures of life instead of *reacting* to them, and pain signals are interpreted as warnings that something need's the Spirit's attention. "Reactive Mind" is then an accurate label for the buried programs which dictate one's habitual or automatic interfaces with the outer world. In the *reactive* mind we find the 'flight or fight' programs, and pain signals bypass the Aware Ego, directly operating the defenses. The contents of both sections of the mind become available for conscious examination and update, all this by skilled application of our centering methods.

The most effective methods to enter the subconscious layers of mind are modifications and embellishments of a process correctly described as conscious regression in a reverie state. We recommend against general use of hypnosis because of the high probability that the conscious mind is less able to control, monitor, observe and participate in the subjective processes of review and reassessment.

THREE APPROACHES

Three effective tools available to the mental health practitioner are introduced here. A comprehensive listing of their variations would be tedious, and new versions are being 'invented' every month. The Old Masters taught going into The Silence to make contact with their recordings, there confronting them the best way they could. The approach was rewarding, but it took a lifetime of dedication and special preparation to achieve success. An apprenticed chela or student-trainee spent years in emulating his Teacher or Guru or Master. It still takes a lifetime of dedication to become a master. Paramhansa Yogananda is a recent example of the Old School. His accomplishments and teachings are well documented for today's Western aspirant. For many contemporary aspirants the religions lack appeal because they are poorly understood and do not go in depth, and private instruction is still found very useful and is available.

A generation ago Ruth Carter Stapleton taught and practiced a useful regressive approach she called "Healing of the memories." Used in a religious setting, it was successful in bringing relief to many ailing souls. While similar to ours, her approach was seldom used to become 'Clear,' largely because of lack of the concept of 'clear.'

Dr. Arthur Janov popularized a powerful method under the name *The Primal Scream*. He facilitates good contact between his client's conscious mind while focussing on the client's buried feelings toward the traumatic events recorded in the subconscious memory. He helps maintain the inner contact and examine the details of still active recordings, reviewing them from the vantage point of Present Time. Fundamental causes of deep-seated conflict are discovered when the client is comfortable in reliving and reporting who is doing what to whom, the feelings being experienced by all parties in the recording, and in assessing justice in the light of the ethics at that ancient time, compared to the ethical standards from today's point of view.

Forgiveness for past-life aggressions is often necessary and is accomplished through understanding the forces at work. The Energies of Resistance and Pain are discharged by the focus of attention on feelings, leaving the client free to face Life as it is in the Here and Now. Those released energies are available for self-expression. Janov's method opens access to early-life trauma and may be studied in *The Feeling Child*. Perhaps his greatest contribution to the medical and mental health communities is his carefully documented research on the correlation between psychic therapy and resulting blood chemistry. [Janov and Holden].

Dr. Fritz Perls of the Big Sur Esalen Institute perfected a powerful 'mind cleaner' and consciousness raiser which he called Gestalt Therapy. [26]. By his 'two-chair method,' Perls established the power and credibility of Creative Visualization as a method for two-way subjective communications with 'the other guy' or antagonist. A beautiful aspect of Perls' approach is that 'the other guy' need not be present physically for the client to gain benefit of his or her contributions and feelings. The 'other guy' can be in Timbuktu, or deceased...it matters not. Observable results are immediate in terms of changed energy flows and/or relationships. The insights thus available are limited only by the skill and imagination of the client and/or the Psychic Psychologist. In fact, once learned, the process can be administered without a Facilitator present, by one's self, but to do that requires being fairly stable and centered.

For a therapist who is a bit less metaphysically inclined the author recommends the approach developed by Dr. Cecil G. Osborne. Called Primal Integration, he has trained a nationwide cadre of well-qualified practitioners and facilitators. Certificated graduates find employment in the holistic and mental health communities, and in the broad field of ministerial counseling. Osborne's Integration program is accepted by prominent universities for doctoral dissertation [including this author's dissertation].

L. Ron Hubbard [19, 30] has contributed a landmark work toward healing the human mind of trauma (engrams), producing what he calls 'Theta Clears,' volitional persons who are no longer controlled by Reactive Mind. Training for certification as an "Auditor" is available to dedicated persons, and includes instruction in use of the Electropsychometer.

These three approaches are recommended for in-depth study and application by holistic mental health practitioners of all types. Psychics need to become Psychologists, and Pastors need to become more effective as Counselors, and Psychologists need to become Psychics! There is a crying need for persons who are dedicated to helping clear the typical confused and badly programmed human soul-mind. And...in almost every case there is also a strong correlation between diet and exercise in the process of attaining unto and maintaining one's Awareness and Centering. Further details in each method are becoming available in the open literature to anyone who would like to go deeper, clear his akasha, and to awaken his total soul-mind, but there is nothing better than training under an expert. And as for customers, it is like the Bible said two thousand years ago, "The fields are white for harvest; you can name your pay, but the workers are few!"

PRECAUTIONARY CONSIDERATIONS

Formal training and certification in these psyche technologies is necessary for control of practitioner quality, and to assure that recognized practitioners will reliably and responsibly discern when a client is a 'basket case,' or is a potential 'case of dynamite.' Some unstable clients should be referred to a protected Specialist, such as an M.D. or Psychiatrist for treatment. It must be understood that no therapist-practitioner should expect to achieve full case resolution of any personal problem he or she has not faced and resolved on his own case. Client-Counselor personality dynamics can become greater than the usual 'uncleared' practitioner can handle. Approaches differ, even among big-name professionals, and ethics are sometimes abandoned when the practitioner becomes emotionally involved with his client, causing more damage than he or she came in with, breaking up marriages, causing lawsuits, and long-term karma.

Let us emphasize further why we consider it important to take a medical and psychological profile on accepting a client. As is well documented by Janov, even simple processing is capable of upsetting a delicate balance between a client's state of mind and prescription medication. This can be true especially for mental or emotional and some heart conditions. Janov found that when a client is carefully monitored, in-depth holistic processing makes measurable changes to a client's blood chemistry. Such is the power of these simple-to-apply methods that even when the subconscious diagnosis and engram review has been only partially begun, the mind-body interface is altered, and not only with measurable blood chemistry changes, but with sociological and/or personality changes as well.

We admonish that most Aquarian Age Psyche Psychologists should be wary and hesitant to make any commitment to a client who is known to be under treatment using mind-control drugs. The wisdom of accepting drug addiction and psychotic cases without on-call or staff medical and psychologist support can hardly be overestimated. The neophyte Psychic Psychologist should err on the side of overcaution, in not hesitating to refer 'dangerous' cases to State Licensed practitioners or the Police, even if it means passing up an attractive source of income. Line up your backups early in the game and do not hesitate to use them!

A low-cost but widely available aid to clearing the emotions is to make use of some form of meditation. Persistently and properly practiced meditation on Being Centered eventually yields it as a natural result. With added benefit of visual and sensory practice, a person becomes able to perceive and review any particular recorded trauma, examining the original threat, related trauma networks, and how the body has programmed its resources to defend itself. After all, *you* probably built the original program to protect *yourself* as the occupant of your body-mind complex, wherever and whenever in Time you were embodied!

With skill one can expect to resolve and remove most unwanted programming. In Present Time, today, right *now*, one can review how one's old Ego-Programming Unit produces the decision of whether to 'see or not see' or to 'hear or not hear' a threat, and whether to fight or run. Many cases of non-responsiveness to obvious threats are attributable to protective programming having shut down the normal instruments of perception. The outputs from those perceptic devices *still exist* but are directed to the Ego-Programming Department and shut off from the Personality-Human. Some programs react and operate so fast that the Personality Self is unaware of the threat. One is heard asking "What was *that*?"…or…"How did I get *here*?!

For the record, let it be recognized that subconscious influences or recordings carried over from past incarnations are handled the same as if they were generated in the present lifetime. When working in the regressed or reverie state, one is seldom aware of Time in its calendar sense. All recordings are approached conveniently in the 'here and now.' Their energies are cumulative and grow when similar trauma are experienced in subsequent lifetimes, and can even generalize, but more on that later.

Other approaches to becoming centered by removing the effects of traumatic incidents include variations of the Rebirthing processes. Reiki processing is a hands-on method capable of producing effects on the emotional, physical, mental and spiritual levels. Many forms of diet, exercise, and meditation are valuable in gaining control over blocked emotions and awareness mechanisms. Kriya Yoga is offered by the Self Realization Fellowship as a way to work directly through obstacles to full God Consciousness. Others, like Feldencraise and Rolfing, recognize connections between body attitudes and the psyche. The beginner would do well to investigate whatever approach is convenient, learning of the application, benefits and the limitations of Massage, Acupressure, Acupuncture, Chiropractic, General Medicine, and Homeopathy.

It is well for the aspirant to total Self mastery and to stable centering to investigate everything and to remove every obstacle to perfect health of body, emotions, and mind. The payoff includes being able to live most fully, expressing Human Life *joyously* in the Eden of Schoolhouse Earth.

We now review several specific attention-control exercises which are effective in establishing order and clearing the human psyche so that Spirit can operate fully from its 'throne,' its Center.

CHAPTER TWENTY
PREPARING TO COMMUNICATE THROUGH THE VEIL

Insights of an outstanding and immediately applicable nature are available through communication with the Inner Self, consciously or unconsciously. It is sometimes a matter for conjecture as to whether such messages are channeled from Spirit Teachers or Guides, from Race Mind or wishful thinking, or whether it comes from our own Higher Self, or God, via Intuition. Many cases are of record where messages are/were received from playful or malevolent discarnate spirits. Then learning to sort it all out is of some significance!

There is also the problem, foremost in some Seeker's minds, as to whether one's insights or-hunches come from some programmed machine or recorded response from the "inside" or subconscious mind, or "outside" from some aspect of astral self that works through the subconscious mind. A very real obstacle for the spiritual aspirant to master is to become aware of *which sources* from among several his insights and hunches emanate. Fortunately the differences can be studied and discerned.

It is feasible to discern exactly from whence cometh one's guidance by *learning how to look at,*, and by *practice* in *experiencing one's impressions.* Every human has experienced some of his automatic responses...reactions which are stimulated by conditions in the physical and the psychic environment, also from the feelings radiated by the conscious and the subconscious aspects of other persons around you. Susceptibility to offensive communications may be traced to chakra choking or unbalance, whether caused by foul diet or emotional practice, drugs, or by protective programming.

Ways for discovery and resolution of one's fundamental problem(s) begin with learning meditation, learning to "Enter the Silence," to experience at will the quietness of the soul. There one learns what it feels like to function as Spirit working in flesh, but with enough perspective to know and to assess what is happening!

We label that condition as Being Centered. The state of serenity gained in meditation is brought forward and lived in full consciousness...not an easy thing to do but possible and necessary.

By learning to become habitually Centered one is enabled to work in the reverie condition fully consciously, retaining perspective while in reverie. One thusly becomes fully psychic and better: one awakens his intuition and clairvoyance. All of this results as one becomes increasingly aware of his feelings, and by *remaining aware* of them at all times. It is that quality of *remaining aware of being aware* which enables a person to function as a master, as there is then nothing that can upset or escape said person.

Exercises follow which develop the capacity for fully sensing what one's attention is focussed on, and which help recognize that *concentration IS* focused *attention*. Focussed attention is vital to work in the higher planes. By practice one becomes an excellent communicator through-the-veil and by becoming cleared of his engrams, his emotional and mental blockages to feelings, and by clearing toxic body chemistry. One's aura becomes as white as the biblical snow.

CHAPTER TWENTY-ONE
ON CLINICAL PRACTICE AND PROCEDURE

The techniques and categories of clinical practice and procedure presented here are not to be considered exhaustive. Rather, they are intended to presents means for approaching the more commonly experienced problem areas among the U.S.A. and the English speaking peoples of the Earth. It is presumed that familiarity will be gained with each fundamental form of treatment so that modifications can be created to resolve peculiarities experienced with individual clients.

There is a wide divergence of experience represented in the Homo Sapiens of Planet Earth. Yet there will be only a small grouping of distresses to be eradicated, permitting a nearly infinite number of ailment expressions to be approached in only a handful of ways. Yet we cannot recommend that our therapeutic tools be used by rote. More respect for human ingenuity should be shown than that!

Perhaps the greatest temptation to counselor-therapists will be to use mass-production processing techniques, because more clients coming in the door means more money rolling in. Your Author-Guide Team has found that overemphasis on Quantity over Quality alienates Counselors from the Guides Who are their very sources of subjective help which make this approach so valuable. Quoting, "As interested Guides working with you from behind the scenes, we accommodate the needs of the better and dedicated therapist in his work with our favored spiritually-oriented clients, and lesser so in working with the general population viewed only as a source of income."

A note of gentle admonition is given regarding how a client should be addressed. In treating a client whose fears seem irrational, it is wise to avoid use of ridicule to force use of the counselor's frame of reference. The source of irrationality does not always lie in the client's conscious mind. Hence, irrationality is to be dealt with at its level of origin. To poke fun at a client who is already sharing cautiously from his bank of fears risks lessened self-acceptance, loss of confidence in the therapist with alienation from subsequent cooperation, and risks the possibility of further repression in the area in which his major problem resides. This makes examination and recovery from original engrammatic material much more difficult and risks pushing marginally stable clients beyond the brink. That possibility requires the therapist/counselor to be more clear of his own buried automaticities and inappropriate or aberrant programs than the client he is trying to help.

It is difficult enough to find protected trauma or programs so that Counselor alertness is merited at all times, especially during the exploratory phase of subjective work. As a help to continuing work covering several sessions, we do not encourage the use of audio or videotaping, due less to the expense of the equipment than to the time required to study such recordings. Even so, sometimes either the therapist or client would gladly recapture and review some precious insight. However, to avoid any possibility of future ill will, we find it may be best that nothing be recorded other than handwritten notes.

Every counselor has had or will have a client who is blocked off in an area that seems inaccessible by any known approach. To work around such eventualities some older therapies have broken the client in spirit by use of physical pain. Electric shock and drugs also have been used but are considered here as unnecessary forms of cruel and inhumane punishment, at best a ridding of symptoms rather than curing same, and capable of damaging the human soul. Nothing need be done that would cause damage to any part of the human psyche or body. Conscientious application of pain to open blocked psychological areas has not yet been developed as a science, even though breakthroughs have from time to time been experienced as fallout from the Rolf program of Structural Integration. Sodium pentothal is sometimes used to work behind the human ego-protection system, but such should not be used by Seekers-on-the-Spiritual Path by Aspirants to Conscious Co-Workership.

It may sometimes be necessary for Spiritual Counselors to refer a client to a practitioner who has developed skills in other areas. Because the human is a composite of so many facets and experiences, treatment of the Human should include skilled utilization of fasting, exercise, meditation, and invocation for Guidance.

After each session involving deep work it is vital that the therapist be certain that his client is brought fully up into Present Time. To facilitate same it is well to make a quiet place where the client can ruminate over or sleep off the session just ended.

When particularly deep or heavy material has been stirred up it is sometimes noted that a client may "settle out" or re-stabilize only after several days, as the disturbance to the subconscious mind or "Inner Self" can be severe, even when the client is in good spirits and fine physical condition. Observation and experience will usually forewarn of possibly difficult circumstances, therefore, "cooling off" periods should be planned as a normal part of closing the sessions. Warm water Epsom Salts baths are excellent at relieving aftereffects of intensive therapy. It is reported that a swim in the ocean is particularly refreshing after deep therapy, enabling the client to "feel clean" in a rather subjective but especially satisfying manner.

If we have any last word of advice, it is to *value your hunches*! Your intuition may surprisingly often provide the approach or insight you need right when you need it. At times it may even seem that you are being led by an Unseen and/or Benevolent Intelligence. If you ARE, be grateful, and express that gratitude by learning to work with it. If another explanation be in order, be grateful anyhow! As your case clears and you awaken into the higher planes you become more and more in touch with the Universe of Collective Intelligence, in which lie the answers to all the problems of mankind. That oneness is available on an individual basis! Ask for help, and give thanks that you have received it! Then, *be open to receive it*!

No, God is *not* dead...and neither need we humans be!

RECORD KEEPING

Usually it will be found both convenient and wise to maintain a separate and current file on each client. That file will contain records of the plans, events and notes on engrams and trauma to be approached for each session. It will contain elementary logistics information such as telephone numbers, addresses, records of session dates and payments, family references, on relationships which may be problems to the client, and relevant medical information.

It is highly recommended that the counselor maintain a running log of the individual sessions, giving attention to the special approaches used, to the results, and to capture whatever insights may expedite continuation of particular work in succeeding sessions. That each client merits professional consideration should be obvious. Since session files will be invaluable for reference far into the future, it is recommended that high quality paper and bindings be used, with clear printed text. Any notes made by the therapist during a session are thence available for quick reference and study at any later time.

Occasionally a client's file will contain information of a very private nature, such that it should not be possible for access by persons other than the therapist. One approach to denying unauthorized use of the files is to encypher the entries in such manner that only the Counselor can read them. Development of even a simple encrypting method used even as the notes are being transcribed should be considered. Stenographic shorthand has been used. Whatever the method, it should be easy for the therapist to interpret his materials in a later session.

Often time lapses for periods of 60 seconds or so between counselor commands and client verbalizations, as when searching Time Tracks and probing particular subjective recorded events. Use of tape recorders for capturing fruitful sessions may seem impractical. Voice-activated recording has been found unsatisfactory because of the loss of start-up words or phrases. And, if a session was unfruitful, its tape can always be reused. Having *some* information available is sometimes to be preferred to having none!

THE BREATHE-DOWN

To begin the reverie-entry process, it is suggested that circumstances permit the client to lie on the floor, on a soft pad several inches thick to promote comfort. Use of a blanket may assist the client to keep warm, feel safe, and to be comfortable. Arrange for the client to have tight-fitting clothing loosened. If the client can comply comfortably, it is well to wear a sweat suit. Socks are useful in keeping the client's feet warm. Use of a pillow for the client's head is optional. Arms may be juxtaposed comfortably.

Some clients like to use incense, and some seem not to like it. Sandalwood or jasmine have been found popular. We discourage any use of tobacco smoke at any time. The room should be well ventilated, avoiding stale air to help sensitize the client's perceptive system.

A semi-darkened room is useful, as if the client were about to take a nap. Some clients will like soft background music. Its loudness will be about right when the client is barely aware of it. Taped meditation music is usually better than off-the-air FM radio music because commercials and voice intrusion can be highly distracting when your client is trying to work in reverie.

Depending on the sort of engrammatic material to be worked, it is desirable to have at hand tapes of various sounds, especially those that stir the client's deeper emotions. These may include a wide variety from street traffic, siren noises, jungle drums, war sounds, racing derbies, military marches, American Bluegrass, or whatever other sort sets the mood for the client. It may be prove useful to test a variety of sounds, based on what turns up in your client Pre-session Screening sessions. Allow the place of Intuition to be recognized as a guide.

The Counselor-Facilitator may seat himself on the floor comfortably but close enough so the client can touch the C/F when troubled.

Commence the Breathe-Down by asking the client to close his or her eyes and to take in a series of deep baby-gasp breaths through the mouth, allowing the air to escape naturally through the lips. Doing a dozen or more deep breaths while focussed on the bridge of the nose often is enough to help the client become detached from whatever was going through his/her mind at the time of reporting to the session. There need be little concern regarding hyperventilation. Just ask the client to report "How do you feel now? and *now*, etc.? Judging by the client's tone of voice, breathing pattern, and perhaps skin tone, you will know when to begin the process of investigating the deeper mind.

While commencing the above processes, it may help the client to focus on feeling the air and its effects as it enters and leaves the body, listening as it passes in and out. Help the client visualize the incoming air as soft Life Energy or Aliveness, feeling it coursing through the client, filling the spaces in and around the muscles, organs, tissues and bones. Clients having excellent visualization ability may report seeing dark places and knots of confusion around their body or in their aura from present or previous ailments and/or accidents. Some of these may be treated in later healings.

In a soothing voice, ask the client from time to time how he or she feels. Observe their body language but obtain a verbal response.

One may use Voice Dialogue by talking with the Controller to keep the client from going to sleep. You can use your right or left hand to make gentle abdominal contact, perhaps best restricted to circular motions to avoid sexual interpretation or implications. Satisfy yourself that the client is approaching the reverie state and as soon as that state is reached with stability, begin the formal reverie work.

Ask the client to look for a situation (or a time) when he/she is feeling very happy, or is looking for something pertinent to the session. The client will usually feel himself to be an interested participant somewhere in his psychic recordings! Interjection of helpful queries is often valuable to the client as well as to the Counselor/Facilitator in assuring that the client is focussed deeply enough in the playback mode so that he can tell you *where* he seems himself to be, *when* it seems to be, *what* is happening, about how old he seems to be, and generally report who is feeling what, and who the people and what the occasion seem to be.

The Counselor/Facilitator is to *guide* the session rather than to *control* it, to assist the client to remain observant and reporting in his reverie recording. In other words, the C/F must *avoid* directing the reverie work, if it is to fulfill its potentials and value. It will be found feasible and sometimes helpful to talk to one or more of the Voice Dialog sub-personalities during the inner reviews, especially when little or nothing seems to be happening. [See Chapter 27.]

That approach also is used to look for times when the client was feeling very bad. Help the client look around to gain facility in working in reverie, but also to help the Counselor/Facilitator find troublesome recordings that may be causing trouble up here in today's session...in Present Time. The Counselor-Facilitator also has much to do to learn to read the client's responses to his commands. Remember that 'present time' for the client may be 5,000 years ago to the C/F. Usually Dates and Time will not have meaning for the client.

This approach works well for entering into and working in the reverie state. *What to Ask/Tell The Client* depends on what you as the C/F find in response to *general* probing commands or questions, perhaps such as "Look for a time when you are hurting, or dying, or cannot move, etc...." A wide variety is possible [30]. As the C/F you are looking for specific phrases to activate a troubled situation in reverie. What further to do is treated further ahead.

ENDING A SESSION

Ending a session is sometimes as easy as just saying good-bye to the client, who rises and just walks out the door. A simple..."Well, that does it for today! I'll see you next time at..." is enough when sessions have been conducted in a relatively low key. But there are times when the going has been rough...difficult...with the client reeling in disorientation, emotional turmoil and exhaustion as a result of the psychological beating he or she has taken for an hour or two. We speak here of psychological beatings, of course, as confrontations with some of the recorded but unresolved trauma still active on one's case. It may have been a suppressed childhood beating or rape administered by a parent or another trusted person, with all the kicks and blows, recoiling, screaming and sweating that originally took place. These events usually are experienced as occurring *in the session,* while the client is still in reverie, instead of having happened far back in Time. In other words, the client experiences them in Present Time. S/he will need to be handled accordingly before allowing the client to leave the premises for personal safety reasons.

When much energy has been trapped and is suddenly relived, it is necessary for the Counselor/Facilitator to restore the Psyche's balance in the *Here and Now* or Present Time awareness and energy levels so that the aftereffects of the processing become allayed. The C/F has responsibility for his client safely to reenter the slam-bam pressures of the world outside the safety of the counseling chamber. That balance may be restored quickly but requires exteriorizing the client's attention.

SPOTTING SPOTS

"Spotting Spots" is a simple but very powerful method for exteriorizing one's attention. It involves commanding the client to 'shoot a Line of Attention to...'or to focus his attention on many separated objects in the room, one at a time, and releasing the attention to focus on another. And so it goes until the eye of the client is clear, his voice is again full, and there is no hesitancy in command compliance. If these conditions are not restored, it will be well for the client to sleep off the after effects of the session.

A typical command process may be:

C/F: Spot a spot on the door. Got it?

Client: Got it! (It may take several seconds to locate the door and find something to notice about it)

C/F: Let go of it! Now...spot a spot on the West wall. Got it?

Client: Got it! (Again, for the earlier commands it may take the Client several seconds to find something to look at and focus his attention on.

C/F: Let go of it! Now...Spot another spot on the floor! Got it?

Client: Got it!

Etc...

After some number of spots, the client's response time should decrease. If it does not, continue spotting spots until the client's skin color, tone of voice, and alertness indicate the client is fully back in Present Time. When that happens, the C/F can command the client to Stand Up and touch a spot on his nose, or the wall, or the door know, drink a cup of coffee, go to the bathroom and wash his face, as necessary to assure yourself that the client is again in charge of himself. After satisfying yourself that he could probably go, ask if the client feels back in charge of himself again. Only then let the session be closed.

CHAPTER TWENTY-TWO
ON OPENING UP A NEW CASE

There is always that first personal encounter, whether or not a client faces the therapist before or after taking a battery of diagnostic tests. These may be one or more of the following: the Draw-A-Person test, the Minnesota Mental Profile Index examination, a Graphological study, a Yokefellow's Spiritual Profile, an Electropsychometer scan, a Palm reading, a Tarot analysis, an Astrological study, reference by another practitioner or friend, or just "walking in off the street."

Often a client does not know what to expect of his new therapist nor of the processes, nor of himself. Neither does the therapist always know what to expect of his client-to-be. A therapist who "comes across" as a friend, one with a good "bedside manner," usually can help his client to relax, to become vulnerable better than one who maintains a cold "professional" demeanor. Various methods have been developed to approximate ideal initial contact conditions.

When the social amenities are taken care of and trust and rapport are established, the next step is to approach the client's subconscious store of programming. An excellent approach consists in guiding the client into a "breathe-down". The client is made comfortable, preferably supine, with tight-fitting garments loosened or removed. Deep slow breathing may be accelerated, allowing such spontaneous arm and body movements as head-rolling, leg kicks, torso twisting and verbal outpourings. The intent is to allow whatever is closest to the surface to "boil over" and activate and observe the client's egomatic or automatic coping programs in action.

While the engrammatic initialization and ego coping processes are organizing, the therapist needs to be alert to his client's tics, his physical and mental activity, and to engage in verbal feedback from the client, serving to enable the therapist to know "where" his client is now," and to "how it seems to be there." This approach should be noted to share one of the fundamentals of Gestalt communication, in that both the conscious and subonscious aspects of the client are available and employed for interrelationship examination and interpretation by both the client and the counselor.

If, after some appropriate time, perhaps ten to fifteen minutes, nothing in particular seems to "boil up" to the conscious client-therapist interface, the therapist may attempt to facilitate the situation by introducing certain "seed thought" triggers having to do with hate, misery, fear, or another emotionally laden quantity. Some examples are found in Table I. Since most humans are usually laden down with one or more standard vulnerabilities and defense patterns, and with doubts and fears about his ability to cope with some one or more normal life situations, it is rather easy to recreate or to restimulate some regenerative pattern of response.

Sometimes a client may become catapulted into some level of strong primal response on his first "mat" session. At other times and with other clients it may have been very difficult to elicit a feeling response of any kind. Dry spells may be experienced several sessions in a row as the Counselor and Client learn how to let go, learning how to approach some strongly protected program(s) or recordings, and as the subconscious storehouse organizes itself. Subliminal work often is taking place that surfaces beautifully later, when the ego has been tricked into permitting exposure, believing an approach to be "safe." This can happen because many ego protective devices are networked, so that a block in one area can be operating which is directly accessible only from seemingly unrelated engrams or recordings in another area.

When dry spells are encountered, the time need not be lost in the sense that it can be very useful for data-taking via engaging the client in reminiscing and recounting relationships and present time problems. Running present-time relationship problems can be especially effective if the therapist is using an electropsychometer to monitor subjective level activity, but usually a lot of digging is still required to "open the tomb."

Difficulty or reluctance in reaching into the subjective or feeling levels can be indicative of a "head-tripper," a client who is intellectually oriented to the point that he or she is far out of touch with his feeling-self. In such cases it may be fruitful to approach the client through a retrogressive search along his Tine Track looking for incidents of the most basic or primitive emotions. As given elsewhere, these can include fear, pain, loss, abandonment, hunger, cold, inadequacy, being buried alive, dying, being born, being elated, etc. The contents of the human mind usually are cross-filed, so the task of finding a sore spot is eased by the ability to enter the filing system (memory) on any of several dynamics, such as pain and pleasure, fear and doubt. et cetera. If one dynamic is found unresponsive, the therapist tries another.

Typical seed thought phrases, triggers, and dynamics useful for "file ticklers" appear in Table I for "starters." While these are being used, the client should be watched for verbal hints and tics which suggest contact and evasion, possibly other entries being needed. Any response at all will often suggest other approaches. Because so many subconscious recordings are laden with sin, guilt and fear, ask the client to put all the emotional reality energy he or she can muster into those qualities. For example, as the therapist gives the command to look for recordings and feelings of "I am cold," suggest the client to imagine that he is *being* cold, assisting in the assumption of *feeling* that condition. Usually a client will have experienced that condition many times from infancy and will have little difficulty to "recall a time when you are cold." Familiarity with processing can be gained easily on any dynamic, with or without including correlating electropsychometric readimgs with physical and clairvoyant manifestations.

1. "I can't take it any longer!"
2. "I am no good!"
3. "It hurts!"
4. "I am afraid!"
5. "I am *cold*!"
6. "Nobody loves me or wants me!"
7. "I am *so* hungry!"
8. "I am so *tired*!"
9. "I am *angry*!"
10. "I do not know what to do!"
11. "I am dying!"
12. "I cannot move!"
13. "*HELP!*"
14. "I want my mother!"
15. "I am *drowning*!"
16. "I cannot *breathe*!"

Table I. "File Ticklers"

Many other seeds (triggers) have been collected in the following and other sources:

(1) "A Phenomenological Typology of Intensive Meditation" by Maliszewski, Truemlow, Brown, and Engler in ReVISION, Fall/Winter 1981, Volume 4, Number 2, pages 3-27.

(2) "Self Analysis" by L. Ron Hubbard by Hubbard Dianetic Foundation, 10335 Magnolia Blvd North Hollywood, CA 91601 Phone (818) 763-0220

Once success has been achieved on any dynamic, entry into similar areas others should follow relatively easily. This encourages the client to become familiar with viable processes, so that less time and effort need be expended in reestablishing the inner contact from one session to another. It is advisable that the Counselor allow enough session time so that the client does not feel pressured for performance.

Successful seed thought entries should be recorded in the Therapist's Session Notes, so that the wise therapist will save much time and effort. Additionally, when picking up areas needing further work, liberal use of previously successful entries is encouraged, and probably will used by the Counselor anyway out of boredom through repetition! After all, even making money can be boring...so one often opts for seeing optimum progress.

CHAPTER TWENTY-THREE
MORE ON CASE ENTRANCES

When feelings cannot be reached except with difficulty, and then only weakly, better use may sometimes be made of Gestalt inner visualization confrontations, ala Perls. In such cases symbolic picture representation usually provides information about the area which is being or should be studied. Facility gained in picture 'reading' leads inevitably to a well-developed intuition, to direct 'knowing,' even though the emotional feeling realm has not been fully awakened. Perhaps learning to read the pictures seems like going 'all around Robin Hood's barn' to get there, but eventually the feeling level is available, and the former powerful inhibitory forces are released. In our experience, those who study the Gestalt approach become vastly improved social beings whose lives take on increasingly deeper meaning as a consequence of learning to use it.

Entries are usually attempted via the classical common denominators and dichotomies likely to be found in the Race mind, and hence in the typical human being. Some are readily recognized and identified in Table II, but many others also exist.

Approach and entry into any of these areas may sometimes be enhanced remarkably by utilization of background sound effects, odors, and/or other related stimuli that appeal to the client's emotions, and perhaps associated with the engram category. One can 'know' instinctively what specific emotion might be triggered by certain sounds, like Australian Bushmen drummers, but a Psychic Psychologist should not be surprised if significant deviations in the resulting response are triggered, depending on who the client is.

Based on what is found in Reverie, it would seem at times that some of us have come from different countries, cultures, or even different planets at vastly different times, so varied can be our responses. The modestly equipped counselling center or office may obtain and have on hand a supply of cassette tapes or other props providing a large range of sounds related in various ways to the feelings engendered by the above and many other basic categories.

As given, these will include but not be limited to jungle sounds, drum rhythms from primitive societies, and accident-related sounds such as sirens and crashes with screams of agony, sounds of the torture chamber, bell sounds from distant mountain herds to monastic bells, funeral tolling, romantic songs, impressionistic symphonies including Wagner and Debussy, old church hymns, the sounds of running water falls, rapids and rain storms. It can include sounds from astral realms, the ocean surf, and many others limited only by the imagination and experience of the counselor/therapist. Assorted selections of these are sometimes offered for sale in metaphysical trade magazines, and even in the lobby or office of the typical therapist/psychologist for just the above purpose. And of course, some tapes and sounds and odors will not be as effective as others, or at various times.

> 1. Fear
> 2. Hunger and Starvation
> 3. Pain
> 4. Grief, Dying, and Death
> 5. Inadequacy and Failure
> 6. Loss and Deprivation
> 7. Love and Hate
> 8. Revenge, anger, Hostility
> 9. Lust and the Appetites
> 10. Joy, Pleasure, and Fulfillment
> ...and others.

Table II. Common Denominators in the Race Mind

It is understood, of course, that the objective in using sound tracks is to facilitate the client's entry and work in his reverie state. Use of hypnosis by a counselor, in our view, should be a method of last resort, to avoid its observed dependency-building trends. However, skilled guidance by a hypnotherapist may still be fruitful in enabling a buried recording to be brought up to the surface for examination in Present Time. The client will still remain conscious and in reverie, observing, evaluating and dialoguing, reporting his situations from Present Time.

Another form of entry in contacting repressed caches of anger or buried aberrations is through the use of feigned violence. It is sometimes feasible to engage the client to defend himself from mock attack or battle via use of battacas (soft baseball bats) or other instruments not normally capable of inflicting physical damage. These are engaged only for the purpose of arousing and working through patterns of fight or flight.

Production of rage and tears often accompanies giving way to the actual possibility for safely express anger. Or the counselor may trigger a descent into apathy! Sometimes it is possible, depending upon known and unknown factors, to ridicule a client into physical self-defense as a way to break through to and update childhood patterns. Badgering as a way to suggest violence may best be tried to arouse the childhood coward fight-back role, but be sure your client is not a 250-pound former neighborhood bully or wrestler!

Use of a padded and/or soundproofed room has brought freedom to express "life" by screaming, shouting, and uninhibited profanity into stalemated sessions or blocks to obtaining client release. This works with both male and female clients as antagonists, especially well with quiet nice little old ladies! Sometimes even the threat of violence will trigger off a buried engram and afford great release through physical expression, screaming and shouting with marvelous recovery of feelings of self worth and regained ability to cope.

A client is fortunate when working with a Counselor or therapist who has a battery of personality profile tests to use for gaining feedback on the effectiveness of his/her work. A particular reason is that progress over a period of counseling and processing may be valuable to obtain Progress Reports, to find where change has occurred, and to show where further work is merited. Useful feedback may be gained via some computer programmed questionnaires. A familiar and easily administered example is the Minnesota Mental Profile Index (MMPI), available through the Yokefellows people.

Another simple and effective indicator introduced elsewhere is the "Draw-a-Person" (DAP) test. The client is given a blank sheet of paper and crayons and is asked to draw a representation of whatever scene (thing, place, condition, or person) cones to mind. There is to be no restriction as to quality or time limit placed upon the artistic product. Everything from stick figures to abstracts is useful, since a person trained in interpretation, or having a good intuition, will find clues jumping to his attention. Sometimes changes or modifications to original drawings will point out changes made in session.

The DAP and MMPI seem less sensitive to changes over shorter periods of time, but will certainly catch major changes in attitudes occurring over any long counseling interval.

Graphology, as classical Hand Writing Analysis, is capable of providing immediate and accurate insights and updates to the eye a trained interpreter. In larger cities, the "Yellow Pages" may list such services under the heading of "Handwriting Experts" or "Handwriting Analysts" if not under Graphologists. Such experts provide services to police departments, to courts and lawyers for probate of wills, even to validating the signatures on documents. Handwriting analysis also can be done by mail if either a Counsellor or a Client should elect to do so. Janov goes so far as to use Graphology immediately following regular sessions to indicate the changes that took place in a client as a result-of the work done. He and this author also report excellent results from Graphology as a fundamental diagnostic tool. Janov and Holden find excellent correlation of client attitude change from blood analyses taken immediately before and after Primal sessions.

When based upon accurate date, time and birthplace location data is carefully drawn up and skillfully interpreted, a natal horoscope is capable of revealing fundamental insight into the inner state of a client. When birth statistics are questionable, often the case with older clients, use of a natal horoscope may be partially successful for diagnostic purposes. Lacking the personal skills and instant access to a thoroughly competent astrologer at reasonable fees, the authors sometimes use Astrology derived from a relatively simple computer-based horoscope to obtain useful insights.

Post-session follow-up is available "on the spot" and "as you go" to the counselor/therapist who has an electropsychometer and is skilled in its use. The meter provides instant feedback as to the client's case status as it is being worked. For completeness, the psychometer dial and meter readings should be recorded for reference, both pre-and post-session.

Bio-feedback was not used by these authors as a method of determining client change and growth status because of the difficulty in obtaining quantitative results, and a skilled Electropsychometer operator and Counselor was at hand (Dr. D. R. Schaffer).

Success in using the Tarot, Runes, Tea-leaf readings and others depends more on the perceptive skills and intuition of the Psychic Psychologist-Counselor than on any innate capacity for rendering absolute or even relative readings of change. Their value is limited by he/she who uses the techniques.

It comes down to the fundamental fact that each therapist must develop his or her own "bag of tricks." It should be recognized that a particular therapist may have difficulty with a certain personality type but will succeed with others. Therefore, it is well for professionals to offer references to other known therapists and to refer the mismatched cases appropriately. A "clear" therapist, counselor, or psychologist would have little difficulty with personality type.

Feedback of another type is available through analysis of client blood chemistry. So-called "forty-point" blood analyses can be requested with the assistance of an interested physician and/or a medical laboratory. Blood testing will be most meaningful when a full analysis is made at the start of a case, is made periodically, and about a week after major breakthroughs have been made in session, so the readings will stabilize. Dr. Ida P. Rolf used blood chemistry change analysis in the mid-1950's. Janov and Holden have published their research as reported in "Primal man". This author recommends blood testing as direct validation of the concept and relative efficacy of any and all of the mental-psychological therapies only if he/she and/or the client are willing to pay for the additional laboratory work and to undertake the extensive study required for meaningful blood sample analysis.

Routine use of blood testing is not vital to any part of the psychic psychological counseling itself, but provides documentary evidence of significant changes attributable only to the therapy, beyond the changes that can be made through diet, exercise, and to pill taking. Often, however, changes in dietary patterns and in levels of medication will be merited to facilitate mental health as a direct result of efficacious releases. Changes in appetites are also observed upon occasion as a result of deep releases, but are often necessitated when a client is found to be eating or drinking in such a manner as to cause or perpetuate his own malaise.

CHAPTER TWENTY-FOUR
ON SESSION PREPARATION

"This morning we are going to work more along the lines of getting one's clientele prepared for their sessions. It is not to be difficult work, but necessary work, that all shall proceed with dispatch in getting their cases resolved.

"There will be times when the client is willing but unable to receive the ministrations of his counselor. At such times it may be possible for the counselor to work around the impasse, but what to do is not always obvious. Your experience with 'Big John' (pseudonym) up at Burlingame is a case in point. He wanted so intensely to get opened up, but could not let himself respond to any of the conventional overtures. His subconscious mind was bound tightly by protective ego defense patterns so that entry and release was impossible: he was 'up tight' to the extreme. Occurring perhaps ten percent of the time, it is probable that any given counselor may find himself facing just such a client. Therefore, we would find and offer case openers that will prevent or avoid loss of time when confronted by an otherwise willing but unable client.

"Some aspects of case opening often go unnoticed by the well-intentioned counselor bent upon establishing his own individual style. In his missionary zeal to move out, he overlooks that any particular session will not respond to the same approach each or every time. It is unlikely that any particular client will be approachable the same way each time. For example, observation of the client's manner of entering the counseling room will usually indicate clearly what should be the counselor/therapist approach most likely to initiate that day's session successfully, getting it off to a good start. Whereas cookbook approaches will often produce desired results, we do not intend to dictate to the reader any particular ways, but elect instead to indicate that certain signals will be noticeable when there is to be trouble.

"We find, for example, that the manner in which the client shuffles into the session will indicate clearly when he is not up to par, not having the spontaneity with which the intuitive process will be available. An antagonistic condition is signalled before the first word of greeting is expressed. It is therefore imperative that each session be viewed as a new time, that all previous successful encounters were indeed held as if with a different client. Such new approach makes it easier to woo those changes in cliental attitude which will produce most immediately the conditions the counselor desires for doing his best work. This is not to say that the counselor cannot prepare in advance certain alternate procedures to run that day, based on findings in previous sessions. He must not, however, always expect to rerun the same old processes, or to continue where he left off the previous time without checking to see if his preparations are adequate for the setting.

Determining the client's mood is the most important element as soon as he steps in the door. The use of casual conversation as openers is perhaps even required to relieve the client and provide opportunity to unburden any present-time problem. For most clients this will be necessary before anything at all can be done in session. There may be petty pressures still remnant upon his arrival, such as difficulty in parking his vehicle, or getting fired after a battle with his boss, or his wife left him. Or perhaps there is *good* news that he is bubbling over to share.

We suggest planning in advance for a pre-session icebreaker, perhaps offering to share some beverage or a cigarette, fruit, or crackers and cheese. These will of course vary with the client, as we find that certain types of personality and certain approaches to the present-time problems may require to forego their use. Conversely, they may be required to raise the client's blood sugar level to support a high level of mental activity. Counselor/Facilitator sacrifice of tobacco, alcohol and sugar may be essential preceding the session when high levels of intuitional sensitivity is required. It is always wise to be prepared for any eventuality.

In our form of Applied Psychic Psychology the higher bodies of the client also need to be relieved of tensions and quieted so that its occupant can devote his full attention to the session. Therefore, getting the body physically, emotionally, mentally, and chemically quieted down is the first order of business. "Entering The Silence" then may as well be made part of the opening ritual, giving both the client and the counselor an opportunity to observe and to assuage hostilities from whatever causes. After the client has become

A Spiritual Psychology For The Aquarian Age

comfortable and has had his present-time problem stress relieved, his outer mind silenced and his blood sugar level raised to par, then his total powers can be focussed upon the work for the session, if there is still time enough remaining!

It is not to be forgotten that each session is likely to be different from those preceding, even when having been in the midst of rather productive materials the preceding time. When a client leaves the counseling room he is leaving a protective shelter to return into an environment of hostilities of a rather different order. He is apt to lose the benefits and insights derived in the recently established consanguinity of the counseling room. It is often necessary for the counselor then to review the events of the preceding session(s) to regain benefits discovered but not yet made a part of the client.

It is, therefore, not unusual when a client is unable to carry forward with the results of one session before he returns to the following session as if he had never heard them before, resulting perhaps in loss of effectiveness otherwise available in the therapeutic process.

A counselor seems to lose valuable time when he has to rebuild an atmosphere in which he can resume a former productive session, so that he can re-enter and continue where he left off a previously successful approach. Yet, there is nothing to say that any particular approach must be continued. The client's deep subconscious mind probably has continued to reorganize itself over the material stirred up in the preceding session anyway. For several days after a fruitful heavy session there may be subtle changes observed in the mental outlook or/and reactions to the client's environment. He will not be the same when he returns to later sessions.

In other words, it is natural that a client's subconscious ego department will be found to have been doing work on his case between sessions below the level of-consciousness. That's good! Such work cannot be stopped, nor should it be. It does mean that the counselor must take his client right where he finds him, each session being a New Time as far as the inner workings of the client are concerned. Therefore, it is necessary to the success of each session that the client be studied by the counselor the moment first eye contact is made. The eye is literally a window to the client's Soul. There will be clues that the counselor can use to save both his client's and his own time and money.

Certain standard types of problems have standard types of approach which normally may be expected to bring about a desired level of rapport and responsiveness between the client and the counselor. The counselor will benefit greatly from possessing familiarity with those opening forms of approach, by establishing quickly the basic rapport that brings/creates the trust and the cooperation necessary for the client to permit exposing his deeper levels of consciousness. Not until that basic trust has been established can much productive work be accomplished.

Then the counselor must find *himself* calmed down and peaceful within, in order to be able to perceive the inner condition of his own client, and to respond to available intuitive or Inner Guidance. If the client is already quieted down but the counselor is upset, not much productive work is likely to be accomplished. The counselor, therefore, needs to have his wits about him before he can be expected to employ the full focus of his own personal psychic or intuitive processes in sensing and guiding his client's problems in the more productive planes needed to work subliminally.

When a client has become established in the serenity required to access his unprotected memory banks, he is open to attack by the counselor. Therefore, particular attention must be paid to the maintenance of a safe atmosphere, lest further access to the client's subjective realms be closed to any and all Counselors. Without that access there is not much by way of inner revelation available from the upper (deeper!) levels of consciousness for examination and review.

When a client has conflict in some part of his Beingness, it is difficult for him to confront his feelings about it, even to look at it at all, to examine it in the light of reasoning mind. When this initial difficulty is present and the client has entered the chambers for his new session, is it any wonder that there is difficulty in getting down to business without first restoring a proper working atmosphere? It is thus vital that the counselor easily and quickly interrelate with each of his clients, being habitually trusted, having gained the unspoken confidence of the client, and thus to enjoy maximum levels of subjective guidance and support.

Without having the full trust and confidence of the client, little significant subjective work is accomplished. Therefore, stated once again, more important than any technique is development of the Counselor's ability to perceive his client's state of being and to be

A Spiritual Psychology For The Aquarian Age 173

able then to acclimate himself to fit it, or/and to modify it without seeming to be controlling the client overtly. Perhaps even half of the counselor's career may be spent in returning his client's system of attitudes to "normal," to "Being Centered," so that the client can even *begin* to face his "normal" self. By so doing, the Counselor is helping the client confront his outer world. Confrontation of the inner world then is followed by ability to confront the outer world successfully, in full waking consciousness. With that ability gained, the client becomes increasingly able to function in his or her environment...a great victory for many aching souls.

Perhaps the greater job for the counselor is to become skilled at restoring equanimity within the counselor's personal world and teaching the client/ how to re-establish his own, for himself. An aid to attaining that objective is to use Voice Dialogue with one of the client's Sub-Personalities, say the Child, or The Controller. The Counselor-Facilitator asks for and receives permission from the dominant subpersonality to proceed with the more subjective or reverie work.

When a counselor has restored his client to being in charge of his inner worlds and attitudes, he will have contributed greatly to his client's ability to enjoy life *That condition as a desirable and possible outcome of counseling should not be overlooked.* It is important, yes, to have gone into the inner recordings to have repaired and regained control over certain of the troublesome automatic patterns, but how well it has been done is reflected in how well the client has gained control over his reactions in his own outer world.

When enough control has been restored so the client is again master in his daily life, it is possible that he will cease the sessions, long before he can be considered to have become cleared of aberrative programming. This leads to a similar situation, in which a counselor has had the immediate task of preparing the client for confronting his counseling sessions successfully, so that inner work could be accomplished, only to find that the client feels able to cope with his or her life once again and quits the sessions. If he feels he has been amply rewarded by his sessions with the counselor, and does return successfully to his world, permanently to disappear from the counselor, that is "not all bad!"

It is possible that a counselor may never have the pleasure of delving deeply into the inner workings of some clients. If by a "quick fix" they feel amply rewarded for the effort and time expended and can face themselves, they have won! Being able to face one's own personal/total self is more formidable than anything the world "out there" can throw at him. Therefore, if you would become a Counselor, do not feel that you have necessarily failed when your client does not want to stay around to become 'cleared' of inner ills he has not yet become aware of, even though *you* know fully well that he is anything but clear. The primary objective of our clearing processes is not necessarily to reform every incoming client into a full functioning God-Self. Your job, should instead be considered to be one of preparing the client more fully to live his daily life, rather than to prepare him for functioning on both sides of the Great Divide—working transveil—as wonderful as that would be, and as much as We and The Hierarchy desire that.

Perhaps this situation is as it should be, because we can usually discover and reestablish our Real or Inner Selves only when and at the same time that we are *balanced* well enough to confront our *outer* worlds. As Counsellors we would then let the chips fall where they may. Even though it may be that the typical Counselor rarely finds a client who wishes to pursue total release, he can offer Humanity the gift to live a greatly improved life without expenditure of the time and effort required for Total Release.

While desirable, Total Release, is not necessarily desired nor to be required of every client. Perhaps only the rare and exceptional client—the Hierarchically selected trainee-candidate for conscious Co-Workership through the veil—will seek development of or to manifest his full spiritual characteristics. In any such case, we must take our client's as they come. The more people to whom we can show their potential, the more we can help the Human Race. But to help anyone genuinely to improve his case is to have been of great value to that client.

We would then learn to be happy therewith.

CHAPTER TWENTY-FIVE
ON SEARCHING THE TIME TRACK

When and as the client and the therapist learn to work in Reverie as a team it becomes possible easily to regress the client backwards in Time, from Present Time into the early years of life and prior. One manner of approach is to ask the client to recall events filed under grades of school, rather than asking for specific age or date categories. One reason for that approach is that chronological age and time recordings are not always reliable, seldom being used as file headings by the human memory system, since the human is designed to function only in *now*, in Present Time. Therefore, a client who has received a command to "Be fifteen years old" in his present incarnation may be found responding to such a request by looking for a reference to some special or memorable event that occurred at or about that age, perhaps via some verbalization such as the following

"Let me see...fifteen years old...I would have been 15 in 1936...Oh, yes. I am spending the summer on Grandfather's farm, and find myself pitching hay and enjoying myself."

In some cases, regressive file search commands might be more easily accommodated by use of the more powerful command:

"Look for a time when *you* were..." where the dotted line may be filled by nearly an infinitude of variety in the dichotomies of Table II. An partial listing of candidates could include:

"...drowning."
"...seeing or being in a bad fire."
"...hungry, tired, cold, lonely."
"...trapped, cornered, chained, or tied up."
"...very ill, dying, being born."

Another powerful entry is created by substituting Present Time terminology for Past Time terminology, such as:

"Recall a time when you *are*..."

When nearing the end of a productive session, especially one in which the going was heavy, it is wise to restore the client to a sense of well-being. This may be enhanced by use of such commands as the above, for example:

"Recall a time when *you* are feeling *happy*," or
"Recall a time when you are feeling pleased with yourself."
"Recall a time when 'they' are saying 'you are a *good* boy,' or 'You are good girl or a fine person.'"

Using tones of voice which suggest the desired condition will assist the client to find such times and speed up the return to Present Time. Another way to restore Present Time and to full occupancy of the physical body is included under "Spotting Spots." [See pages 155 and 156.]

CHAPTER TWENTY-SIX
COMMUNICATING AND COMMUNICATIONS PROCESSING

Communicating *meaning AND feeling* by energy flows is *real* communication, whether done by touch, word, or telepathically!

The inability to communicate effectively is one of the greatest symptoms of a serious problem in human relationships. It is caused by an inability to relax and work from an expansive state of awareness and to feel intuitively. It is not unusual to find people who are unable to communicate (from) their feelings. In this section the authors discuss means found by which such persons, in private practice or at large, may be enabled to communicate both from and with feelings.

In considering the dual aspects of effective communication it is necessary to include being aware of one's own thoughts and feelings, sending both their intellectual and emotional components, and then responding to the intellectual and emotional contents of the communication returning from the other person. Good communications should be seen to result from mastery of the process of consciously being at Cause Point, creating a desired effect upon another person, and then exchanging roles, willingly being at Effect Point for the answering communication. It is therefore to be realized that good interrelationships with our fellow Human-Humanoids require awareness of the existence of and skill in the practice of these communication processes, since they occur in varying degrees in every life interrelationship.

Many criteria may be used in estimating the probable degree of success of any communications exchange. These may be exemplified by the following: 'Is your other terminal really there?' Is he in Present Time? Do his eyes indicate comprehension, fear, doubt? Are they glazed? Is he being hostile? Is his skin flushed? Is he on drugs? Is he angry at you or at somebody or something else? Is he receptive? Accepting? Is he all tied up in a knot, or is he in a relaxed state? Is he in an expanded state of awareness? Can you see and feel his level of feelings and response to your expression? Can you accurately and fully sense your response to his originations and responses? Can you sense what and where the barriers are to the ongoing process of intercommunicating? Is poor communication *his* problem, or is it *you* problem? Who is in control of the communications process? Are you a part of the problem? Is it a communication process problem or is it a conflict of some sort, a confrontation without any specific accomplishment? What is his body telling you? Is he livid? Are his fists clenched, his teeth gnashing? Are his arms folded, or his legs crossed, or both? Is he pacing nervously...calmly...? Is he looking you in the eye?

What are *you* doing? What are *you* telling *him* or *her*?? These and other indicators, including voice inflection, the way he grasps pen or pencil or shuts the door, etc., all are readily available as signals that communicate What is going on inside a person.

If the counselor/facilitator is more aware of what is transpiring than the client, then the C/F is in control. Conversely, if the client is more aware than the C/F, the client is in control of the situation, and can outmaneuver the C/F, especially if the client is game oriented. The same phenomenon is true in encounters of nearly all kinds, such as boss-employee, wife-husband, teacher-pupil, etc. Many people take these character signals into account during their communications but are not usually particularly aware they are doing so. For lack of that awareness they may get caught up in a mutual button-pushing contest, in which both parties are triggering off defense-offense patterns in each other that are preventing any kind of harmonious communication, transaction or achievement.

Awareness of such signals can be developed by practicing being centered and by observing their focus of attention. Again, he who is most aware of the energy flow in thoughts, feelings, and attitude signals in a confrontation is in charge of it. It is mutual benefit to engage the client in various communications exercises, so that the therapist or C/F can regain and maintain control of his own sessions, and so that the C/F can help his client to be in control in the client's personal world.

Here are certain fundamental drills which will develop and enhance the client's ability to communicate much more effectively by developing awareness of the process.

1. On command, establish, hold, and release client contact with external objects in the immediate environment, and with parts of the

A Spiritual Psychology For The Aquarian Age

client's extended environment, i.e., with parts of his body, with his feelings, and with his C/F as a representative of the human race.

2. Become increasingly aware of the many nuances which establish the personality of the person or object with which the client is communicating. These will include color, temperature, texture, odor, weight, feelings of like or dislike toward the other terminal, etc.

3. Observe what actually is transpiring in communicating at both the intellectual and the feeling levels, objectively and subjectively by finding where the communicants are coming from.

4. Be aware of true intent versus statement of intent.

5. Assist the client to make many small decisions deliberately and consciously, and to execute them upon command. Examples of process by which these may be implemented will be found elsewhere in this epistle.

When engaging your client in the conscious communications processes, practicing the above and related extensions thereto, many hours will usually be necessary. These necessarily will be spread over the duration of the client-therapist relationship. Their use will also be found a valuable aid in restoring a client to Present Time after deep introspective sessions.

When working in depth with one's client it is important to minimize distractions caused by other people, telephones, radios or television or background music unless used as an adjunct to moodsetting, and the sounds and odors of eating, drinking, and smoking. When threatened, the C/F and client alike may "hide" behind any of the latter three gestures, obscuring communications signals rather than abetting them. It is therefore good practice to declare "time out" perhaps at hourly intervals for personal comforts, especially if the session has been difficult.

Many clients are unable to hold their attention focussed on the drills even in a quiet session, and may not be able to "stay with it" longer than an hour without a break of some sort. The client usually should not be allowed to break or interrupt the session if he gets uncomfortable, if it is apparent to the C/F that the client is having his escape button pushed and wishes to run away or hide.

Every command directed to the client is to be acknowledged by an appropriate answer from the client each time given, further confirmed or acknowledged by the therapist, regardless of the quality of the client's response. Each command and response pair is to be treated as a separate and complete new transaction, i.e., each communication is to be treated as a "brand spanking new" time, independent of all previous commands and communicated responses. Does this not suggest and require the need for simple communications practice?

The first series of commands is used to build conscious control of the client's ability to direct his attention...to enable him to develop the ability to *be aware that he is being aware* by establishing contact with an object, finding what it feels like to be in intentional/real contact with something and even with inanimate objects. He will usually be surprised to find that there is genuine feeling, an energy flow, associated with being in communication with a stone, with an ashtray, a picture, a book, etc.

After gaining the client's tacit approval or agreement to proceed with this form of exercise, the commands may begin somewhat as follows:

"Establish a line of communication to...," where the dots allow insertion of anything visible in the counselling room, for example including the door knob, the light switch, the wart on the therapist's cheek, the pencil on the floor, the spot on the ceiling, the nail holding up the picture, and myriads of others which will suggest themselves.

If the client seems confused, is not certain as to how to initiate any required effort, command the client to "Imagine a line going variously from your (the client's) head, eyes, or heart, etc., out to the object. Experimenting may be required until the client is able to fulfill a command with facility. To maintain the client's focus of attention, especially if the client is troubled, follow each command with simple questions such as: "Can you do that?" or "Did you do that?" and "Now, are you doing it?" The client is expected to reply with a verbal indication that s/he has or has not accomplished or complied with the command, perhaps saying "Got it!" The C/F/therapist would follow with an acknowledgment such as "Thank you!" and then proceed to establishing good communication with the next object.

Some clients may experience difficulty in letting go of the other communications terminal, once established. Having experienced difficulty in establishing the line of communication in the first place, the therapist/counselor or client may find it necessary to change the subject in order to let go of his previously mocked-up line of attention. Experimentation on the part of the therapist will yield one or more ways to help a particular client release or "let go of the object" on command easily and completely.

To close out a particular communication as an accomplished cycle of action, give the command: "Now let go of..." followed by the query "Did you do that?" When the client has acknowledged release of the contact, initiate another cycle by stating:

"Now, establish a line of communication *to*...and observe whether the client proceeds accordingly. This may be continued for as long as the client shows hesitancy or inability to respond. Many hundreds of hours may be required, spread over periods of several years. No standard number of sessions devoted to Communication Drills is applicable to all clients. Perhaps the best indicator for length of treatment is the relative degree of Present Time 'presence' exhibited by the client while running the communications processes.

Yawns by the client are a good indicator that a cache of push-button communications engrams or programs has been found. To "run off" such a cache may require extended sessions, or even a marathon or two. To undertake such a program will, of course, require agreement by both the therapist and the client. A good indicator that the problem is being worked through will be an alert client who responds brightly and to the point, without squirming, evasion, or getting groggy.

When a counselor is unable to accomplish the desired release in a few hours it may be useful to alternate the above with a seemingly rather insignificant but useful extension of the above. The command becomes:

"Now, establish communication *with*..."

When some proficiency becomes evident, the therapist may enter another and more abstract element-of communications, that of getting in touch with the realism or concepts of Thought and Ideas.

The original form of communication among humans was picture transfer, and is acknowledged by the phrase "Get the picture?" It implies clairvoyance and an ability to "feel subjectively into" the scenes being offered and interpreted, To help restore that native ability (and to practice communicating with the World of Spirit) the client (or Aspirant) is requested to repeat verbatim phrases of gradually increasing complexity, being certain to note and to repeat the therapist's exact and varied inflections. In doing so, one becomes aware of the picture behind the words, developing the capacity for communicating telepathically.

This subtle exercise has a marked effect upon the ability of many clients to lengthen their attention span, and to pay attention to what is really happening. This may be seen as a very useful tool to help people who have attention-span problems, quite regardless of age. Many people have not learned to control their sensory mechanism and hence find it difficult to stay in communication in most normal relationships, as in a classroom, in business, and especially in marital relationships. This method of treatment is recommended for use in relieving psychological causes rather than to correct certain chemical/dietary causes and blood toxicity problems.

When the client accomplishes the above with some notable degree of ease, he may be introduced to the process of consciously contacting and communicating the contents of his inner memory bank. This is also knowable as the Time Track or the Metaphysician's Akasha, and is useful for past lives review. It is often contacted without recognition.

The basic command to enter the deeper levels is to "Recall a time when…" Scenarios for filling in the dotted line include the gamut of human experience, such as "when you got fired", or "when you got an 'A' on your homework," or "when Daddy said you were a good girl or boy," or "when you drove a spaceship," or "when you lived and swam under water," and so on ad infinitum.

When the client is comfortably in some scene you can guide his focus of attention by asking him to observe and to relay information to you, such as:

"Look around and just observe how it makes you feel."

"Describe what is happening around you: what is taking place? Where are you? Who is with you?"

"Describe what time of day it is, what you are wearing, the season of the year, who is standing near you, who is observing, how it is making them feel"…and other commands as become appropriate to relieving the trauma of the situation."

A possible trap exists here of which the counselor needs to review to be aware. It is sometimes difficult to get some clients disconnected from their subjective or mental-realm adventures and back into Present Time. To avoid programming him how to "woolgather," and to avert any observable tendency to wool-gather, the counselor must follow each command to "Recall a time when…"

A Spiritual Psychology For The Aquarian Age

with another command, or with commands of another type, and must receive acknowledgment from the client that the command has been received, is understood, and is being acted on.

When a command has been given, the counsellor should wait a few seconds, during which he observes whether the client is having difficulty in understanding and complying with the command. To assist the client, ask questions such as "Can you do that? Are you doing that? Have you done that?" Allow time for the client to make a verbal response. If none is forthcoming, the therapist may follow up with "How does it seem to you?" and "How does it seem to you *now*?" The client is expected to make some response to indicate he is still in Present Time, even if slowly. The ultimate in going out of Present Time is for a client to escape by falling asleep, as when one is experiencing an exteriorization from the body.

When the therapist C/F desires the client to withdraw from a scene, perhaps to proceed with another, he may issue the command by indirection:

"Now let go of it."
"Can you let go of it?"
"Have you let go of it?"

If the client seems stuck in the scene, commands which usually produce the desired severance are:

"Hold on to the scene and do *not* let go of it", or
"Hang on to the scene and do *not* let it change, or
"Keep it from going away."

Try as he may, the client will find that the scene does slip away, and the more energy he puts into retaining the scene, the faster and further away the scene recedes. The reason for the above observable process is that energy is trapped by the emotional content of the recorded "scenes." Directing a stream of attention to that energy recording [hologram, ala Pribram] drains its emotional energy content. The harder the client tries to keep the scene from going away, the faster will the recorded energy be released. The scene may be contacted later for review of just how clear the recorded incident is and how free the client is from being controlled in Present Time by its former energy content.

In subsequent sessions it may be found that a cleared or neutralized scene has become difficult to contact even though it was more or less readily contacted in the first place because of its high energy content. The recording is still there, and unusually sensitive psychics or an electropsychometer may still be able to find it. Facility adequately gained in this manner can lead to recovery of events that took place in what seems to be other times and spaces in which the client knows his present body did not partake, yet which he feels he was or is being a participant. The therapist must not negate any such experience(s) or Reality being reported by the client.

When material comes up that seems to be occurring in a past life, treat it exactly as if it is happening *now*. Help the client to confront it, running off the charge accompanying the situation, real *or* imagined. Whatever its true origin, it is actively influencing the client, being restimulated by events in the present-day life of the client, or it would not "come up" at all. Religious convictions must be set aside, at least temporarily, when dealing with the inner world, if they interfere with the ability to confront a counselling situation in real time. It is presumed that the counselor-therapist is psychologically stable and experienced enough not to be shaken by *anything* that comes up in a session. If the situation is otherwise, the counsellor should engage the services of a colleague who is competent in this area!

CHAPTER TWENTY-SEVEN
VOICE DIALOGUE
Prepared by Lora A. Lytle on Request

Among the most recent techniques for alleviation of human distress and integration of the Personality, we have met, used, and are impressed with a process labeled "Voice Dialogue," developed by Hal Stone, Ph.D. and Sidra Winkleman, Ph.D. Their books, *Embracing Each Other* and *Embracing Our Selves* are current, useful, very informative, and enjoyable to read.

Voice Dialogue is a dramatically effective, and frequently humorous, tool for entering into direct communication with an individual's complexes. It offers the opportunity to separate out these complexes, or sub-personalities, and to deal with them as interacting psychic units or energy systems. Thus, when we speak of using Voice Dialogue, we mean that we directly engage the sub-personalities as Voices in a dialogue without the interference of a critical, embarrassed, or repressive Ego. Each sub-personality is addressed directly with full recognition of both its individual importance and its role as only a part of the total personality.

While the Ego is given its own central physical space within the body of its Owner-Spirit, the sub-personalities play out their conflicts around it. Thus, the individual will have his own chair and will discuss his problems, e.g., "I don't seem to be able to do anything right and I'm constantly depressed." This alerts us to the existence of a troublemaking sub-personality. We will then ask to speak to the "Voice" or complex that is operating by saying, "I'd like to talk to the part of you that feels that you can't do anything right. Please move to another place and let's hear what *that* Voice has to say." Before you can believe it's happening, we're deep in conversation with a critical Voice that is discussing endless physical, emotional and intellectual shortcomings. When faced with this overwhelming catalogue of its inadequacies, the Ego, which is listening, begins to disclaim identify with the critical energy or sub-personality and to interact with the constant bombardment of negative feedback in a more conscious and effective fashion.

Disclaimed or disowned selves are directly engaged in the same manner as are troublemaking selves. As we become aware of a missing or repressed sub-personality, we consciously seek to find it. For example, when dealing with a person/client who is aggressively intellectual and blocked emotionally, we might say, "I want to talk to the part of you that gets hurt." When we as Counselor/Facilitators note the absence of Vulnerability Selves, or a Sexuality Self, an Aggression Self, A Spirituality Self, a Creativity or Power Self, among others, we night be alerted to find them by asking to speak directly to them.

These sub-personalities, as ego-constructs or Voices are constantly operating within everyone. The Voice Dialogue gives us opportunity to objectify them—to elevate them into Units of Consciousness, to name them, to understand them and to work with them creatively. By thus using Voice Dialogue as a tool, we sensitize ourselves and others to the drama played out by these myriad subpersonalities which have accumulated around the ego-self. It is necessary for a Facilitator to become able to identify these various sub-personalities because, in the beginning, the Facilitator is more sensitive to the subtle psychological and physiological changes that accompany the activation of different Voices. As one becomes more accustomed to listening for these Voices within himself, use of a Facilitator becomes less crucial: you can process yourself!

There are many different Voices—each individual client having his own unique combination. The search for these Voices and the attempt to understand their functions (both positive and negative), and to balance them, are the joint task of the Facilitator and the Ego; and Voice Dialogue is the basic tool for accomplishing this task. Since clearing a subconscious mind is now a joint exploration, it is not necessarily limited to a therapeutic setting, but can be used in a variety of interpersonal or healing interactions.

CAUTIONS IN THE USE OF VOICE DIALOGUE

The primary caution in working with Voice Dialogue is that it should not be pushed upon a client indiscriminately. The basic integrity of the client should be respected and if, after an explanation of the rationale behind Voice Dialogue and the nature of the technique, there is still client resistance to its use, this objection be respected and other methods should be employed to contact the recordings.

The secondary caution is that this method of working with inner egoic constructs or recordings must not supersede the relationship between the therapist and the client. To maintain a happy working relationship, a basic client rapport should exist before Voice Dialogue is introduced. Said rapport should remain as a stabilizing influence throughout the Dialogue work.

The third caution rests with the degree of comfort and operating facility the Therapist-Counselor has developed with the method of Voice Dialogue. Respect your own concerns about the kind of clients with whom you wish to work in this fashion. Dialogue work has been effective even with very fragmented personalities, when the therapist was comfortable working in this way. There are no restrictions, insofar as Stone and Winkleman are concerned, as to the type of client patient appropriate for this technique, but each therapist must evaluate this for himself.

APPLICATIONS OF VOICE DIALOGUE IN DAILY LIVING

As one becomes familiar with one's own Voice systems, it is possible to introduce them into relationships. In any significant relationship, it is less threatening if one deals with, or speaks of, anger, vulnerability, judgmental qualities, fear, etc. as Voices rather than permitting them the privilege of taking over one's Ego entirely.

Each member of a relationship can take turns talking to, or working with, the various Voices of the other member. For instance, if one's anger is blocked and needs releasing and it is threatening to explode inappropriately and do damage to the relationship, the anger can be addressed directly, given a chance to express itself and its needs, and then the Ego can decide what to do with it. This is far more effective than continued repression or suppression followed by an unscheduled explosion.

Similarly, if there's been a good deal of stress, perhaps at work, the vulnerable Voice may need some attention. Just giving it a chance to state its discomforts and its desires releases the tension and facilitates constructive behavior.

The principal guidelines are the same for the therapeutic work. Individuals in close relationships can sensitize themselves to an imbalance in the sub-personalities of one another and can actively pursue those that need re-balancing. This is an exciting, loving and non-threatening way of helping ourselves to meet the needs of all the constructive sub-personalities that make up our marvelously complex psyches.

Instead of worrying about solving anything or subduing anyone, if we as the therapists simply engage the Sub-personality in a Dialogue, helping it to unfold as though we had discovered a new plant or a flower that needed caring, a very different kind of response, reaction or result takes place. As mental health clinicians, as soul therapists and healers, we are Gardeners of the Soul. The opening and unfolding of sub-personalities is a process, and it is the awakening to this that is our goal.

Having gone this far in introducing Voice Dialogue as an available direct approach to reestablishing harmony in one's soul, one can gain further appreciation only by trying the processes. Still a relatively new technique, it may be difficult to find instructors or persons qualified to teach the methods and build the skills to become a qualified Counselor-Facilitator. Having worked in the new field of Voice Dialogue ourselves, we attest to its value as an integrative process, and valuable to building a greater appreciation for one's own evolution accelerated as Spirit in Flesh.

We then respectfully suggest you to read their books, making due allowance for different use of key words like Ego and our 'ego.' We recommend you contact them for appointments for personal private consultations in your area. We believe you will be pleased that you learned how to make Voice Dialogue work for *you*.

[Voice Dialog is highly useful in working out the meaning of dreams Each player in the dream represents some aspect of the dreamer anyway, so Voice Dialogue offers an unmatched opportunity to discern the inner workings of our psyche by direct discussion of and the message It has for our conscious or 'aware ego' personality-self. Editor]

Reverend Lora Lytle may be reached via the Publisher and/or via our sponsoring agency, The New Age Fellowship (see front pages).

CHAPTER TWENTY-EIGHT
ON RUNNING PRESENT TIME PROBLEMS

When a client is having severe problems in his personal life, be it family, financial, professional, health, or other, it is possible that his or her attention is occupied to the extent that "Everything proves I'm in Hell!" The client may need a confessor figure...a real listener...as contrasted to a judge. He may need a sounding board, an impartial ally, with whom to play the game of "He said...and then I said..." Here is another opportunity for the Counselor/Facilitator/Therapist to make use of a technique built around "How did that make *you* feel?" and "How does that make you feel *now*?" and "How did it make the *other* guy feel?", "How does it feel to now?" and "How does the *other* guy feel *now*?" These are alternated as appropriate to understanding both points of view and gaining new viewpoints. Resolution may involve Gestalt or/and Voice Dialogue or/and other techniques.

Situations in which namable antagonists can be identified are grist for application of the Role-Playing concept, except that the problem may be sufficiently personal so that it's use should be restricted to private sessions, as contrasted to group work. In the absence of a clear antagonist, the Counselor may agree to be the "Bad Guy" for the purposes of working through a difficult situation and giving the client a new set of viewpoints, whether the client is or is not at fault. Usually there is learning which is invaluable to future relationships.

When forms of role-playing are to be tried, it is recommended that the approach perfected and advertised so well by Fritz Perls be used [26]. In this approach an antagonist need be present only in the mind of the client. An empty chair is placed before the client, on which the antagonist is placed in imagination. Charges and counter-charges then flow between the client and the antagonist, with the Counselor acting as Observer-Facilitator. The grievance is aired by the Client to the Antagonist, and the Antagonist is allowed to present his side by switching chairs with the Client, the Client now becoming the Antagonist. From time to time the C/F will ask the Client to note and to report "how the situation seems to you now." All combinations of roles are played, so that the Client has the opportunity to observe the Antagonist's feelings, and to observe what the Antagonist thinks about the feelings S/HE has regarding the probable feelings that the Client is having.

It will be evident when the proper time has come to terminate the confrontation between the client and his invisible opponent, based upon observation of the relative amounts of Light versus Heat generated by the proceedings. It is often reported that relations between the opposing factions are wondrously changed in their very next meeting, as if a psychic connection has been mended, which we know it has!

Sometimes it is possible to maneuver a client into an emotional outburst while running Present Time problems. Energy released during such outbursts originates from triggering a highly charged program element, from a "line charge" stored somewhere in the egoic subconscious) memory. If it is possible to keep a client aware of and "looking at" his outburst and the incident or situation producing it, keeping himself in present time relative to the original incident or facsimile thereof, full relief may be achieved in a short time. It is usually safer to help the client blow off steam in the presence of and with the assistance of the counselor than to blow off the same quantity in public with the boss, with his loved ones, or other antagonist. Encouraging the client to give vent to his feelings in session *while being fully aware that he is feeling them* will usually lead to permanent relief. However, going into "blind rages" at certain triggers is nonproductive for counselor and client alike. Until such time as the client is enabled to be aware of the onset of such "attacks," *staying alert and aware throughout them,* little permanent good will result.

When a client has gained the perspective to observe his method of expressing a tantrum, it is safe to assume that he will control their onset slowly enough so that the client, by working subjectively, can observe and release the original pressures and their feeling content. It is possible and the natural result that the pressures will gradually subside, leaving that whole category of tantrum cleared. To find if such is the case, the original trigger may be modified to be approached from other psychologically similar angles. The degree of release and remnant energy usually may be measured on an electropsychometer used as a psychological "Richter Scale" device.

When the client has "run through" several traumatic or engrammatic incidents successfully with his therapist/counselor, he often becomes so interested in the methods and their effectiveness that he will encourage further encounters "in session," until he gets the hang of it well enough to practice the processes in his daily life. At this point, his normal associates will probably comment on the change which has come over him, and the client will report an improvement in his relationships and in his general well-beingness.

In summary, with any new client it may be necessary to do an initial scan for "on the surface" releases before getting into the deeper areas. When present-time "bombs" have been defused, enough relief may be realized so that the client is never seen again, having chosen to terminate his relationship for the case gains already made.

While the ability to produce "Quick Fixes" is perhaps an ideal ability, to become known for rapid client turnover may become somewhat a dubious distinction, considering the fees that such a good Counselor may forfeit. However, that is a condition which rivals becoming known as a Specialist, both categories being entitled to higher fees accordingly. A good reputation should bring in many clients, so that we would opt for excellence as the cause for rapid turnover and charge or scale our fees accordingly to our needs.

CHAPTER TWENTY-NINE
ON RUNNING GUILT AND FAULT

Casual reference to the diagram of Figure 3 as representative of the inner workings of the Human-humanoid, will reveal no God-given or "designed-in" repository of or necessity for that mysterious quantity or quality labeled "sin" or "fault." Guilt feelings arise from internal conflict between the software or programming within the Human-Humanoid, as between two or more of the implantations required or accepted by the person, family, or society of which the H-H is expected to be a normal and functionally acceptable element or member. Race mind, tribal customs, and even family patterns and local area cultural patterns over a long period of time usually dictate what special conditions and circumstances are to prevail, along with the expected societal responses thereto, and are therefore programmed and entered into the subconscious as the 'thou shalts' and the 'thou shalt nots' of the Bible, conveniently labeled 'psychic software.' The software then proceeds to dictate the relationships and responses of the human all his subsequent life until later revalidated and removed accordingly as they cease their utility or cause trouble.

Sometimes certain programming seems to have been brought along at birth into the life of the client, from odd characteristics reported by parents when the client was a very small child. Often the counselor will have a client who seems to contact experiences such as hanging, drowning, or otherwise experiencing the death processes or other events that obviously did not occur in his present lifetime. Perhaps the theological concept of "Original Sin" requires reexamination and revision in the light of contemporary counseling experience accumulated during this research project, before and since. [See also Kubler-Ross, Blavatsky, and Cayce.]

The Conscious mind and its recorded attitude programs are kept active to enable the human to become and to remain an accepted member of society, a business organization or family. As seems to be commonly experienced, those familiar "Rules of the Road" that are so easily recited as the Biblical "thou shalt nots" are many times rather easily overridden by urgency or desire. It should also be noted that one program is often implanted more strongly than another conflicting program and momentarily wins control seemingly without conscious participation of the "faulty" or "guilty" program, at least at the time. Enter here another theological convenience, the concept of demons and devils to explain away personal responsibility, perhaps best typified by the phrase "The devil made me do it." Probably all that was needed or operative was a computerlike "override" ala a strong desire to indulge in the "sin" situation with great gusto but without compunction, blaming it on 'the devil.'

To establish whether demons and devils be of psychological or of religious origin is not within the intended scope of this material. However, the author does make the assertion that too many religion oriented Human-Humanoids do indeed use the 'devil' concept as a convenient scapegoat for avoiding personal responsibility. As is very apparent in contemporary society, and unfortunately so, any H-H can find an abundance of one-day-a-week religious institutions that are willing to trade 10% of one's pecuniary resources for protection and support of his belief in his vulnerability and inherent weakness to devils, principalities, and powers which offer and sanctify the all-too-welcome belief that "something out there" has the power to torture and test him, and is ever seeking opportunities to do so! We admit that for some people, there are dangerous forces at work in the ego/Ego, but that there need be none such.

To remove and/or mitigate the effects of Guilt, a client is brought into his reverie or Alpha state and stabilized therein. The Counselor-Facilitator-Therapist may be of assistance to the client in the stabilization process by giving commands such as those of Table III. This technique may be used until the client is comfortably holding all eight corners of the room. It leads to an expanded feeling which we shall call being "centered" [refer to Chapter 19].

Be sure to wait for the client to discover how to implement each command you give, and then to formulate a verbal response and deliver it. Observe carefully his mental attitude as reflected in the tone of his voice, and by any visual facial or body expression changes. If an electropsychometer or polygraph is used, observe the tone scale reading for level, whether rising or falling, and note its stability. When the client has stabilized, introduce the following technique for familiarizing the client with directing his attention while in the reverie/Alpha state. Have your notebook handy to jot down comments or occurrences, as they will often be grist for use as seed thoughts and commands during later work. Table IV indicates possible scope in client-peculiar triggers.

Give support and validation to the client as seems opportune or appropriate. Repeat the above commands in whatever varied form is necessary to help the client find, hold onto and reexperience the engram or trauma recording(s) and thus resolve or neutralize his feelings. It may be desirable or necessary to test for degree of client release by rerunning the incident in later sessions, checking for presence and strength of remnant response.

If the client seems hung up on Guilt or Fault, give the following or a similar command(s):

"Look for a time when you felt terribly guilty (at fault)."

"Hold on to the event. Feel the feelings and keep them from going away."

Do your best gently to help the client remain in Reverie and verbalizing her/his feelings. When the client seems stuck on some point, you can suggest s/he look around it to see what else is happening, how the battle is going (if applicable), etc. These will assist greatly to maintain client-contact and forward motion toward clearing whatever is being examined and/or reassessed.

Explore more deeply and request feedback by cautiously repeated use of an expression such as:

"How does it seem to you *now*?" or "What is happening now?" "Describe your surroundings, the people, etc." Engage in repetition of the commands as long as is required to keep forward motion and to clear or/and to de-energize the incident. Sooner or later the client will lose hold of the situation and come up into present time when an incident has been cleared, perhaps sidetracking into another incident of related character. Control of the situation is dependent upon the logistics of the session, and sometimes it is wise to let the client control his own viewing and feeling situation.

SOME STABILIZATION COMMANDS

Use of these commands is dependent on what sort of situation the C/F/T finds, so may require judgment.

> "See if you can find (sense) the ceiling of this room...can you do that?" (If not, see next.).
>
> "Now see if you can find (or sense) the in upper left corner of the ceiling. Can you do that?"
>
> "Now see if you can find (or sense) the upper right corner of the room...can you do that?"
>
> "Now see if you can hold on to them both...just hold them gently and tell me how it seems to be holding them."

Table III. Some Stabilization Commands

Guide the client in going around the eight corners of the room until he can comfortably hold them all in his attention focus, and still be responsive to the Counselor in Present Time. The process has other values also, such as for Exteriorization and Perspective training.

SOME CLIENT-PECULIAR TRIGGERS

These suggestions are usually sufficient to open and keep alive an invasion into the subconscious mind, for doing work on the Akasha. Note carefully that some clairvoyants are able to see what the client is doing when in Reverie so can lead the review, but most are not. It is then essential that the client be held gently on the borderland between waking consciousness and the sleep or trance state. Ideally the client should remember all he or she did while 'down inside' the recording.

> "Now...look for a time when you are feeling guilty."
>
> "Who or what is making you feel guilty?"
>
> "How are they making you feel guilty?"
>
> "What are you doing in response to that present situation?"
>
> "Describe how it seems to *you*."
>
> "Describe how it seems to you *now* (a new time!)
>
> "Now, look for a time when you are told that you are a good girl...or a good boy: Can you do that?"
>
> "Now, find another time when..."
>
> "Now, find one more time when you are told you are *good*."
>
> "Now look for a time when you feel (are told) that you are a sinner or a bad girl or a bad boy..."
>
> "Have you found such a time? Look around to find who or what is making you feel bad or naughty...just keep looking... Have you found such a time?... How does it seem to *you*?... Are you enjoying it? What are you doing? Who else is there? Are they doing it with you?" What do *they* feel about doing it?"
>
> "Just keep looking at it and observe the feelings you experience. Describe them to me."
>
> "How does it seem to you now?"
>
> "Allow the situation to change as it will."
>
> "How does it seem to you *now*?" etc.

Table IV. Some Client-Peculiar Guilt/Fault Triggers

ENDING A SESSION

A "heavy trip" or session may require repeated visits to a particular event or type of event, dissolving a little more in each session. After a session has come to an end, regardless of whether or not it has become cleared, and/or before you elect to go into new areas, be certain to reestablish or check the client's psychological location by asking probing questions, or giving commands such as these:

"Find the upper corners of this room." Can you do that? The client attempts to do so. Continue issuing the question until the client is able to do so brightly.

"Can you find your body's head? Your body's feet? Your body's rump? Can you feel your body's heart beating?

"Let me know when you have found them...and just tell me how they feel or seem top you." Continue until the client is able to respond easily how they seem to him with a clear voice.

"Now...are you here? Wiggle your body's foot...now wiggle your body's fingers...now your body's legs and arms and torso and head."

"Now, listen for the sounds in the room and describe them to me. Client should be responding clearly by this time. If not, repeat body-awareness commands.

"Now, slowly open your eyes and look around the room. Now, *Look me in the eyes!*" Client should be clear and responsive.

You may now wish to share a cup of coffee or other stimulant, and perhaps discuss what happened in a Session Summary. You may wish to discuss the time and date of the next session. While doing so, you as the Counselor-Facilitator-Therapist will have enough time to determine whether the client is in Present Time, if it is therefore safe to release the client to the outside world.

If the client is not sufficiently back in touch with physical world reality, run Spot-A-Spot mixed with small talk to speed up the process, giving you enough time to reestablish his client's awareness and stability in Present Time.

[See also the material on Reestablishing Reality in Hubbard.]

CHAPTER THIRTY
ON RUNNING INERTIA, BODIES, AND DEATH

This material has to do with processing for removal of *inertia*, because Inertia is the antithesis of life itself. This process reestablishes a person's freedom to function with lessened dependency upon matter or mass, Things, and Bodies for security and builds a sense of Beingness, Lightness and Existence. In the limit, one becomes able to live in and exit from the human body at will. Listed herein are processing entrances typical of those found useful in accessing this class of programs and accompanying attitudes.

The first commands are patterned after: "Where could you have *strings* on your freedom?" In using this command, expect a period of puzzled confusion until the client understands the command. The theme of the second command is similar to these:

"Examine your Memory bank for a situation having strings and describe it to me." Client responds. "Now, find another." Continue. This command may be run productively for several hours.

"Now, look at your giving. Do you see any strings attached to your giving?"

Ask the client to look for symbols having the meaning of *attachments to things*, such as cargo tied all over the deck of a ship so heavily laden that one more item would sink it. Examine the straw that broke the camel's back...as typical examples. Look also for correlating symbols which might indicate that *freedom to travel* is tied to or prevented by excessive baggage, weight, size, Fear, or unwelcomed responsibility, or any and all of these characteristics.

Typical entrances into *freedom* might include the following commands, depending upon what *freedom* means to the client:

"How could you be *free*?" (Describe them to the counselor.)

"What is tying you down?" (Look at and describe them)

"How could (being tied to) *things* prevent (reduce) your mobility?" (What things could...?)

"Now, look at times when you were giving gifts. How could you not let go of a gift?" Client responds.

"Now, look at times when you were unable to accept gifts. Client responds.

"What ties you to gifts?" Run until clear.

To run this dynamic may require many hours in session. As a method for approaching the general categories of mass, things, physical assets, etc., the following opener might be employed:

"Mock up a pile of your physical assets, goods, hobbies, things, and tell me what you see as you pile them right in front of you in the middle of the floor. Now, just observe the pile. How does it seem/feel to you? The Client tells how it seems from several locations and points of view.

..."Now, imagine yourself trying to pick up the whole pile in your arms...Can you do that?...How does it seem to you? Just keep feeling into the pile and describe any changes you notice...Now, let the pile grow in size...Now, let it shrink to half its original size...Let it grow again...Now, shrink it to one fourth its original size...How does it seem to you *now*?"

"Now, look around you and realize that you can no longer touch, have or use any of that accumulation. See other people noticing that you cannot prevent them from stealing items from your accumulation. See them stealing items and misusing them, breaking them, and ruining them. Observe carefully how this makes you *feel*. Does it make you feel dead? Just look at the feeling...How does it make you feel?...(The C/F/T waits for a verbal response).

"Now, feel that you are alive again. Can you mock that up?...(Allow time enough for the client to get the 'hang' of it and to report having success in making mock-ups of being alive).

"Now, see yourself selecting a gift from your pile of treasures. See yourself picking it up and giving it to someone less well provided for than you are. Tell me how it seems.

"Observe carefully how their acceptance makes the receiver feel. Now, observe how that makes *you* feel...Are you expecting a reward? Look carefully at the situation and tell me how it feels.

"Observe carefully...Is your gift truly a gift, or is it a *bond*?...What attachment do you feel to the object you just gave away? Do you feel *real*? *Alive*? What do *you* expect of the intended recipient?"

"Now, this is a new time. Go back to your pile of possessions. How does it seem (look) to you now? Now, select another object. Give it to someone else, and observe *your* feelings about *it*. Report them, please.

"Now,...find a 'man on the street,' or a little kid, and try to give him your treasure, but s/he refuses it. Note what happens when you try to give him your treasure...just keep trying and observe *his* feelings, and *your* feelings about *his* feelings." Repeat the process if the client has any reality difficulty in releasing the gift items. Repeat the above process, seeing the treasures alternately rejected and accepted. Let the recipient be alternately poor, rich, child, adult, drunk, ill, etc.

The above process enables examination of the degrees of freedom a client has from his attachment to things of the physical world, of his ability to be free emotionally and *spiritually*, by observing at first hand his dependency upon physical and psychological *mass* for his actual feelings of Beingness and Reality.

When the above process can be run without hesitancy, with real freedom, so that there is no undue withholding or disability to give away things of moderate or even great value, it should be possible to begin running *Attachment to Body*. Such processing proceeds as follows:

"Take a deep breath of fresh air and stretch. Do it again, and again.

"Now...mock up your body out there in front of you...about three or four feet away. Can you do that? Tell me how it seems to be observing your body out there. Wiggle its face, its fingers.... its feet. Now, imagine that you cannot make it respond. How does it seem not to control it any more? Tell me how it seems to you. Hold the feeling and observe it. Now, carefully test to see if you can again wiggle that body's toes. Now wiggle a finger...an arm...Do you again control that other or etheric self body? See and feel it responding to your command. How does it *feel* to be back in control of your body? Open your body's eyes and look around. How does it feel to again be in your body controlling it? Now...again mock up your body out there and imagine that you can no longer control it and describe the feelings."

NOW...note your silver chord and see your body lighted again. Be back in control over your etheric body and have it bend over, turn its head, lift its arm to shake hands with you. Let it rise and fall and move away from you and back to you. Are you in it? Now, merge it again with your body, and examine how it feels again to be one entity.

It is of critical importance that the process be ended with the client running in control over his vehicles, and that the client *likes* having his body surrounding him.

This process is continued until the take-it-or-leave-it feeling seems genuine. However, before risking actual loss of the client's body...seeing the client's death...it is imperative for the client and the counselor/therapist to have previously prepared by running *giving*, starting with small objects of trivial worth. Gradually shift to objects of increasing dearness to the client, building up to include giving away one or more of his most favored possession(s). Then include giving away *people* who are precious to the client. To have done the preliminary work sufficiently well will avoid the trauma or shock due to the usual vivid vision of loss of his body at death. This also will avoid risk of possession of the client's body by discarnate entities which may be interested in gaining entrance to the client's auric field at the time of running the technique.

WARNING! Because of the possible danger in running this technique, it should not be run on any but the advanced client who has already achieved control over his ability to make mental mock-ups and can relate to them on a feeling level. When the client is ready, he will have no difficulty running the "gift" and "giving" process, which must necessarily precede this technique. By the same token, the process should only be run by the *thoroughly trained career practitioner therapist.* Ideally a trained akasha-reading clairvoyant will monitor the session to avert any danger of psychic interference before it can arise. The client should always be able to find his silver chord, and see it connected to his body-self.

When beginning to run processes relative to the client's ability *TO BE*, whether with or without a body, it will be well to punctuate the mock-ups with frequent references and suggestions to the ability of the client to manipulate his physical body at his behest. He must experience, by deliberate activity, however subtle, be assured that he has and maintains continuing control over his body, mind and feelings, and thus knows he is remaining alive while possessing full use of his etheric body.

If this process is run successfully, it will be possible for the client to become psychologically independent of mass for his security, including his physical body temple. He then could find himself, other considerations met, able to leave his body and travel at will, returning with full memory of his travels. This represents an ultimate in the attainment of Freedom on Earth. When accompanied by adequate development of his intuition, the client will then find himself in possession of a priceless treasure, that of being able to go anywhere and perceive and to know anything he desires. It is not the essence of wisdom to turn a client loose with such power until he is reasonably free from old abortive programming and has developed his God-self characteristic by being in complete control of his case. Unless he has attained to such control, he is even more subject to manipulation by forces outside his normal sphere of consciousness than when he started this special development.

The capability for "out-of-body" travel is then more or less a graduation gift. If it is desired that a more detailed instruction be given than the above, in more or less the exact form that one would use in private session with a very advanced client, then the following material will be found invaluable. Ridding one of dependence upon *mass* and on Human Bodies for security will generally be successful, then, if patterned on the following procedures.

1. Make a small part of the pre-clear's body come and go, i.e., make it disappear and reappear. At first do this with small objects and mock-ups, either with or without eyes open, depending upon the client's reality, graduating from inanimate objects to the small body parts...from ash trays to fingers, for example.

2. Mock-up and allow some parts of the body to get larger and smaller alternately, while staying in charge of that process. Observe and report on the feelings associated with the process and its results, to assure good communication in Present Time with the client, and between the client and his body.

3. Most clients should be started with small inanimate objects first, followed later by plants, small animals, and then by small parts of the client's body. It is suggested that trivia be utilized at first, until some certain skill is attained in the process. Eventually it could be extended safely to larger and more abstract objects, such as the stars, the moon, sun and ideas.

4. A typical command sequence might be as follows:
"Get the idea or conceptualization of...(an object)"
"Now make it smaller."

"Now make it larger."
"Now make it much smaller."
"Now make it go away."
"Now bring it back."
"How does it seem/feel/look now?"
"Now let it disappear and reappear."
"Now see it neutral."
"Now, ask what *it* wants to do."
"What is it doing now?"

5. The objective of this process is to assure that the Thetan or God-Self is able to function either *with* or *without* dependency on a physical body (and/or physical objects at will) to give him his reality. He can develop familiarity by learning to function with as well as without small things having mass, graduating to larger items. Item density should become increasingly larger without leaving the candidate dependent upon that particular item for his safety or his reality until he can function without having a planet to live on or/and control.

6. When the time comes that the client/candidate is able to function without mass, he should be expected to be able to move into other spaces with safety and consciously, his "silver cord" remaining intact to permit return at will [Leadbeater, Heindel].

A CONCLUDING NOTE
FROM OUR INVISIBLE CONSULTANCY

"Successful application of this technique of observation should result in a high degree or state of Clear, approximating that of the religious Master, or ideal Thetan-Humanoid incarnation. It results in a state approaching Serenity on the Scale of Being. In fact, it even *requires* a fairly high state before the process is allowed to be run, and before a Candidate/Aspirant can respond to the process.

"This technique is seldom run, and few therapists may ever have occasion to use it. Its successful application requires a therapist and a client both to be very high in stability and perception, that condition in itself being a high order of attainment. Therefore, before running this technique, it is highly recommended that the therapist and the client both request assistance and guidance from *WE* who are sponsoring the release of Humanity from its bondage to the Earth Plane. Therefore, the occurrence of this processing should be considered and handled more as a sacrament than as a typical therapeutic technique. It is therefore fitting that We shall administer and supervise the sessions in which this process of final release to Earth bondage is accomplished.

"So let the work stand."

"Amen!"

CHAPTER THIRTY-ONE
THE TRANSVEIL TRAVELER

This unusual communique is offered as it was received by one of our research team associates—of unimpeachable credibility whose personal history is of record, and who has participated in this project from its inception. Also, the credentials of the Originator of this letter have proven above question, His unseen guidance and encouragement having proven invaluable to extending the depth and power of the creative therapies we have assembled in this treatise. This item is included for the dual purpose of expressing gratitude for his ministry and to offer specific assurance that persons who have risen above self are provided the same breakthrough to Higher Intelligence.

Sentences containing personal pronouns such as "we" and "our" are usually presented verbatim as received from our Unseen Consultancy. His method of verbal expression transcends in clarity and brevity what has otherwise ken attempted by way of meeting traditional "dissertation English" requirements. His style serves well to indicate his depth and wisdom of guidance during the project and which is continuing throughout the years since. Our success in this research program acknowledges his wisdom, excellent guidance, and company. The following quotation is directly as It was received.

HIS MESSAGE

"There is so much more valid information than most people's attention span will allow them to think about, or that their thoughts can encompass, that we hesitate to advise anyone his best avenue of approach to understanding any particular aspect of the Heaven worlds. There seems to be no end in sight, for everywhere we ourselves have been inclined to investigate, there is still depth beyond what we have attempted to fathom. Therefore, we would neither say nor tell anyone that the Kingdom of Heaven is or is not in any particular Way, thing or place, or consists of any particular form of pleasure or pain, love or hate. Overflowing in it all, however, is to be found that *life* is expressing. Life goes on without end up here, somewhat as it does there on Earth, but up here things are so much greater in variation than we could expect you down there to understand, or even to begin to be able to appreciate, that we have decided not even to attempt telling all we see. It is therefore likely that you will best be able to allow your own minds to mock up whatever is your own version of how a Heaven should appear, and then to let you go on from there with your own aspirations and growth processes.

"Certain things are more obvious to us than to you, however, for when it comes to functioning Up Here, we find it rather straightforward and simplistic. There is more or less only one way allowed to us, in which mode we are able to perform our tasks, interrelate and grow. *All* is consciousness, Dear Friend, and without that element nothing would exist at all. So that we are able to continue with our life expression, there is One Form, One Life, One Plan. There are several methods, but only One God manifesting through it all. We are *HIS*. In the usual theological sense we are indeed all "made in *HIS* likeness and image" as you've been told these past eons. It is not obvious as to the meaning of that phrase until one obtains the broader view of what it is like up here by virtue of having tried to *live* up here. For those who make the grade, who make a successful adjustment to this region, there is no limit to the variety in which he/they can be accepted, as to what this place is, and as to what it is not. Therefore, we have thought it worth while to begin sketching certain aspects of how life up here may be accomplished successfully, generally finding that such method will apply across the board, and for that matter, applying equally to any who come Up Here at all, whether they stay or whether they go back to Earth or to another planetary system in the galaxy.

"There will accordingly be found certain qualifications for permanent "membership" in this aspect of the Universe of Intelligent Life, requirements, quite literally, which must be met. In order that continued membership or citizenship up here be sustained, there are indeed certain qualifications without which it is not possible to maintain the mental-emotional or psychological stability necessary for this place to appear real or stable for those personalities who have just come up from your planet, as by way of physical death. There is certain to be dismay when such a one arrives, already to meet his God, to meet Jesus, or to meet another saint, when upon arrival it is actually found that nobody at all, or perhaps another being meets him or her; that Abraham or Moses or the Master Jesus whose bosom is sought is not available at that moment, that certain waiting periods of purification or preparation need be undertaken before The master can or will appear, or is able to be perceived or recognized at all.

"To those persons who have learned anything at all about this side (the upper realms), the death transition is made smoothly. To those who have not experienced any sort of study or training while on Earth, the transition can be traumatic. It is therefore wise, even necessary...and certainly it is *far* more than merely desirable...that the man of Earth be trained in what to expect before he arrives Up Here, so that it is therefore much easier on those of the upstairs "Welcoming Committee" who have the duty to greet and indoctrinate the successful arrival.

"Hordes will be arriving up here in these next few decades, generations having been dispatched by the Earth's activity relative to its cleansing (Ruth Montgomery, *Strangers Among Us* Chapter 17, Fawcett Crest Books. 1979, and other authors), in which so many will meet their deaths by climatic and geographical changes, by wars, famine, and pestilence, that it is neither to be found attractive as a place to visit, nor is it to be easy upon the resources We have available up here for that mass entry.

"For those who would take it upon themselves to prepare by study of our normal activities, the theory of our operation up here is available, and for having studied it, the new arrival will find himself stable, not "lost" in some foggy territory in which there are neither signs nor paths, no roadside "hot-dog stands" or gasoline stations at which he may inquire of directions. He therefore would be Wise *now*, while incarnate at this time, to take charge of his own personal edification to the extent that he read some of the copious materials already available down there. We do not really need to duplicate that material at this tine, nor need we give fresh new statements of what to expect up here. But we do recommend that interested persons begin their education concerning familiarization of anything and everything they can find about Life Here Above in the mental-spiritual realms.

"Kubler-Ross is probably as good a place to begin study as most persons can find and accept. She has written from her technical experience, descriptions by those who have actually made the Transition and returned to tell coherently of the adventure. Since it is written about the experiences of "normal people" rather than composed of the foggy inventions or wishful thinking of a well-meaning ecclesiastic or science fiction writer, her writings present a more accurate and correct evaluation than is otherwise likely to be available anywhere else, and therefore acceptable to the Laity.

"Another excellent and readily available source is Ruth Montgomery's recent work entitled *Threshold To Tomorrow*, put out by G.P. Putnam and Sons, New York, 1982. It is available in most large bookstores in the U.S.A., and will refer to other fascinating accounts of messages from This Side, intended specifically for the enlightenment and information of those Earthlings who are at all interested in the larger aspect of this Universe. We can recommend any of her works highly.

"One of our objectives is to prepare the minds of the general population of Earth, of the United States of America and all English-speaking nations in particular through this channel, and through other channels as we find them available. Since it is our good fortune to have found a channel having a typewriter, a trained scientific mind, enough time, and a natural curiosity, we can entertain your curiosity as well as proceeding with our assigned and accepted tasks of elucidating the populace. This is therefore likely to be more pleasant for you than otherwise is possible, but it is to be lots of work for us both, Dear Reader, before you are finished with us, or we with you! There will increasingly become more that we wish to tell people who are interested, as the variety of what we have to tell is infinite in extent, so that there is no real end possible in our descriptions of what is available.

"To you, our many forthcoming discourses may seem to ramble at times, but such is not without purpose, as the style of our presentation is apt to be more easily assimilated when given in different styles, as has already become noticed by you in this manuscript. It is not your transcriber's inability to copy us, but is instead due to our attempt to cross many disciplines, by varying approaches to this study to find different methods of explaining our philosophy, so that no one need be missed, or need find it difficult to encompass conceptually. We shall prepare our materials for assimilation by the average twelve-year-old intellect from the mid-section of the United States of America, as found in the U.S.A. middle classes. So that our information is interesting, and therefore likely to be read, we have taken the tack of rewriting everything which was formerly put forth in the highly technical jargon of the old Sanskrit or Hindu-Indian language, for consumption by the contemporary American-English speaking world. Later there may be translations into other tongues, but for now it is our intent to proceed with addressing a specific audience through this particular channel, as he already speaks and writes English in the American idiom.

"If you do not clearly understand what we are trying to put forth, you are encouraged to tell us, so we can try again from other points of view in later publications. There is no particular best way to express what we have to say, even though there is but One Truth. Since no one usually is able to recognize All Truth, different facets are apt to appear differently to various observers, much as in the familiar story of the three blind men and the elephant. So that *you* will be allowed that honest difference of opinion, we have attempted here to express much which should be found within your common experience, so that The Elephant will tend to have uniformly similar characteristics, especially when it comes to those important aspects and matters of "returning home" Up Here at so-called Death.

"We offer this treatise partly by way of easing the transition of the newly-arrived or newly-deceased, as well as for making life easier for our ever-attending staff function Up Here, which is devoted to caring for the needs of the bewildered traveler who suddenly finds himself cast into territory totally outside his lifelong experience. On arrival it will be the common experience to be met, whenever possible by an old friend known already to have come across the Great Divide of Death. This will serve the double purpose of hastening acceptance of the traveler's new state of being, as well as to inspire trust that he is in good hands. Then, for the moment at least, the new arrival, the Transplanes Traveler as we shall prefer to call him, is quiet and not stirring up a storm in this otherwise peaceful place.

"*Fear* is disorienting in the extreme, Dear Friend. When one arrives Up Here in great fear, he is able to and usually disrupts the mental and emotional fields of other newly-arrived Travelers, and therefore upsets them in their own attempts to attain peace. Tranquility is much to be sought, so that the very busy reception process, the indoctrination process and "checking in" to the new residence, introducing them to their circumstances as a way-station is accomplished peacefully, if at all possible.

"To achieve this end it is therefore desirable that we shall have given utmost attention to promulgation of these views, given from *our* point of view, as is witnessed in the heavens rather than from traditionally speculative sources down there in the Earth, from people who are otherwise well intended but who lack the genuine experience from which we are informing you in these works and words.

"There is no end to the variety of human experience we have introduced, so that there is no end to the study which could be levied upon the topic of the death transition and/or transveil experience. It is all a part of the Grand Design of Life that there be these periodic transfers from one place to another, but it does seem that the traveler would retain some of his previous experience, remembering some part of the transition process, since every Traveler has been back and forth, has reincarnated on Earth and returned many many times. There should by now be nothing new to any part of the short trip, a transition then being merely going from one gate through to another, as if catching another train, although even with this example, there is no other train to catch or miss

"Similarly with they who can lay down the body and pick it up again at will, the Great Transition should be a casual thing, done on decision, except that the Traveler in one case does not sever the silver cord until the last transveil passage. One thus goes through the gate, and except for a very brief change of luggage and clothing, he will find himself already in familiar surroundings, and therefore able to be at peace within himself. Therein lies the greatest part of our goal in writing these opinions of Ours, as to what WE believe the Transplanes Traveler should be apprised of and prepared for in advance of his next out-of-body trip.

"If the Traveler across the Divide would be well prepared, he would consider the nature of his trip, determining what he wants to take with him and what s/he hopes to leave behind. Crossing The Veil is made exceedingly difficult when one attempts to take certain chattels of property, attitudes, and attachments with him. For his transition to be the most harmonious, he should be able to feel that nothing of Earth importance need be brought along, that all his needs will be met as he goes. Approaching his transition from the point of view of an all-expenses prepaid trip, with all arrangements having been made in advance for his comfort, and then trusting that all is thusly so, makes life for all concerned much the easiest, and then the trip can be a pleasant experience. Then, in advance to lighten one's caseload by study is of tremendous value, out of proportion to its cost in effort, time or money.

"To have not prepared for his transition otherwise makes some travelers arrive already Persona Non Grata, we and they alike wishing that the traveler had gone somewhere else, or had stayed at home on Earth! There are those people who have the absolute knack of causing trouble from the instant they arrive on This Side. We are therefore inclined to shunt them aside while the more peaceful members of "the tour" are helped to pass "through Customs" quickly.

"There is thus an element of quarantine Up Here, a period which is usually referred to as Purgatory. In that phase, which for some is quick, short, and reasonably pleasant if noticed at all, others will find to be disquieting, as they impatiently attempt to force the "Immigration Authorities" by rushing the waiting room provided them while their case is being reviewed in Spiritual Customs. When a "Between Planes" traveler has taken the trouble in advance to study the new country and to familiarize himself with its customs, its people and coinage, just as on Earth, he will find himself that much better accepted and able to get around successfully with neither muss nor fuss, much more so than he or she who relies on bully and bluff on arrival, making life unpleasant for himself as well as for all about him.

"Therefore, you could say, Dear Friend, that we have selfish motives in giving this material today in the form and of the type by which you are receiving it. It is not all in your head, Dear Transcriber, as you are being concerned, but is *our* real attempt to get across our ideas of what we would *like* to have for the regular state of affairs Up Here between planes.

"When we consider the hordes of invaders, perhaps up to two-thirds of the world's population, coming all at one time up from the physical aspect of the Universe, i.e., from the planet Earth, which we see coming up in only a few more years, we are almost inclined to throw up our hands and take off for remote parts of the Galaxy. To do so would accomplish little, however, except to saturate those dedicated souls up here Who would remain faithful to their assumed tasks, assumed in Love rather than having been accepted grudgingly. For them to have the most possible success in handling what is to be an all-time record number of returnees, and in such a short period of time, it is therefore *vital* that this message get across the Great Veil.

"Dear Reader, and Dear Transcriber alike, you are at liberty, nay, are *requested* to put this material in the hands of publishers. We can assist you in finding good channels for widest circulation, so think not how to offer it. We shall take care of that aspect. You shall just prepare the text, and even there we will guide your hand. So, you can see how serious, how earnest, how intent we are on getting our story across to as many of the future Troupe as possible in the short years that remain before it cannot be done. While it may be another twenty years (circa 2010) before the rush Upstairs begins, it is just sufficient time to accomplish what we wish to accomplish, with little time to spare.

"We do not recommend that people start coming up early to avoid the rush! Stay there in your body and continue to experience the opportunities for growth, and finish your obligations while it is still possible to do so, avoiding any need for another incarnation or return trip to Earth. Use your tickets to the fullest while you have them down there, please! There is no money-back guarantee policy available. One can return to Earth only upon having made prior application and arrangements with the Upstairs management.

"You cannot be guaranteed an identical repeat journey, since the territory (Earth) will have changed. Also, the prices and cost of the entertainment will change, as will everything else which the Traveler formerly had relied upon for his comfort and familiarity on his previous tour through the countryside. Therefore, it behooves the wise Traveler to study up on his itinerary, even while he is traveling through Earth on his present trip. His pleasures and benefits will be the more enjoyable for having taken full advantage of the offerings as they become available, so that he shall have no desire to return to take care of things left undone previously, or to have experiences once missed, or having missed opportunities to properly finish his relationships. There will be so many people with whom he had relationships of a living-loving nature that he did not properly attend, that unless he took special care, he will leave the country/planet with regrets at having not given fully of himself to their lives while he was yet incarnate with them.

"Thus is it that we would admonish the Between-Planes Traveler to take time to be holy while it is yet possible. Holy, in the sense we use the term, does not mean religious as that term is used down there. Up Here, to be 'holy' is to be whole, complete, integrated, entire, fulfilled. *It has nothing at all to do with sanctimony*, nor with putting on the outward show of piety, sweetness, and harmony while all along the Personality is inwardly seething with hates, desires, and rage. Success does not lie in overcoming the world with 'sweetness and light' in preparing for the next leg of The Trip, but in overcoming the inward feelings just described. The outer manifestation of Light is a natural reflection from Within, originating from the Inner Self, from The Christ Within...the God Within...that is so important a product to be cultivated while in the Earth planes.

"It is a mark of the successful traveler, having journeyed his itinerary from one end to the other, that he has no desire to return, nor regrets at having to leave the Earth. He will have made a sufficiently good adjustment within himself and his surroundings of things and people and attitudes that he has experienced all that was important, plus earning a few bonuses for unusual behavior.

"Note please, that one can come and go across the Veil, traveling both ways at will, when that similar adjustment has been made, the Traveler then being freed from addictions of all kinds and sorts!

"However, to arrive 'back home' in such a wonderful state of serenity requires careful attention that the fine print in his original 'contract' or Life Plan has been fulfilled. Opportunities for getting copies of that original contract abound in properly drawn and interpreted natal horoscopes, as all Travelers to Earth purchase pretty much the same basic tour. Some have paid in advance, for more comfortable quarters, having previously accumulated Treasures in Heaven, while others have accepted more austere 'pay-as-you-go' accommodations in their haste, on their available budget, or having desired a more specialized adventure. However, the fine print, as found available in the Christian Bible for the general Western Traveller, in the Koran or in other documents for trips to other portions of Earth, contains all the instructions necessary for a wonderfully successful adventure.

"In your planned travel through the incarnate planetary life, occasionally a bridge will be found washed out as if due to a local flood, or some other unscheduled event may have inconvenienced your tour. Perhaps another tour which was to meet yours may appear to be late, or may seem otherwise to damage or modify your itinerary. However, it is also in the fine print that satisfaction is guaranteed. Contingency plans are built into the system, into The

Tour package. Therefore, no traveler need feel shortchanged unless he has not taken the time to become adequately familiar with his Bible, Koran, of other Book of Instructions from The Management on High.

"Upon proper study, one may extend his travels into deeper mysteries of The Galaxy, into deeper reaches of the Kingdoms of Heaven, with assured success and happiness. It is our purpose to point up these truths so that none need miss the glories of the many available side trips, nor the accomplishments of the main tour as he goes from one Life to another perhaps a level higher. Going from one level to another requires different outfitting, changing into garb more properly fitting whatever territory in which the Traveler will find himself. Then, he and she who have studied, who have done their homework will find interesting delights all along the Way, and will be prepared for and even understand what is befalling them in their travels in unfamiliar parts of The Trip(s). No better preparation is possible than to study to Know One's Self.

"He who would go on from this point should avail himself of one of those rare combinations of Therapist-Counselor whose background includes Bible, is skilled in the more prosaic or conventional methods for confronting Life, and who is well schooled in Psychology and Metaphysics, plus having a well-developed Intuition. He would be skilled in use of clairvoyance as an aid to or substitute for diagnostic instrumentation, assuring proper case treatment for guidance of his clientele. Such persons, cleared from their own subconscious trauma, coupled with genuine desire and compassion for alleviation of the ills of his fellow Mankind, will find ample reward for the effort expended in preparation. Such persons become further elevated in consciousness as he or she travel along the pathway, and become increasingly able to elevate those who are sent to him by Us for preparation as Counselor-Therapists or Specialists, as incarnate Conscious Co-Workers in the Higher Services.

"We now rest, Dear Friend. We sincerely hope and trust that you have enjoyed reading this "through the veil" team venture. There will be other volumes for your assistance in Self Mastery.

"Rest assured that you are of interest to us, even by virtue of having noted your interest in having read this far. Persons having done so are already predisposed to wend their trek along The Path with us successfully. As we go on, you too shall be further enabled to go on with us as Conscious Co-Workers. Ready yourselves, then, by continuing to decipher the mysteries which we may have presented to you, unraveling that greatest mystery of all, *yourself*. Join our conducted Tour! We shall be happy to help you gain the most from it.

"Offered in Love and signed by our Constituency Above."

CHAPTER THIRTY-TWO
ON DEVELOPING HUMAN CREATIVITY

There are at least two fundamentally different categories of intelligence—human and non-human. Intelligence may be further subdivided into the divine, the superman, human, animal, organic or amoebic, and non-organic. Of the non-organic, there may also be several types, divided into Computer-Electronic or artificial "machine" intelligence, perhaps into the simple impulse-response cells, crystals, and devices. Included is a model accounting for certain interface problems between Spirit and the Human Body, for technical convenience diagrammed in a robotic sense. [Figure 3].

Artificial Intelligence is marked by limits set upon the creative functions which may be accomplished through imposed "programs" or patterns as commonly understood and accepted relative to human intelligence. The limits created by man are set by the limits to which the creative impulse of the human designer can mechanize his thought processes in present-day computer software and hardware. Therefore, the limits of Artificial Intelligence must be equal to or less than the intelligence of "they" who create the hardware and software "machinery."

Should faulty operation be detected either in the computer hardware or in the software intelligence units, the cause may be located and corrected. The superior intelligence of the human, working in his "creator mode," makes that possible, since the limits of the device are finite and known to the designers.

As of today the limits of Human Intelligence are not really quantified. By general agreement it seemingly is not possible for a human being to fathom the limits of that special category assigned to "Divinity," a level to which we humans are apt to consider ourselves distantly capable, although having been "created in the image and likeness" of the gods themselves (Bible, Genesis 1:26).

A wide spread in the levels of intellectual achievement is readily observable among the members of the human race. There also seem to be definite limits to the accessibility of whatever intelligence capability a human may possess regarding present levels of understanding of the *location* of human intelligence, i.e., whether situated in the aura or super-conscious mind, in the convolutions of the brain, and/or wherever else resident. The various factors which may be used to categorize limits of intelligence or creativity or to explain them are treated in different frames of reference by present-day schools dedicated to studying the inherent characteristics of the human being, mind, and soul. Their differences in approach and their sparse intercommunication should entitle one to question the qualifications of each of those various schools of behavior analysis as to their individual authority for assessing and treating *any* human capability or distress at all!

When careful attempts are made to define and to measure the fundamental intelligence-bearing characteristics of the human mind, it is soon discovered that there is a fundamental difficulty or inability to validate anything which may be quantified. Our contemporary inability to provide verifiable dimensions of the human mind prevents Humanity from coming to grips directly with methods for evaluating its relative performance in terms which may be considered in any way scientific in the usual Engineering or Mathematical senses. Yet, it is well understood that some definite situations and circumstances operate to prevent the-human from functioning at his full capacity. Some of these are chemical, some dietary, some are psychological and others are not yet well understood, if at all. Contemporary holistic schools consider that food chemistry, diet, and exercise in proper relationship will greatly enhance the ability of the human to approach its maximum creative capacity. And yet, because of carefully-drawn observations and conclusions, it is also perceived that there are further impediments capable of preventing full realization of the natural intelligence of the human mind, whatever be its ultimate capacity. Those factors do not seem to manifest equally in each human being.

As with equipment which is man-made and operates by virtue of designed-in or artificial intelligence, the human intelligence can, when experiencing a limited range of difficulties of either organic or inorganic nature, sometimes be repaired or treated so that some degree of normal operation is once again restored.

In a dissimilar vein, but true of both man-made intelligence units and human intelligence units (the mind, for example)—various levels of sophistication and types of troubleshooting or analysis are available. These depend for their effectiveness on the basic equipment budget, the available time, the test equipment, and on the training and experience levels of the practitioner who has the task of restoring acceptable levels of performance. It is usually possible to restore a faulty piece of machinery to "brand new" performance levels, so that such piece lives up to its original guarantee or 'intelligence level,' and sometimes higher!

This is to suggest that without major redesign an ailing item of *man-made* equipment, an artificial intelligence unit once repaired, has no further or higher limit in intelligence to which the unit can be pressed nor to which it can "strive,"...barring, of course, incorporation of factory upgrades and the like. Yet, a *human* intelligence Unit *may* rise *without limit*, given proper consideration, assessment, and treatment!

There is an emerging school of thought, now comprised of several religions and avant garde psychological institutes, which says that the ultimate limit of the human intelligence approaches the "divine" level of its Creator, and therefore it should approach that "built-in" potential in the 'beginning.' Several approaches to actualization of that potential are offered, classically including one or more meditation methods and other programs of self development drawn from the Ancient Wisdoms.

If it is indeed possible for the human intelligence or creativity level to be raised, it would seem *most* profitable to investigate any and every method or means by which any sort and type of human intelligence malfunction could be discovered and then used for correction or outright removal of whatever distortion source accordingly was found suspect.

It was on the basis that the above premise was correct that this particular study was initially undertaken. A study of digital computer intelligence, quite apart from any immediate application to a study of human intelligence, shows some behavioral patterns duplicated in human intelligence networks which parallel certain processes in the design of computer or artificial intelligence. The author and many other persons, long engaged professionally in the Engineering and Computer aspects of Electronic Communications, had long suspected that similarity and began looking for common approaches to the diagnosis and resolution of *human* "operating difficulties" which might be responsive to still appropriate computer diagnosis methods. Several methods were found, tested, and are here made available to the extent that they now form solid bases for a new approach to the alleviation of difficulties in the human psyche without sending the human 'back to the factory' for upgrade to *higher levels* of intelligence.

With sustained and proper application of these methods for repair and raising of human creativity and/or intelligence, it can become more or less routine that a client, under a skilled practitioner, can be relieved of a wide range of human debilitations and miseries of predominantly a subconscious and/or mental-intellectual characterization. It is our experience, using the methods here expounded as results of our researches, not only to remove socially-engrammatic and inappropriate relationship traumas but also to *open up higher or extended levels* of extrasensory perception, such as clairvoyance. Also observed were increased awareness of the thoughts and feelings of others, generally tending to allow entry into the psychic domain typically held sacrosanct by the religionists as characteristic of individual divinity or as restricted to sainthood.

One goal of this particular treatise is to expand upon the premise above, leading more into an exposition of the origin and application of the method discoverd, rather than to delve more deeply into the theory of the method itself. One reason for that choice is that people generally are much more in need of personal *application* of the principles of isolating, repairing, and restoring Human functionality than they are in hearing how it works. Therefore, we have written you a "How To Do It" book intended for use by the interested practitioner already employed in the mental health field.

We propose that further research will eventually reveal ways to go even deeper into an ailing human soul, finding what is required for greater enhancement of the human ability to function at *any* level of awareness, Human *or* Divine!

In the coming centuries, further research will undoubtedly become accelerated by judicious practice of these methods propounded and explained in the present treatise. As more people of higher levels of accomplishment and standing in the intellectual community benefit from practice of what must now be recognized as a fledgling Soul Science, it will be possible for Humanity at large to bridge the present wide gap between Humanity and Divinity with the ancient Antakaranah, but the *motives* of the human race must and will become purified long before that result is widely experienced.

A Spiritual Psychology For The Aquarian Age

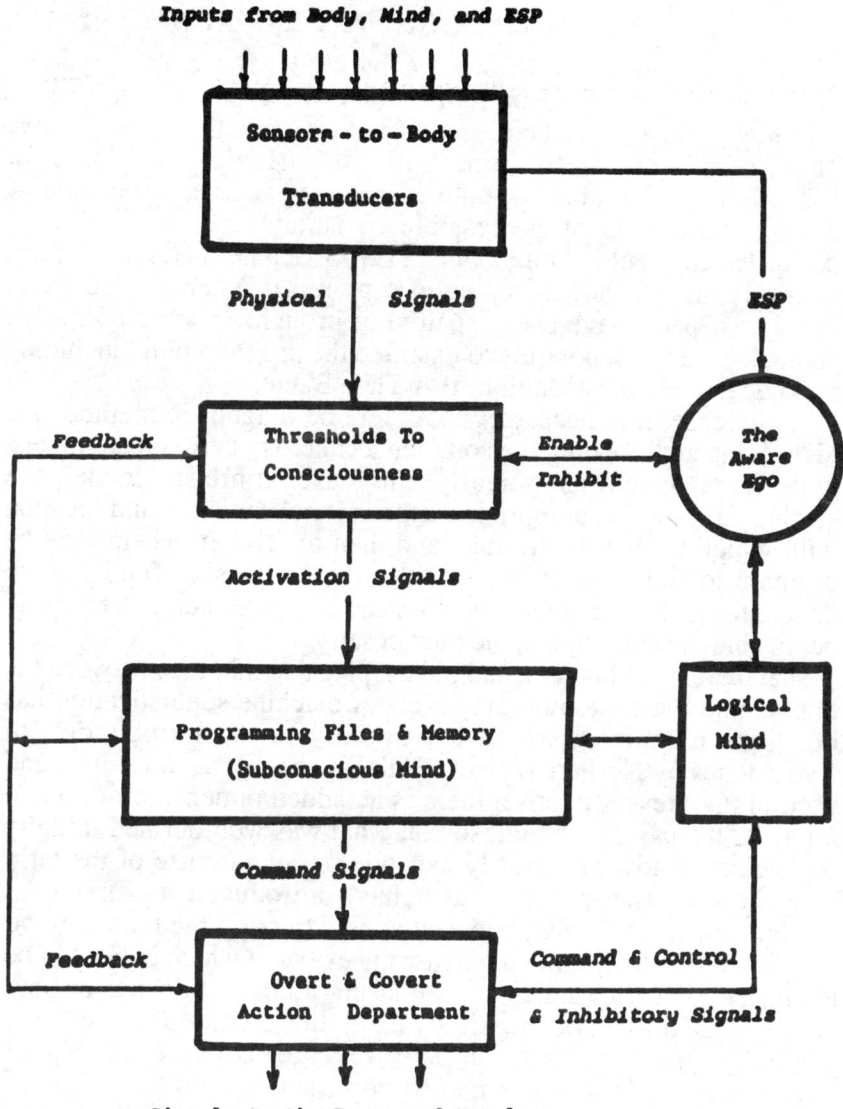

FIGURE 3
CIRCUITRY OF THE PSYCHE

SOME PSYCHOCYBERNETIC IMPLICATIONS

Figure 3 tries to represent the parallel between the type of intelligence manifested by humans and the types of intelligence seemingly capable of being manifested by machines. Both have "hardware" or "body" and both have logical software or "programming" as entered routines or habit patterns. Upon suitable examination, it is often possible to isolate the cause of poor performance in either or in both types of "machine" and to treat them similarly, as was noted in the basic premise. When the hardware "health" aspects have been repaired or brought to some norm—or "cured"—it is then possible to examine the programming, including its logical operators as Inhibit, If A Then B, etc.

In any case, it is necessary that there be diagnostic methods for identifying and isolating the common technology between computers and humans; philosophically they are similar. Hence, the "technician" needs appropriate methods for observation and location with which to find the trouble, and then to "fix" it, whether he be oriented to fixing machines or to fixing humans. A fundamental difference is that we do not ever see the computer being "creative," being able to synthesize in the human sense.

That there were fundamental philosophical similarities between the human and the contemporary levels of machine sophistication has not gone unnoticed, which led initially to the introduction of Cybernetics by Norbert Weiner. With his concept as developed and used in the present treatise, there is an added dimension of human mind, as the psyche or soul, so that what was well-defined initially by Weiner is now necessarily expanded to require use of the term "Psycho-Cybernetics." We then have introduced a convenient reason for differentiating between and addressing the human mind and the human soul, limited only by the extent to which either can be identified. Thus, treatment of the ailing human at deeper or soul levels is being made possible using the techniques we have advanced through creation and investigation of "artificial intelligence." We thus are indeed contributing to a new field of human endeavor by integrating and hence augmenting the power available in Religion, Psychology, and medicine, not to omit Robotics!

Please note clearly that our discourse is aimed principally to treatment of the human Soul rather than to treatment of the human

A Spiritual Psychology For The Aquarian Age

body. There will be 'fall out' in improved levels of body functioning when faulty mind processes are cleared. This is observed already through the imperfect art of Psychosomatics, although it is not the immediate intention to further address that field.

It has so far not been found necessary in application of our method to differentiate the human "Mind" from the "Soul." It is not even necessary to attempt their location in order that this particular technology shall become accepted and used effectively. Taking this position avoids any necessity to further defend concepts introduced from less well-accepted metaphysical and psychic sources and realms. That makes it possible for the professional "Mental Health Troubleshooter" to identify "trouble" even when he does not know immediately what to look for. All he need do is to *learn how to look* for it, and how to treat what he finds for its reduction and removal, even when having only "system-level" symptoms to go by. Sounds a bit like the M.D. and Medicine, aye?

Because of the power in the techniques and the sensitivity of the human psyche, extensive and intensive Practitioner training and experience are needed. Based upon the cut-and-try experience of most practitioners it is believed all mental-health technicians should be required to have been a client and student for at least 1,000 hours, being processed and also doing supervised processing of others under a skilled tutor, one already trained in cause-effect relationships with the public Development of a judgment factor cannot be avoided, as basic variations among clients may cause unusual difficulties for the 'Cookbook Counselor.' An experienced practitioner often can identify onset of a difficulty and avert or cope with it harmlessly by referral to proper professional aid. That aid may be in the form of on-call staff medical expertise, a Psychiatrist or Psychologist, a Lawyer, an expert witness, or a "bouncer" if physical protection should be needed.

To minimize possibility of surprise abuse from the client or to the client, the would-be Counselor/Facilitator needs to have experience as to signals which can be encountered during processing a client, and assessing quickly from these whether the situation needs immediate action. Therefore, skills in communicating with a client are required, through use of intuition, body language, tone of voice, manner of response, delay in responsiveness, etc. Tied in to this is that your effectiveness as a C/F when judged by the apparent ease with which you are able to see a difficulty and resolve it. To enhance his effectiveness, a practitioner is often required to modify a command from those listed as entrance commands, in order to suit a particular client and to fit his client's vocabulary and emotional condition.

One effective safety measure is to dismiss a session or cancel it in midstream, sending the client on his or her way without charging for the session. You can blame it on your own in disposition if you need to state a reason.

It is well known in the Psychology and Metaphysics fields that the human subconscious mind works in picture language or symbols. When attempting to translate them into words, different verbalizations yield different interpretations with different clients, although the original pictures may be expected to remain stable from time to time in the same client. Therefore, the practitioner using these techniques does well to be familiar with the *meaning* and *intent* of each command he gives, so he will do well in correct interpretation of the responses. Fortunately, much can be learned from a study of contemporary documentation on that subject.

ON THE NEED FOR BETTER COMMUNICATION

While these instructions appear simple, even elementary at times, their implications are of major significance to anyone who would be successful either as a client or as a practitioner, in public practice or in private. Communication between client and C/F is difficult until both parties understand the processors and each other. Communication between researchers has often come about via personal correspondence rather than by opportunity for funded study. Hence, the work being done by The Institute For Noetic Sciences and The Association For Transpersonal Psychology takes on an especial value.

That a fundamental divergence in approach to Life exists between the bastions of Electrical Engineering (right-brain) and Psychology (left-brain) is freely admitted, and is necessary for good reasons, and a truce was negotiated to produce the dissertation on which this research is based [31]. Curiosity and the necessity for good communication will long continue to drive the golden spike of compatibility into an area that is not yet well understood by either field's entrenched hierarchies. A marriage is being developed successfully as specialists in each other's field arise and are willing to be counted among the black sheep who jump the traditional fences.

Boundaries defining the present subdivisions are Information Theory and Artificial Intelligence, and of course Cybernetic Engineering, as a branch of Medical Engineering. In the U.S.A. the military research establishment is presently much better financed and researched than is the relatively less explored field of Human Creative Intelligence Theory. The latter is the subject of indirect study and much speculation among leading software philosophers and hardware humanitarians. Further technological research for the elements of commonality are required before either discipline can reap the rewards of a marriage of the two, perhaps mechanized as the mind-reading supercomputer, or the genius personality.

Each of these particular ends seems to require different types of quantization for labeling and identification of the characteristics to be observed, creating problems particularly in establishing a common meeting ground for interdisciplinary communications. Perhaps the most fundamental and common problem aspect is the traditional problem of attempting to communicate *meaning between humans*. While the ability to define information per se has become rather straightforward and can even be quantified via applications of Shannon's Law, [University of Michigan Ph.D. dissertation] the correct *interpretation* of that information by another human varies considerably, and often differs greatly from the originally intended message. Perhaps this is one major reason for the presently observed expansion of the profession of Law into interpretation of fundamental human communications. The reasons for differences between information originated and information received are worthy of considerable effort at discovery and alleviation.

In transferring information between a sender and a receiver it is a common experience that distortion enters the process. This is especially true when electrical and electronic equipment is used to transmit messages between any two points. But in electronic communications the amount of distortion can be quantified, can be *measured* electrically, and coding can be used to reduce the error to arbitrary levels.

However, the distortion which enters through differences in the "human equipment" characteristics of he who sends and s/he(!) who receives and interprets the message are much less readily quantified, partly because each terminal does not use identical vocabularies, so the meaning is even less perfectly identified. Who or what shall constitute the example of the "ideal receiver" is also poorly identified, and depends largely upon who does the actual evaluation.

Research into the causes of faulty human communication, as well as discovery of distorted communications and their correction, form a great unresolved problem in human relationships at all levels, even from Heaven to Earth! Cataloguing its proclivity, its identification, minimization, correction, and removal looms as a *most* important factor in this era of high-speed mass electrical telecommunications. One example of a vital area is when one human agency attempts to communicate successfully some of today's military and political messages around the world to enemy and ally alike. Especially is this true when the correlation process upon which interpersonal communications rely is based upon minimization of or correction for differences in background of personal experiences logged in the respective subconscious memory systems. It is even difficult for both parents to agree on all the individual family member character traits because of differences in how and when their family life was experienced.

Nearly anything which can enable a researcher to "put a handle on" and then resolve the problems of distorted human intercommunications and achieve successful sociological relationships will be very valuable as tools for any therapist engaged in treating human difficulties.

Perhaps one of the most immediately important areas accessible to approach was taken in this project, where it was accepted that the sources of distortion for interpersonal communications purposes are the same which damage or prevent good general sociological interrelationships. We know that certain experiences found in our human subconscious mind color our use of words, and as well color our evaluations of those experiences we have, even to the extent that no two people ever "see" the same parent identically, the same picnic, or whatever other common experiences people share. Our methods were presented in such form that they may be applied directly in encountering the general public, taking into account the importance to successful relationships gained, considering also the necessity to regain and retain inner peace in one's own self.

Therefore, the discoveries which have resulted from our researches are given in the frame of reference of a handbook for improving human communications and interrelationships by eradicating the causes of distortion resident in an ailing soul or subconscious mind, for example. It was done this way because in The Sciences, problems of human interrelationships are all but ignored as intangibles. Many technical problems are also left untreated in the fields of Psychology and Psychiatry, or are made to "go away" with administration of drugs for convenience, by institutionalization, or are merely ignored as unresolvable for lack of knowledge of a suitable technology.

The present discourse then has the fundamental purpose of *offering a working methodology for direct treatment and release* of those human distortions which plague Homo Sapiens the world over. With that introduction, we have entered into the formal body of the methodology itself. It is hoped that the user/practitioner will appreciate this work as a technical manual giving a brief introduction of the theory and the processes involved within the Cybernetic Human Being, going on by showing how the engrammatic distortion sources are brought up and then how they may be relieved.

For having freed the human of his predilection to distorted relationships, we have as our goal to free the trapped human soul to reach its greatest heights as a creative individual, a Conscious Co-Creator with God.

To enhance doing that we have provided a basic block diagram that attempts to show a working relationship between the various sensors with which the Human Psyche and Body-Mind are equipped. From inspection of Figure 3 we find the usual sensors along the top block, representing Feeling, Taste, Smell Hearing, and Seeing, with allowance made for their spiritual octaves, like abstract Thought/Intellect and Intuition. Each sensor is equipped with a transducer, a device that converts a particular form of sensory input signal to an electrical signal that can travel along the nerve communication lines between the various places and functions which must be included upon which the sensor evaluation and programmed responses are based.

Note that each sensor signal goes through a thresholding device. When an input signal is below some predetermined electrical signal strength, it is passed along to the *awareness ego* and to the little Programming Department ego as part of general information, where it is usually ignored in the typical human. If the signal is strong enough to overcome the threshold, it indicates the possibility of damage or the threat of an attack or damage. The attention of both egos is also dependent on what is going on elsewhere with other sensors. If a threat pattern requires an immediate response, the subconscious Programming Department will pick it up and automatically react. If there is need for conscious *aware ego* participation, if a reasoned response is called for and the threat is coming in slowly enough, the expenditure of the relatively slow Conscious Mind Department will evaluate and assign corresponding action as needed.

Exactly how and where the functions are distributed throughout the human psyche is not clear, but it could appear that the memory uses every atom in our beingness. It is perhaps readily accepted that the chakras and their circuits are in themselves connected to their respective endocrine attachment points along the spine. In that manner one can picture the Spiritual Currents interfacing the Human body circuitry with chakras as the Transducers that down-convert Spirit frequencies to their correspondingly lower frequencies for body energizing. That same consideration implies that our physical health has a direct correlation to our spiritual health, and perhaps vice versa!

Chakras are known to spin at different frequencies on the outer rims and slower at the inner spine end. If a chakra spins slowly or is blocked, the physical body and psyche is unable to support its incarnate Spirit, which in turn is unable to do in the body what it incarnated to do. Then what can be discerned in Figure 3 is conceptually correct, in that blocks anywhere in the network produce hindrance or other effects elsewhere. Then once recognized, it matters little where the actual restriction is in the structure, as we still can confront and remove it.

We are thus able to approach the human as a structure of complex logic circuits or symbols such as *and*, *or*, *If A and B and C and D then E*, and other standard computer logic functions. We have provided a way for the *EGO* to be supreme in its own house by inhibiting Defense action, or Enable, *on decision*. As given earlier, the little battles or skirmishes are usually handled only by the Programming ego-self, feeding the results up to the *EGO* if there be a need, or if the *EGO* is interested.

Suffice it to say that in Figure 3 we have a suitable working model to see how our previous explanations of programming and its place in the overall scheme of things is useful to the point of demonstrating that our Reverie Search is valid. We look for and at the results the programming produces rather than at the actual programming itself. If we do not like a particular result, we can still discharge its self-contained program energy and be freed from it. Usually the review process brings that function up to the *EGO* for future resolution unless it is a response to an unresolved traumatic recording, which once discharged, remains discharged.

It is easy for the client and his/her C/F to work through the maze, once understood, even though some of the unresolved areas might be very tedious and difficult to work, or to open for resolution. Then, given the tools contained in this tome, properly applied with Patience and caring, most humans will significantly change their Creativity and Intelligence Quotients, making satisfactory adjustments to incarnate Life.

It remains only to try it. The Guides are ever ready to support the sincere Student and Counselor/Facilitator.

Amen!

CHAPTER THIRTY-THREE
RECOMMENDED READING

This listing includes special resources for anyone who wishes to peruse Aquarian Age Psychology research in depth.

[1] Ashby/Conant, *Mechanisms of Intelligence: Ross Ashby's Writings on Cybernetics*. Edited by Roger Conant. Available from The Systems Inquiry Series, Intersystems Publications, Seaside, CA 93955, U.S.A. Copyright 1981

[2] Jahn, Dr. Robert G. *The Persistent Paradox of Psychic Phenomena: An Engineering Perspective*, an invited paper. Published in "The Proceedings of the IEEE," Vol 70, No. 2. February 1982.

[3] McNichol, Andrea and Nelson, Jeffrey, *Handwriting Analysis—Putting It To Work For You*, Published 1991 by Contemporary Books, Inc., 180 North Michigan Avenue, Chicago, IL 60601

[4] Wilber, Ken. *The Holographic Paradigm and Other Paradoxes*. Edited by Ken Wilber, Shambhala Publications, Inc., 1920 13th Street, Boulder, CO 80302

[5] Gray, William *General Systems Theory and Psychiatry*, Edited by William Gray et al. From The Systems Inquiry Series, 1981. Intersystems Publications. Seaside, California 93955.

[6] Bailey, A. A. *The Light of the Soul—Its Science and Effect*. (A paraphrase of *The Yoga Sutras of Patanjali*), Inter-Lucis Publishing Company, 11 West 42nd Street New York, New York.

[7] *The Brain/Mind Bulletin*, Interface Press, P. 0. Box 42211, 4717 North Figueroa Street, Los Angeles, CA 90042. Phone (213)-223-2500.

[8] *ReVISION—A Journal of Consciousness and Changes*. Available via Re-VISION, P.O. Box 316, Cambridge, MA 02138. Published biannually.

[9] Heindel, Max. *The Rosicrucian Cosmo-Conception*. Available from The Rosicrucian Fellowship, P. 0. Box 713, Oceanside, CA 92054-0112 (many titles).

[10] Janov, Dr. Arthur *The New Primal Scream* 1991 Enterprise Publishing, Inc., 725 North Market Street. Wilmington, Delaware 19801

[11] Osborne, C. G. *Understanding Yourself, The Art Of* and eight other titles. Published by Zondervan Publishing House, Grand Rapids, MI 49506.

[12] Fox, Emmett. *Stake Your Claim.* and other titles. Out of print. Dates not available.

[13] Schuler, R. *Possibility Thinking* and other titles. Available via The Crystal Cathedral, Garden Grove, California 92640. Telephone (714) 971-4000.

[14] Peale, Norman Vincent. *The Power of Positive Thinking*, and others. Available in most religious and psychology bookstalls. Originally published in 1936.

[15] Montgomery, Ruth. *Threshold to Tomorrow* and others. G. P. Putnam and Sons, Publishers, 1982. New York

[16] Leadbeater, C. W. *The Inner Life*, and others. The Theosophical Publishing House, 306 West Geneva Road, Wheaton, Illinois 60187.

[17] Stone and Winkleman *Embracing Ourselves—The Voice Dialogue Manual* 1989 DeVorss and Co., Marina Del Rey, CA

[18] Sutphen and Taylor *Past-Life Therapy In Action* 1983 Valley of the Sun Publishing Co., Box 38, Malibu, CA 90265

[19] Hubbard, L. R. *The Dynamics of Life* 1988 Bridge Publications, Inc., 4751 Fountain Avenue, Los Angeles, CA, 90029

[20] Deepak Chopra, M.D., *Quantum Healing Workshop* tape set, 1990 Available via Mystic Fire Video, Inc., PO Box 1092 Cooper Station, New York, NY 100276 Phone 1-800-727-8433

[21] Berne, E., M.D. *Transactional Analysis in Psychotherapy*. New York: Grove Press, 1964.

[22] Rogers, C. R. *On Becoming A Person—A Therapist's View of Psychotherapy*. Boston: Houghton Mifflin Company, 1961.

[23] Hubbard, L. Ron, *The Dynamics of Life*, 1988, by Bridge Publications, Inc., 4751 Fountain Avenue, Los Angeles, CA 90029.

[24] Piaget, G. W. and Binkley, Barbara. *Overcoming Your Barriers: A Guide to Personal Reprogramming*. New York: Irvington Publishers, Inc., n.d.

[25] Cayce, Edgar and others. *A Search for God*. and others; Association for Research and Enlightenment, Virginia Beach, Virginia 23451.

[26] Perls, F. *Gestalt Therapy Verbatim*. Moab, UT: Bantam/Real People Press, n.d.

[27] Lytle, A. C. *So YOU Want To Be A CHANNEL!"* First ed 1988, Falcon Press, 7025 E 1st Avenue, Scottsdale, AZ 85251

[28] Hills, C. and Rozman, D. *Exploring Inner Space*. University of the Trees Press, P.O. Box 644, Boulder Creek, California 95006.

[29] Krishnamurti, J. *The Wholeness of Life*, and others. New York: Harper and Row, Publishers, n.d.

[30] Hubbard, L. R. *Self Analysis*, Bridge Publications, Inc., 1414 North Catalina, Los Angeles, California 90027.

[31] Lytle, Arthur C. Jr.,1983, *Psycho-Cybernetic Principles and Practices Applied In Treating The Human Mind*, Doctoral Dissertation, University of Beverly Hills, Los Angeles CA.

[32] Grof, Stanislav, M.D., *Spiritual Emergency* and others. J.P. Tarcher, Inc., Los Angeles, California. Distributed by St. Martins Press, New York.

OTHER VALUABLE REFERENCES

A Course in Miracles		
Assn for Humanistic Psychology	Books and Courses in Humanistic Psychology	Assn for Humanistic Psychology, San Francisco
Assn for Transpersonal Psychology	Journal of Trans-Personal Psychology Psychology	Assn for Transpersonal Psychology, Stanford, CA
Bailey, A.A.	Esoteric Psychology	Lucis Publishing Co., New York
Berne, E.	Transactional Analysis in Psychotherapy	Grove Press, New York
Bible	King James Version	Nelson and others
Boole, Dr. George	Laws of Thought	Dover
Braddeson, W.	Scientology For The Millions	Sherbourne Press, Los Angeles
Branden, N.	The Psychology of Self Esteem	Bantam/Nash, Los Angeles.
Brown, B. B.	Stress And The Art of Biofeedback	Harper and Row, New York
Brown, B. B.	Super-Mind	Harper and Row, New York
Capacchione	The Creative Journal	Swallow Press
Fredericks, C.	Psycho-Nutrition	Grosset and Dunlap, New York
Gerber, Richard, M.D.	Vibrational Medicine	Bear and Co., Santa Fe, NM
Goldstein and Herden	Handbook of Psychological Assessment	Pergamon Press
Grinder, De Lozier, and Associates	Neuro Linguistic Programming Books, Training, and Certification	Grinder, De Lozier and Associates, Santa Cruz, CA

Hastings, Arthur	With The Tongues of Men and Angels	Holt, Reinhart, and Winstonn, Inc.
Heindel, Max	Rosicrucian Cosmo-Conception and others	Rosicrucian Fellowship, Oceanside, CA
Hills and Rozman	Exploring Inner Space, Awareness Games For All Ages	Univ of the Trees Press Boulder Creek, CA
Hofsttadter and Dennett	The Mind's I	Basic Books, Inc., Pubs, New York
Holmes	Science of Mind Magazine and text	Science of Mind, Los Angeles
Hubbard, L.R.	Dianetics, The Modern Science of Mental Health	Grossett & Dunlap New York. See also [30] above.
Janov and Holden	Primal Man	Croswell, New York
Janov, A	Prisoners of Pain	Anchor Press-Doubleday, New York
Janov, A	The Feeling Child	Anchor Press-Doubleday New York
Janov, A.	The Anatomy of Mental Illness.	Anchor Press-Doubleday, and The Primal Institute, LA
Janov, A.	The Primal Scream	Delta, New York
Janov, A. M.D.	Imprints	Coward-McCann, Inc., New York
Klimo, Jon	Channeling	J. P. Tarcher, Inc., Los Angeles,
Korzybski, Alfred	Science and Sanity	Institute of General Semantics
Leadbeater, C.W.	The Hidden Side of Things and others	The Theosophical Publishing House, Wheaton, IL

Leichtman, R.R. M.D.	Active Meditation: The Western Tradition	Ariel Press Columbus, OH
Lewis, N.	Psychosomatics	Pinnacle Books, New York
Maltz	Psycho-Cybernetics	Science of Mind, Los Angeles
Mathison and Hubbard	Electropsychometry	Out of Print
Mathison, V.	Creative Image Therapy	Out of Print
Ornish, M.D.	Reversing Heart Disease	Random House, NY
Osborne, C.G.	Understanding Your Past, The Key to Your Future	Word Books, Waco, TX
Perls, F.	In And Out Of The Garbage Pail	Bantam/Real People Press Moab, UT
Perls, F.	The Gestalt Approach & Eye Witness to Therapy	Bantam/Real Life Press, Moab UT
Pritikin, N. and McGrady, Jr	The Pritikin Program for Diet And Exercise	Grossett and Dunlap, New York
Roberts, Jane	The Seth Books and others	Bantam/Prentice-Hall Englewood Cliffs, NJ
Robt Graves	The Greek Myths	Penguin
Rogers, Carl	On Personal Power	Delta/Dell, New York
Roman and Packer	Opening To Channel	H. J. Kramer, Inc., Tiburon, CA
Satir, V.	Conjoint Family Therapy	Science and Behavior Books, Palo Alto

Satir, V.	People Making	Science and Behavior Books, Palo Alto
Seale, E.	Learn to Live: The Meaning of The Parables	Wm. Morrow and Co., New York
Solomon, Paul	Books, Tapes, Readings, Courses	Fellowship of the Inner Light Virginia Beach, VA
Stapleton, Ruth	The Gift of Inner Healing	Word Books Waco, TX
Stevens, J.	Awareness	Bantam/Nash, Los Angeles
Targ and Harary	The Mind Race	Institute of Noetic Science Sausalito, CA
The URANTIA Society	The URANTIA Book	URANTIA Foundation, Chicago
Toben	Space, Time, and Beyond	E. P. Dutton, New York
Unity	Metaphysical Bible Dictionary and "The Twelve Powers of Mar"	Unity School of Christianity, Lee's Summit, MS
Wilber, et al	The Holographic Paradigm and other Paradoxes	Shambala, Boulder, CO and London
Worral and Worral	The Gift of Healing	Harper and Row, New York
Zinker, J.	Creative Process in Gestalt Therapy	Random House and Vantage, New York

APPENDIX A
DEFINITIONS OF TERMS

1. A full solar zodiac cycle takes approximately 25,800 years. The *AQUARIAN AGE* is that 2150-year portion of astronomical time when the Sun, by precession, travels through the zodiacal Sign, or Age, of Aquarius. Each such Age parcels out the lessons assigned to we humans in Schoolhouse Earth allocated for incarnate Humanity to learn during each such Age. Man's lesson for the Aquarian Age is said to be Altruism, or Transpersonal Love.

2. The terms *BARRIERS*, *BLOCKS*, and *ENGRAMS* are used more or less interchangeably in this book for the purpose of identifying trauma which have the effect of blocking Life Energy flows through the human composite of Soul and Body-Mind. Restoration of normal energy flow or COMMUNICATION throughout the human structure enables Life to be experienced more fully and on and in higher planes of consciousness, with feeling and intuition and clairvoyance.

3. *CHANNEL* and *CHANNELING* are used to mean transfer of insights, information, and knowing between one Source, usually invisible, and one or more receivers. The medium or channeling person may be doing the channel-communication by allowing temporary possession of his vehicles, by overshadowing, or by telepathic exchange or transfer of pictures into the mind of the receiving/transferring person. Messages can also be transferred by writing and by speaking fully consciously, except that some clairvoyants witnessing the channeling process claim that the medium always experiences some level of altered states of consciousness, even when the medium or channel feels perfectly clearheaded. In that latter case we prefer to call the process "overshadowing."

4. *CHAKRA* is a term used to label the morning-glory-like funnels that arise in the endocrine system of the human spine, and appear at the outer periphery of the human electromagnetic body or aura. In a

spiritually developed person those centers are seen as multicolored and bright. Lesser levels of development can produce the appearance of little activity and energy, usually traced directly to some shortcoming experienced by said lesser or afflicted person. A Chakra is a transformer of frequency, spinning in the colored spiritual spectrum, reducing in speed and diameter as the energy drifts downward and into the appropriate endocrine centers. As a complete set or system of seven energy transducers, each of the chakras needs be balanced, else an unbalanced personality is experienced.

5. The terms *EGO-Self* and *ego-self* are used respectively to differentiate between and to label the Incarnate Spirit and the personality or Controller-self. The Controller-self is that collection of programs and habits assembled to operate the human body-mind structure, but which has effectively gained almost total control of the incarnate spirit, reducing the spiritual evolution and expression intended by that EGO just prior to its latest incarnation. The EGO-Self is properly labeled as that God-in-You or Christ Within, but which is so difficult for Man to discover and accept.

6. *GUIDES*, *TEACHERS*, and *ANGELS* are among the names and descriptions used to identify the Spiritual Beings which constitute the Brotherhood of Light which has the responsibility to attend the spiritual development and to manifest divine purpose and order in the lives of we incarnate Earthlings. The Guides and Teachers have experienced and mastered life incarnate on Earth, whereas the Angels have not. Guides seem to be most directly involved with particular humans, as if assigned throughout a lifetime. Some sensitives are able to communicate at will with the Guides, and may have direct contact with a Teacher for special occasions or purposes. Personal contact with each is encouraged, even though such Beings will not live our lives for us, but guide us as best They can so that we shall make the right decisions and hence live harmoniously and abundantly, even perhaps Joyously.

7. *PRACTITIONERS* are that collection of interested and talented persons whose interests are in providing spiritual counseling to Earth Persons needing or desiring Spiritual Guidance and Counseling. That group may include formally trained and psychically talented Psychologists, Psychiatrists, Advisors, Mental Health Clinicians and reader/interpreters of special means of

Divination, such as Tarot, Runes, et al. Usually the successful Practitioner is skilled in contacting the Akasha and can help his/her client do so during regression. Whatever its name, reviewing one's recorded trauma and habit patterns and programming enables resolving energy-binding recordings as barriers and blocks in the human, driving a person to inappropriate activity, and preventing persons from attaining and experiencing their highest good. To be a successful Practitioner a person must have resolved most of her/his backlog of similar engrams and blocks and barriers. A practitioner can usually only help a client resolve problems that the Practitioner has himself resolved.

8. *GESTALT* is a term of German origin that is used to enable workings with abstract concepts and is associated with describing and labeling programmed or related mental-psychic and spiritual activity and performance. Contact is made in and work is done with the human ovoid and Inner Worlds by learning to work with the energies and inner resources of any particular gestalt. The term was used initially as a collective label for the entire panoply of spiritual-psychological phenomena observed by Freud and Jung.

9. *PRESENT TIME* and *REAL TIME* are convenient labels for describing when an event occurs. Present Time means "here and NOW!" It is the seeming now-ness when events are being observed to occur either in subjective realms as during past-life regressions. A familiar parallel is how the observer feels when becoming absorbed in the on-screen activity in a cinema. Similarly with prehistoric or akashic recordings of events that to the observer are occurring on the spot! *REAL TIME* is a term used to define event occurrence by reference to clock time and calendar time, and may or may not have a definable relation to a subjective occurrence in Present Time. When a person is normally alert and participating in his/her social or business world it is said that Present Time and Real Time are identical. Then *TIME* is frequently observable by the human Spirit as a variable quantity, rather than as an invariable or independent variable as used in correlating classical Physics and Engineering processes.

10. *SOUL* is a word used here to mean that accumulation of experience recorded on each individual Spirit's Akasha, registered in what some religions and bibles refer to as The Book of God. Our soul is then of supreme value to we Earthlings, containing as it does

the distillation of all the Joy and all the unhappy events, experiences and situations which we did or did not master in Time Past. Perhaps one now better understands that a natal horoscope is a fine way to find what we have done in past lives by seeing what lessons we have yet to learn, or have chosen to learn this time around, and by seeing what we liked and/or did well at in previous times. Most persons among us then have usually earned their position in incarnate Earth-Life. Let it be recognized that we plan in advance of our incarnations what we will strive to do throughout each incarnation, and do indeed have access to that Plan. We are not left alone, as Guides and Teachers and Friends and Angels come with us to help those who are receptive, and who are sincere at prayer, at working with their Divine Helpers.

11. *KARMA* is that word taken from the ancient Sanskrit that is variously interpreted in The West as both as a process of Cause and Effect, and as the carried-along accumulation of debts to be paid off and rewards to be collected. In that sense, *KARMA* as a process permits a person to carry along with self the good and the yet-to-be learned or not-so-good lessons, problems and talents accumulated in former human incarnations here on Earth. It goes without challenge that most persons would bring their old baggage and talents with them from other Life Systems, perhaps from other galaxies. How an incoming soul chooses to work off certain lessons, using other accumulated skills and talents is said by Hierarchical Sources to be dependent on decisions made Jointly by the candidate returnee and a Board of Superior Intelligences Who have the responsibility to keep the entire Earth School System operating constructively. Because of the participation of such all-wise August Beings, it is therefore considered a very bad sin indeed to attempt to avert pre-incarnate agreements by suicide. More on this may be found in the URANTIA Book

12. *PSYCHIC PSYCHOLOGY, TRANSPERSONAL PSYCHOLOGY* and *TRANSFORMATIONAL PSYCHOLOGY* are terms which are being heard increasingly and merit some formal introduction. Each term is a synonym for the other terms and operates by considering a vaster understanding of the Human as an incarnate Intelligence working through a Mind that in turn operates on and in levels of awareness that conventional psychology and psychiatry do not yet recognize. As members of the mental health

community increasingly take into account the oft-reported but seldom heeded accounts of Near Death Experiences, and correlates these with the findings and observations of the better psychics, they come to admit that there is more to Life and Living than has been accepted. The dimensions and description of the human Spirit and Soul take on increasing strengths and Reality as they are researched outside of the conventional barriers adopted by Religion, Psychology, and Medicine, coming together in recognizing man as a wonderfully made integrated being. It requires that Religion, the supposed bastion of Spirit, expand its understanding beyond superstition to include the concept as fact that the Divine Beings spoken of in the various bibles and religious lore are but representative of the capabilities of each and every human incarnate on planet Earth. Then these new Spiritual Psychologies are oriented to bring about the literal transformation of human intelligence to reveal and nourish the innate spirit locked away in the human breast. The approaches offered in this our test are tried and tested true approaches to release that imprisoned splendor, leading to the individual christing here-to-fore shown us by the shamans of today and the holy men of the past. We shall sooner know that we are indeed gods ourselves!

APPENDIX B
A TIMELY EXAMPLE OF SYNCHRONICITY

Here is an address presented at the Church Of Inner Light in Los Angeles May 3, 1992. The scheduled speaker was suddenly called to Brazil, so at 9 AM on Wednesday, April 29, 1992, Joel Longenecker was asked by COIL's Pastor Trudy Jarno if he would substitute. Several hours later that same day the Los Angeles riots began. Joel is an attorney and a candidate for an advanced degree in Transpersonal Psychology. He channels and is being ordained for a Spiritual ministry. He is well qualified to have been chosen for delivery of this timely topic. The majority of his presentation follows.

As the title for today's presentation I have chosen

LAW and LOVE

We humans have Law, which is essentially society created, and we have Love, which is engendered by God. We have the Old Testament of Law, and we have the New Testament of Love. The Apostle Paul in his letter to the Romans addresses those residents of Rome who were interested in a belief system which came to be called Christianity. In the salutation Paul writes "To all God's beloved in Rome." Then he goes on to present Romans 13:1-10 (RSV), which I quote here.

> Let every person be subject to the governing authorities. For there is no authority except from God, and those that exist have been instituted by God. Therefore he who resists the authorities resists what God has appointed, and those who resist will incur Judgment. For rulers are not a terror to good conduct, but to bad. Would you have no fear of Him who is in authority ? Then do what is good, and you will receive his approval, for he is God's servant for your good. But if you do wrong, be afraid,

for he does not bear the sword in vain; he is the servant of God to execute his wrath on the wrongdoer. Therefore one must be subject, not only to avoid God's wrath, but also for the sake of conscience. For the same reason you also pay taxes, for the authorities are ministers of God, attending to this very thing. Pay all of them their dues, taxes to whom taxes are due, revenue to whom revenue is due, respect to whom respect is due, honor to whom honor is due.

Owe no one anything, except to love one another; for he who loves his neighbor has fulfilled the law. The commandments, "You shall not commit adultery, You shall not kill, You shall not steal, You shall not covet," and any other commandment, are summed up in this sentence, "You shall love your neighbor as yourself." Love does no wrong to a neighbor; therefore love is the fulfilling of the law.

In short, Love does no wrong to one's neighbor. Therefore Love fulfills the Law. I say it again... Love fulfills the Law. If we treat our neighbors with Love we will not hurt them. Therefore the only law we need is the Law of Love.

Religion has too often departed from the Law of Love, caught up in other laws, rules, dogma, and doctrine. But a new Spiritual Psychology emerges combining Religion with a psychology for human behavior which is connected to and is a part of God. God and humanity are intimately connected at all times.

We are talking about a new model (paradigm) for how we perceive ourselves and how we behave. Oneness of self. Growing up spiritually into our higher expression of ourselves which inevitably connects us to God in our body in this dimension *now. Law merges into love. It a new way of life.*

We have for too long now lived in our lower chakras or energy centers, those we usually regard as being more of our animal heritage. However, we have always had four additional primary chakras of the higher expression of God within us. But we have ignored these higher centers. Most twentieth century psychology has been ego-oriented, concerned with strengthening our ego, our third chakra. Furthermore, our permissive society focuses on the sexual and other "appetites" of the second and first chakras.

We must now "grow up" spiritually into our higher expression of our human potential as God-connected spiritual beings. We *must* now become adults—mature adults—and this means spiritually mature as human beings. We *must* grow up now, collapsing our personal separations and dichotomies and *uniting* and integrating ourselves into personal oneness. This means *personal* transformation.

For over twenty years a new psychology has been emerging, a transpersonal psychology, a spiritual psychology. Expanding the sense of self beyond the personal is what is involved. It is the study of consciousness, spirituality, and the integrated development of Self. It moves beyond ego to that which is shared, not just God consciousness, but god connection, that is, connection with and expansion into these other four chakras. It is oneness with an expanded sense of self on a personal level which inevitably leads to oneness with God, therefore oneness with others and oneness with life. It is called Love...the Law of Love.

It is largely through the prompting of my spiritual mentor that I have been able to be in contact through the veil with members of the Spiritual Hierarchy, the group known as The Brotherhood of Light. Thru-the-veil communication has become an increasingly frequent phenomenon for more and more people. Once one accepts that there is indeed life after so-called death, and once one accepts that there are other spiritual dimensions, dimensions not accessible to our usual senses, then one may open his or her awareness to those spiritual beings who are available for communication through the veil. This veil does not divide us or separate us from these spiritual beings, but it does challenge us to develop our spiritual awareness and abilities.

This is the first time I have publicly shared my personal Thru-The-Veil communications. I usually do not pose questions, but this time I did.

My opening Question to the Guides was:

> "I ask for your help! Los Angeles is in chaos and flames since the Rodney King verdict Wednesday afternoon (4/29/1992). I have been asked to give the talk on Sunday (5/03/1992) at the Church Of Inner Light. I plan to talk on LAW & LOVE. Do you have suggestions?"

Their response was:

"Good morning, Joel. Yes, we are here and we bring you love and affirmation. The current situation in Los Angeles, dreadful though it is, has long been anticipated by those of us who have access to the Akasha. It is unfortunate, of course, that there is so much injury to both persons and property, even death. From our perspective, however, this is a predictable and anticipated consequence of life distortions, not only by those directly engaged in lawlessness but by the large numbers who have impeded spiritual awareness.

"Planet Earth—Schoolhouse Earth—is a place for potential evolutionary development and despite notions and evidence to the contrary, human awareness is making significant evolutionary progress. What is now occurring is an essential aspect of such development.

"Do not be dismayed, even though there may be similar confrontations in a variety of ways, including on the personal one-on-one level between associates and those of direct relationships.

"What is occurring is a clash of ideas and basic perceptions of such magnitude and intensity that it will literally rock the world. Out of this clash will emerge whole new premises and paradigms for human behavior, and how the human being perceives itself, others, and the world. The dualities that have predominated in Western thought are giving way to new concepts of unification and wholeness.

"Your talk on Law and Love is especially relevant at this time, and we remind you of our part in guiding your choice as the speaker. While you do not need to speak directly about the present crisis and its social implications, an indirect reference will connect law and love to lawlessness and to the absence of love, tolerance, appreciation, and acceptance of one another. Functioning limited to use of the lower chakras must be replaced by higher spiritual and physical concepts and behavior. The duality and split between mind and body has included a duality and dichotomy between spirituality and physicality.

"A new spiritual psychology for human behavior and interpersonal relations shall now emerge increasingly. Keep in mind that the old will pass away, but with resistance. The new will predominate in time, after a period of pronounced confrontation. This confrontation is a real war and must be regarded as such.

"Over Time, unity in diversity will not be as alien as at present. Difference without division will be accepted as routine. With 20th Century technology, Planet Earth is now reduced in size. Travel and communication compels close cooperation. The need for a larger concept of community contributes to the new basic philosophy of underlying brotherhood and sisterhood, regardless of ethnicity or culture. Religiosity will be replaced by a spirituality with structure but without the rigidity and isolation which has characterized religious matters for so long.

"We deem it appropriate to say that the Western philosophies of many, many centuries have served human kind in beneficial ways even though it is now anachronistic in large measure. Art's and Our new book *A Spiritual Psychology for the Aquarian Age*, addresses the subject of new models for human conduct and association. Ask Art what the book's primary premise is and use it in your talk. It is directly in point.

"Law, as practiced, adopted and used, has served to alienate. It must now be reinterpreted to unite into the Law of Love. Law as a divider between those inside—i.e., 'good'—and those outside, i.e., 'no good,' must now be a means to implement/promote harmony, not to create or stimulate or extend differences into adversarial or confrontational behavior models.

"As you prepare today for your talk, be assured and therefore comforted that you will be guided by us. This is part of the defining moment in these matters. Your words will be part of a universal message of change of basic philosophy of life, of law, of love. As the inexorable push of love is exerted, law must be redefined to encompass, not exclude, to unite, not to separate. And while there will be those "outside of the law," those "inside of the law" will be dramatically enlarged.

"Yes, Joel, speak of Law & Love and of the higher expression of human potential now exerting such pressure for expression that it will not be denied. There will be those who are unable or unwilling to adapt. And those who live by maladaptation shall perish by maladaptation.

"This birth of a new way of Life involves pain—great pain for some—but the *new* will not be denied. A new paradigm shall increasingly assert itself and this means a new spirit of cooperative human behavior, a behavior not of exclusion but of inclusion. That is wholeness, Joel—inclusion. All life inclusively in harmony—in concert with a grand design, evidenced in the natural order. Humanity is part and parcel of the natural order, not an exception to it!"

"That is your basic theme, Joel, Humanity as an harmonious part of the natural order, not an exception; a spiritual psychology which unites the individual in personal transformation; a concept of Law which promotes commonality while honoring diversity; Love as the underlying philosophy as first expressed so long ago."

(End of response)

In closing I'd like to quote Romans 12:1-2;

> "I appeal to you therefore, Brothers (and I add Sisters), by the mercies of God, to present your bodies as a living sacrifice holy and acceptable unto God, which is your spiritual worship, Do not be conformed to this world; but be transformed by the renewing of your mind, that you may prove what is the Will of God, what is good and acceptable and perfect."

God bless each one in this endeavor.

INDEX

Abstract aspect of the Universe 19
Accelerating personal evolution 128
Acupuncture 45
Addictions, releasing; freedom from 19, 26
Air signs 113
Akasha, The 63, 133
Alpha Waves 105
Alternative Medicine 71
Ancient Wisdoms updated, The 31, 57
Antakaranah or Rainbow Bridge 17
Anti-Christ, The 26
Applying for Divine Assistance 130
Aquarian Age Counselor, The 10, 135
Aquarian Age Psychic Psychology 27
Aquarian Age Religion, The New 27
Astro-diagnosis 109
Attacks by client 190
Aura, The electromagnetic 135

Back home 215
Bad habits, demons and devils 27
Being born again [See also Reincarnation] 64
Being Centered 173
Benefits of clearing 32, 133
Beta waves 105
Between Lives Reception Committee 209
Between planes travel 213, 214
Biofeedback 168
Blind rage 190
Blocks and barriers 43
Blood testing 168
Brain: right, left 226
Brainwave analysis 105
Breathe-Down process 152, 157
Brotherhood of Light, The 9

Cayce, Edgar 193
Chakras 40, 46, 230
Chopra, Dr. Deepak 17, 234
Church of Religious Science 71
Clear, as a state of awareness 57, 70, 123
Clearing thought forms 64
Coffee grounds, reading 103
Color swatches in diagnosis 101
Communication 113, 147, 148, 221, 226, 227, 228
Compatibility by chart overlay 122
Computer-like human 221
Conscious Co-Workership 9, 127
Conscious Immortality 23, 229
Conscious vs. trance channeling 30, 82
Cookbook Counseling 169, 225
Counselor, requirements for becoming 137
Creative Imagery 86, 97
Cross of Man, The 24
Curricula of the Future 28
Cybernetics & Psycho-Cybernetics 224

Dear God letters 130
Death, overcoming 217
Delta waves 105
Destiny is mutable 122
Detoxification 77
Devils and Demons 23, 43, 74, 193
Diagnosing personal compatibility 122
Diet critical 20
Diet, simple austerity preferred 20, 40
Dietary Effects of meat, spices and alcohol 20
Dimensions of Life, The twelve 115
Draw-a-Person 98

Drills 178
Drugs of all sorts to be avoided 107, 145

Eating eggs and local produce 39, 40
Eden & Heaven 19
EGO-Self and ego-self 47, 84, 89, 188, 230
Electrical Engineering tie-ins 226
Electronic aids to diagnosing 63
Electropsychometer 15, 23, 45, 106, 194
ELF SELF, The 81
Energy 15
Engrams, blocks and barriers 25, 44, 143
Esoteric Psychology 45
Exercise, Aerobics and Yoga for body/mind rejuvenation 45, 144
Exteriorization 135, 203

Facilitator, Facilitating 9, 135
Fasting 40
Fault 193
Fear blocks Life Energy flows 211
Fear blocks Love 90, 133
Feldencraise 146
Fire signs on the chart 113
Fong, Dr. Herbert 14
Food chemistry 20, 37, 220
Food selections important 20
Freedom 199

Genius, developing 15, 18
Gestalt 163
Goals of Aquarian Age Psychology 8, 29, 133
Golden Age, The 130
Golden Wedding Garment, The 33
Graphology 98, 166
Guides, the place of and function of 8, 13, 15
Guilt 193

Handwriting Analysis 98
Healing versus Cures 69
Heart as Subconscious mind 73
Heaven is within, an attitude 23, 106
Heindel 24
Hercules and The Twelve Labors 26
Hierarchy, The 30
Holographic recordings 183
Horoscopes, Mechanics of 109
Hubbard, L. Ron and Dianetics 71, 143
Humanistic Psychology 28
Hypnosis 85

I CHING 101
Ignorance 25, 28
Incarnation cycles [See Reincarnation] 24
Inertia, running it off 199
Institute for Transpersonal Psychology 29
Integration of Soul Technologies 15
Intelligence, Creation of 219, 220
Interference, Psychic 49
Intuition 79, 170

Jahn, Dr. R.G. 13, 17
Janov, Dr. Arthur 14
Jesus of Nazareth 24

Karma 26, 58
Koran 216
Kubler-Ross 17, 193, 209

Labors of Hercules, The Twelve 26
Law-Nolte, Dr. Dorothy 14
Laws of Mind 58
Laypersons as Conscious Co-Workers 15
Lessons of Life, The Twelve 115
Life is a stage 32
Look for a time when 133

Make-A-List 95

Mallan, Dr. Joan Leo 13
Master of Life 27, 146
Material Aspect of the Universe 62
Mathematics 227
Meat-eating, effects of 37, 38, 146
Meditation 35, 143
Mental aspect of the Universe 19
Millennium now at hand 130
Mind, the Builder 61, 133
Mind-control technology 50
Minnesota Multiphase Personality Inventory 103, 157, 165
Montgomery, Ruth 209
Mystical wedding 134

Name means "nature" 64
Neuro Linguistic Programming 29, 73
New Age Religion 27
Noetic Sciences 29

Original Sin 195
Our Mission 127
Out-of-Body travel 140, 203
Oxygenation as a detoxifier 45, 144
The Occult 28
The Ouija Board 103

Palm Reading 99
Parapsychology 9, 143
Pastoral Counseling 15, 144
Perls, Dr. Fritz 143, 189
Personality Profiles 102
Polygraphy 194
Possession 50
Practices and Processes 77
Practicing the Presence 46
Practitioners, kinds of 31, 72
Prayer 66
Present Time Problems 80, 170
Pribram, Dr. 183
Primal Integration 143
Primal Scream 142
Psychic Interference 49

Psychic Psychology 31
Psychometry 25, 194
Punishment 59
Purgatory 213
Pyschosomatics 70

Qualifications for a Aquarian Spiritual Counselor 10, 75, 130
Quantity versus Quality of customers 149

Race mind 52, 164
Raw foods 20
Reactive mind 136, 142
Recall a time When... 182
Record-keeping 151
Reincarnation as rebirth 19, 25, 63
Religion of The Father 18
Religion of The Son 18
Renewal of the mind 70
Repentance 69, 73
Reverie 154
Right where you are! 131
Rising signs 110
Robotics, Humans as Robots 10, 224
Role-playing 189
Rolf, Dr. Ida P. and Rolfing 13, 146
Rorschach tests 98
Runes in diagnostics 101

Sanskrit 211
Sathya Sai Baba 24
Saved, Being 25
Schaffer, Dr. Donald R. 13
Schoolhouse Earth 128
Seed thoughts 125, 160
Self Mastery 8, 146
Sexual Expression 5, 154, 185
Silence, The 132
Silver Chord, The 201
Sin 193
Sleep four hours a day 40
Soul 63

Spotting Spots 155
Stability and Stabilization 196
Sub-personalities 185, 188
Sugar excess is toxic 20
Sun signs 105

TAROT as a diagnostic tool 95
Theta waves 105
Things in a Material Universe 19
Thought, the Power of 65
Thoughtforms 50, 61
Time Track, The [see also Akasha] 132
Transveil Travel 22
TRUTH, Relative and Absolute 19, 211

Understanding 9, 135

Vegetarian Diet, Changing over to 38
Voices, multiplicity of 186

Water signs 113
Weiner, Norbert 224
Welcoming Committee 209
Wheel of Rebirth 19

Yoga: Hatha, Rajah and Kriya 45
Yogananda, Paramhansa 142

TABLES and FIGURES

Figure One: The Natural Wheel of Life 114

Figure Two: Sophie's Natal Chart 120

Figure Three: Circuitry for the Psyche 223

Table I: File Ticklers 160

Table II: Common Denominators In The Race Mind 164

Table III: Some Stabilization Commands 196

Table IV: Some Client-Peculiar Guilt and Fault Triggers 197